A Creole Nation

A Creole Nation

National Integration in Guinea-Bissau

Christoph Kohl

berghahn
NEW YORK · OXFORD
www.berghahnbooks.com

First published in 2018 by
Berghahn Books
www.berghahnbooks.com

Library of Congress Cataloging-in-Publication Data

A C.I.P. cataloging record is available from the Library of Congress

British Library Cataloguing in Publication Data

A catalogue record for this book is available from the British Library

ISBN 978-1-78533-424-5 hardback
ISBN 978-1-78533-425-2 ebook

I dedicate this book to my wife Sandra and our son Moritz.

Contents

Illustrations

Figures

Maps

Acknowledgments

This book was made possible only through the continuous advice and encouragement of my mentor, Jacqueline Knörr, head of the Research Group Upper Guinea Coast of the Max Planck Institute for Social Anthropology. I am very grateful to her for her support and inspiration. I am also very thankful to Richard Rottenburg from the Institute for Social Anthropology at the Martin Luther University of Halle-Wittenberg for his help. I owe very special thanks to Wilson Trajano Filho of the University of Brasília, who reviewed my manuscript and contributed valuable advice and ideas. Special thanks to the late Christian Kordt Højbjerg of Aarhus University for his critical and encouraging comments. I also thank the other members of the Research Group Upper Guinea Coast, Markus Rudolf, Anita Schroven, Nathanial King, Maarten Bedert, Anaïs Ménard, and David O'Kane, as well as the group's student assistants Céline Mühl, Isabella Voigt, Nina Dreier, Joachim Langner, and Ivonne Willing. Moreover, I would like to thank Peter Mark, Wesleyan University, for his very helpful and constructive comments.

My field and archival research, as well as a language course, were kindly financed by the Max Planck Institute for Social Anthropology, which also supported my participation in conferences and workshops. In addition, I received a grant from the Graduate School "Society and Culture in Motion" based in Halle (Saale). I am much obliged to both institutions for providing fruitful academic (and nonacademic) exchanges. The Peace Research Institute Frankfurt (PRIF) funded further fieldwork in Guinea-Bissau in early 2013 and late 2014.

I am indebted to the archives and libraries that I consulted in the course of my research and all those who assisted me there, notably the Centro de Intervenção para o Desenvolvimento Amílcar Cabral (CIDAC), Lisbon; the Biblioteca Nacional and the Instituto Nacional de Estudos e Pesquisa (INEP), Bissau; the Instituto da Biblioteca Nacional e do Livro, Praia; the Council for the Development of Social Science Research in Africa

(CODESRIA) and the Institut Fondamental d'Afrique Noire (IFAN), both in Dakar; the Instituto Superior de Ciências do Trabalho e da Empresa-Instituto Universitário de Lisboa (ISCTE-IUL); the Arquivo Histórico Ultramarino (AHU); the library at the former Tropical Research Institute (IICT), notably, Ms. Branca Moriés, and the Sociedade de Geografia de Lisboa (SGL), both in Lisbon; the African Studies Centre (ASC), Leiden; and the Gambia National Library Service, Banjul. I am also much obliged to Gerhard Seibert at the Universidade da Integração Internacional da Lusofonia Afro-Brasileira in São Francisco do Conde / Salvador de Bahia, Brazil, for providing me with otherwise inaccessible literature. I owe very special thanks to Anja Neuner, Anett Kirchhof, Lydia Pötsch, Josefine Eckardt, and their student assistants at the library of the Max Planck Institute for Social Anthropology who made the greatest efforts to find and provide me with books and articles from various libraries throughout Germany and Europe.

There were numerous people who were very helpful in the field, and I am not able to mention them all here. Among them were Teresa Montenegro, the late Gabriele Poungoura, Carsten Wille, Marcel Kühne, Lina Gomes, the Nandingna family (Isabela, Midana, Sandra, Fatinha and Dio, Babo, Fernando, Finhani, Finémon, Isa, Alcioni, Bidanssanta, Abna), Fodé Dabo, Seni Mané, the late Luís "Guerra" Vaz Horta Santy, his late father Alfredo, and his mother Nhama, Inês da Cunha, Carlos Robalo, Jamel Handem, Isabela Nozolini, Aurora and Almiro Carvalho, Jasmina Barckhausen, Francisca Pereira, and Jamelia and Francisco Rodrigues.

Apart from this, I would like to thank my colleagues and friends at the Max Planck Institute for Social Anthropology, the Institute for Social Anthropology of the Martin-Luther-University Halle-Wittenberg, and the Graduate School "Society and Culture in Motion," who read and discussed sections of my study, thus providing me with invaluable comments, suggestions, and words of encouragement. These include Joachim Görlich, Regine Penitsch, Christiane Adamczyk, Oliver Tappe, Patrice Ladwig, Kirsten Endres, Merle Schatz, Han Vermeulen, Birgit Huber, Christina Gabbert, Karen Witsenburg, Jutta Bakonyi, Felix Girke, and Thomas G. Kirsch. I am also indebted to Ramão Lucas for his patience in teaching me Kriol, Jutta Turner for preparing the various maps used in this volume, and Oliver Weihmann and Viola Stanisch for providing technical support, as well as the administrative staff at the Max Planck Institute for Social Anthropology. Special thanks to Marina Temudo, Universidade de Lisboa, and Ramon Sarró, Institute of Social and Cultural Anthropology at the University of Oxford, for their encouragement, generosity, and hospitality; and to George E. Brooks, Pascal Gaudette, Ricardo Roque, Cristiana

Bastos, and Andreas F. Weber for their useful hints, as well as to Wolfgang Bender for his support and appreciation.

Last but not the least, I would like to thank my family, particularly my wife Sandra, my son Moritz, and my brother Philipp, as well as Melanie Carl.

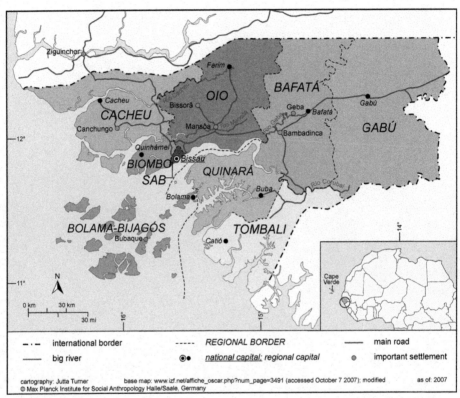

Map 0.1. Guinea-Bissau

Introduction

Creolization has been a widely discussed and controversial concept, both scientifically and popularly, for decades, resulting in numerous different understandings, approaches, and perspectives of the term, evoking at times positive, at times negative connotations through history. Historically, the term was closely associated with the development of colonial societies and exchange networks, and Guinea-Bissau, the venue for this book, was firmly embedded in this unequal colonial encounter and the related travel of traders, slaves, commodities, and ideas and models. Over the last years, Guinea-Bissau has frequently been the subject of media headlines reporting about political instability, corruption, political authoritarianism, coups and coup attempts, and the country's new role as a West African hub in global narco-trafficking, thus often obscuring the country's polymorphic creole entanglements that emerged in the course of globalizing processes since the mid-fifteenth century. Yet, this volume is not merely another study of creole historicity and linguistics that numerous scholars have thoroughly researched. Rather, this book seeks to cast new glances on creolization in Guinea-Bissau, focusing on the interrelatedness of creole identity with other identities and creole identity's significance for postcolonial nation-building "from below," and combining both contemporary and historical perspectives as well as social-anthropological, historical, and political science dimensions. In my study I have sought to explore how creolization processes—and the formation of creole identities—have been conducive to the national integration of postcolonial societies characterized by ethnic and religious heterogeneity. To pursue this path I have opted for a more encompassing socio-anthropological approach toward creolization—hereinafter referred to as "cultural creolization"—because a purely linguistic approach would fall short of explaining social and political implications of postcolonial nation-building processes. In doing so, this book links up with the only recent, ethnographically grounded monograph on creole culture and identity in Guinea-Bissau,

Wilson Trajano Filho's "Polymorphic Creoledom" (Trajano Filho 1998). More than this, the present book does not consider itself to be solely a country case study but instead intends to make a theoretical contribution to a better understanding of processes of cultural creolization in general and the relationship between ethnic and national identity formation and development in particular.

The Setting

Guinea-Bissau provides an illustrative case study of creole culture and identity and their relevance for analyses of postcolonial nation-building, facilitated by the country's geographic small size: spread over an area of almost 14,000 square miles (slightly more than 36,000 square kilometers) and populated by an estimated 1.5 million inhabitants, Guinea-Bissau is one of the smallest West African countries. This smallness, however, contrasts with a high degree of cultural, ethnic, and religious diversity: for instance, censuses enumerate between thirty-two (1996) and thirteen (2009) "indigenous" ethnic groups, the diverging numbers speaking volumes about the controversial character of identity and alterity in the country (Instituto Nacional de Estatística e Censos 1996: vol. 1, table 3.5; Instituto Nacional de Estatística 2009). In terms of religion, apart from Christianity and Islam, local religious beliefs are widespread throughout the country. This high degree of cultural, ethnic, and religious diversity led many of the country's citizens and external observers alike to express doubts about Guinea-Bissau's national unity. They argue that, in fact, this diversity precludes the development of national unity or, at least, a profound degree of intergroup integration.

Guinea-Bissau's varied and changing history is closely related to creole culture and identity. Situated between Senegal to its north and the Republic of Guinea to its east, Guinea-Bissau is marked by riverine lowlands along its coastal areas, which Portuguese navigators first entered in the mid-fifteenth century. Subsequently, Europeans identified the coast as suitable for establishing a handful of small commercial settlements for trade between Europeans, Cape Verdeans, and Africans. Due to intermarriages between all these communities, there emerged creole Kriston (in the local creole lingua franca, from Portuguese *cristão*, literally meaning "Christian") communities that developed their own identity and distinct cultural representations. Continuous migrations of Cape Verdeans, themselves creoles because of their mixed origins, to colonial Guinea-Bissau lasted until the late colonial period. Since the early twentieth century, creoles have dominated the nationalist movements in the Portuguese colony: starting with the "Guinean League" in 1911, creoles were strongly represented in numerous (illegal) political movements founded especially since the end of World War II. After a war for national liberation, Guinea-Bissau gained its independence in 1974, and along with it emerged a left-wing autocratic political system. The regime's state ideology, based on a strong appeal to national unity, proved to be a powerful unifier, since it had been shaped by the charismatic founding father—and long-term leader of the victorious independence movement and enduring governing party, African Party for the Independence of Guinea and Cape Verde (PAIGC)—Amílcar Cabral, himself a creole of Cape Verdean origins. The first successful coup plotted in 1980—interpreted by some observers as directed against the politically, culturally, and economically influential Cape Verdean minority—marked the beginning of political instability in Guinea-Bissau, bringing to power former independence fighter João Bernardo "Nino" Vieira, likewise of creole descent. In 1998–99, the country experienced a short but severe, mainly Bissau-centered, civil war, going down as "Military Conflict" in history books, and ever since then it has been faced with serious political, social, and economic challenges. Since this war, political turbulences have intensified, the intervals of coups, coup attempts, and politically motivated assassinations getting shorter, culminating in the assassination of the state president in 2009. Further, cocaine that originates from Latin America has been channeled through Guinea-Bissau and a number of other West African states for about a decade, and this practice is believed to threaten political and social stability even further. Politicians with creole background have continued to exert crucial political influence in Guinea-Bissau, and in the past years—until an April 2012 coup—Carlos Gomes Júnior, the offspring of an old-established Bissau-Guinean creole family, held the office of the prime minister. Despite manifold patterns of interethnic integration observable on the ground, the exploitation and manipulation of ethnicity continue to rank on the agenda of political entrepreneurs. Populist politicians' agitation has been repeatedly directed against the country's top-heavy bureaucracy and urbanized elite—also comprising a number of creoles—that has been made responsible for the neglect of the interior and its population.

My first encounter with Guinea-Bissau dates as far back as 2004. At the time I had rudimentary knowledge of the country's history and some idea of the political constellations on site, but I was not aware at all of issues related to creole culture and identity in past and present. In that year I completed—supported by Germany's then Capacity Building International (InWEnt)—a four-month internship with Guinea-Bissau's Biblioteca Nacional (National Library) that is attached to the Instituto Nacional de Pesquisa e Estudos (National Research and Studies Institute).

I used this time to make local friends, become acquainted with various parts of the country, further improve my Portuguese-language skills, and even pick up some Kriol, Guinea-Bissau's Portuguese-based creole vernacular. These experiences would prove valuable when I began to conceptualize this book in October 2005 with the research group "Integration and Conflict along the Upper Guinea Coast" at the Max Planck Institute for Social Anthropology, based in Halle (Saale), Germany. After perusing the relevant literature on both creole identity in the Bissau-Guinean context and various theories of creolization and ethnicity, I came up with a number of interrelated research questions, which were finally incorporated into a research plan in early 2006. In the meantime, in January and February 2006, I completed a four-week Kriol language course in Lisbon, the language serving as the lingua franca not only in Guinea-Bissau but also in the neighboring Senegalese region of Casamance and, in a varied version, in the Republic of Cape Verde. The fact that I was already able to communicate in Portuguese aided my learning of Kriol. The course was organized by the Lisbon-based nongovernmental organization Centro de Intervenção para o Desenvolvimento Amílcar Cabral (CIDAC).

Methodology

With these preparations in place, fieldwork in Guinea-Bissau started in late March 2006 and continued—with a one-month interruption—until early May 2007. Short-term stays realized in February–March 2013 and in February 2014 contributed to an update and completion of research data. While in the field I employed "classical" qualitative ethnographic fieldwork methods such as participant observation, formal and semi-structured interviews, and informal conversations. In most cases, interviews were conducted in an informal atmosphere. In order to avoid distracting and intimidating my interviewees, I rarely used a recorder. Some interviewees were afraid of negative repercussions from the state authorities. Therefore, I mainly took down notes during the course of the interviews or immediately afterward. Apart from this, I performed participant observation (Girtler 2001; Hauser-Schäublin 2008) by witnessing ceremonial and ritual events—including, apart from funerals and weddings, carnival celebrations and *manjuandadi* associations meetings, among others— and modes of interethnic interaction. In particular, my participant observations and the more informal conversations concerning my research themes proved to be very useful for obtaining insights into people's daily routines. However, I found it relatively more difficult to gain access to upper-class creole inhabitants. By and large, people living in the countryside were more accessible. I examined creole identity construction and boundary maintenance not only by studying the interactive strategies employed by creoles as well as non-creoles in their everyday life but also by determining the creoles' authoritative "on-stage" identitarian portrayal of themselves. I examined the Bissau-Guineans' attitude toward their nation and state through my informants' historical narratives and contemporary discourses regarding these topics. Patterns of identity performance were explored by focusing on two cultural representations, in particular, that used to be exclusively creole at one point of time but have undergone considerable changes and spread beyond the boundaries of the creole community since Guinea-Bissau's decolonization in the 1970s. One of these cultural representations is the institution of the *manjuandadis*—predominantly female associations that provide for sociability, mutual assistance, and solidarity within the community, mainly by playing music and participating in feasts and other celebrations. The other representation is carnival—a festivity celebrated both in the streets and among groups of family members, friends, coworkers, and neighbors. In addition to attending these events, I discussed the role played by *manjuandadis* and carnival celebrations in the past with contemporary as well as former participants and enthusiasts.

Collected data were triangulated—i.e. information obtained from different sources and methods was cross-checked in order to make visible multifold viewpoints and standpoints—as part of a comprehensive discourse analysis, taking into account interviewees' and participants' social characteristics. In this respect, I also gathered biographical accounts (Lange 2005) to learn more about the individuals' backgrounds, their attitudes toward certain issues, and their assessment of specific matters. Sources consulted during ethnographic research were subject to sampling: I sampled my potential informants in such a way that my data would present a comprehensive picture of Bissau-Guinean society in general and creole identity in particular. Keeping in mind factors such as social class, ethnicity, religion, age, sex, and rural/urban origins of my informants, I began my research by identifying the descendants of established creole families who might like to give me more information regarding their creole identity. In this process I was supported by a number of local acquaintances who acted as "ice-breakers"—and such "door-openers" were initially indeed essential and extremely helpful for a research starting at zero. Using the snowball effect, I was then able to detect further possibilities of entry while simultaneously using other contacts in my vicinity, including my local circle of friends and acquaintances. I also approached many informants on my own, without any prior recommendation or introduction. In order to avoid "anecdotal" impressions, I paid considerable attention to my informants' expertise, for example as contemporary witnesses of historical occurrences or as testimonies of the inner working of associations, contests, etc. The resulting interview data have been rendered anonymous so that the persons are not identifiable; the anonymized interviewees appear on a list in the appendix, indicating their gender identity, their approximate age, as well as the location and date of the interviews.

The field research was "multi-sited" (Falzon 2009), i.e. not focused on one location only but taking place at various settings: I conducted most of my research in the capital city of Bissau, which is generally regarded as the biggest center of creole culture in Guinea-Bissau. In addition, I did some field research in Geba, which was one of the most important trading posts in the region at one time. However, most of the creole inhabitants have left Geba by now, many having relocated to Bissau and Bafatá, where I also conducted research. Some other field sites that I occasionally visited included the former trading posts of Cacheu, Farim, and Bolama as well as Ziguinchor—located in the southern Senegalese Casamance region—which were once foci of creole culture.

As far as possible, I combined written sources with oral traditions, a procedure that proved difficult for at least two reasons. On the one hand, historical documents, especially on issues like (creole) identity, carnival, or associativism in colonial times, for instance, were scarce. On the other hand, the use of oral traditions to "reconstruct" history poses several problems. As scholars like Jan Vansina (1985: 31) have shown, narrations are often "summaries of events generalized," suggesting simplifications, stereotyping, and skipping of generations. Apart from this, oral traditions may be grounded in legitimizing, normativizing, or even ideological considerations; therefore, they are "normative data rather than observed data" and do not need to be taken as historically "realistic." In other words, "statements about situations or trends need not in fact relate to actual events or observations. Often they derive from generalizations made by contemporaries or later generations. Such data testify then to opinions and values held, to mentalities, and that is their value, not as testimony of fact" (Vansina 1985: 31).

Hence, both intentionally and unintentionally oral traditions tend to reinterpret, invent, reconstruct, imagine, reconfigure, or omit past events. Memories and narrations are neither static nor passive; instead, "remem bering is action, indeed, creation" (Vansina 1985: 43). This means that oral

traditions are processes. They must continually change to remain alive. . . . A tension always exists between the two realities people can be aware of: the cognitive reality, which predicts, and the physical reality, which then happens. When the discrepancies between them become too great . . . , the two realities have to be readjusted. The readjustment is the point where permanent changes occur. . . . Therefore tradition is a moving continuity. (Vansina 1990: 258)

Triangulation and repeated inquiries may help to discursively trace and understand past occurrences; yet, the result will never be an "objective" reconstruction of the past. Comparisons with written resources may also contribute to this endeavor. However, scholars like Ann Stoler (2009) and Nicholas Dirks (2002) have shown that written and archival resources, particularly in colonial contexts, are also sites of totalizing, fragmented, yet monolithic knowledge production. Both oral traditions and written sources are therefore expressions of a society's "culture of remembrance" (or, *Erinnerungskultur* in German) that refer to its interaction with the past, thus to the—sometimes contested and challenged—remembrance and reinterpretation of historical events (cf. Cornelißen 2010; cf. Assmann 2002), as part of the "collective memory" (Halbwachs 1980).

Written resources were another component. The archival and literature research for this book was performed at the national libraries of Guinea-Bissau, Cape Verde, and the Gambia, which are situated in Bissau, Praia, and Banjul, respectively. The search encompassed both academic and popular historical and contemporary literature hard to find in Western European libraries, as well as relevant gray literature, census data, and legal texts. In addition, I conducted research at various libraries and documentation centers in Europe and Africa. Apart from this, I managed to refer to a considerable amount of relevant literature by using scientific databases available online.

Partly, the collected ethnographic raw material (observations complemented by interviews, written resources, etc.) was eventually contextualized in what was introduced into social anthropology as "thick description" by Clifford Geertz (1973). This term characterizes "the process of paying attention to contextual detail in observing and interpreting social meaning. . . . A thick description of a social event or action takes into account not only the immediate behaviours in which people are engaged but also the contextual and experiential understandings of those behaviours that render the event or action meaningful" (Dawson 2010: 943). Instead of a "traditional" social and cultural sciences research I chose an approach superficially indebted to grounded theory as proposed by Anselm L. Strauss and Barney Glaser (cf. Strauss 1987). This means that instead of departing from a hypothesis or theoretical framework, I first collected data to finally derive theoretical conclusions, making it possible to react flexibly and rapidly to new insights gained on site.

The general conditions of my field research proved to be difficult. Fears of an upcoming military coup or war were prevalent among Bissau's inhabitants at the time of my fieldwork—their anxieties were fueled by decades of both colonial and postcolonial authoritarian rule, a generally tense political environment, previous coups and coup attempts and the

Military Conflict, as well as the fatal assassination of a popular former high-ranking marine officer, which caused riots in one of Bissau's neighborhoods in early January 2007. As a result, some interviewees were afraid of frankly expressing their views on certain political or politicized issues pertaining to identitarian matters.

Frequent power and water cuts in the capital, a complete absence of public electricity and tap water in the country's interior regions, including the administrative centers, and the time-consuming public transport in the hinterland—either by *kandonga* (a public transport vehicle, also known as *sept-places* throughout the region), motorbike, *piroga* (a big wooden, power-operated boat), or, more recently, decrepit bus—aggravated both working and living conditions and taught me how these conditions shape the lives, perceptions, thinking, desires, and identities of Bissau-Guineans. I used these experiences to better understand the social, cultural, economic, and political contexts.

Research Questions

Based on my methodological framework, I have attempted in this study to address a set of closely interrelated key research questions, which can be grouped into three clusters.

The first cluster is about the making-up of creole identity in Guinea-Bissau and creole boundary construction and maintenance in relation to other ethnic identities. More specifically, I raised the following questions: Who is ascribed a creole identity, when, how, and by whom? How does creole self-designation and the ascription of creole identity work at the grassroots level? Which terms and concepts are employed when ascribing a person creole identity, and how do creoles identify themselves? To what extent does a plurality of creole identities exist in Guinea-Bissau? Which factors served to facilitate or complicate the formation of creole identities during colonial times? What kind of attempts do the creoles make in order to revive and revitalize their "tradition" and group identity? How are interethnic cohabitation and relations between creoles and non-creoles conceptualized and socially practiced? How do creoles distance themselves from non-creoles? To what extent and using which strategies do they maintain their identitarian boundaries?

The second cluster addresses the role played by creoles, their culture, and identity in processes of postcolonial interethnic and national integration as well as nation-building, as expressed by the following set of questions: How and to what extent has the regional and social expansion of cultural representations that were previously exclusive to the creole minority contributed to Guinea-Bissau's national integration since independence? How have non-creoles appropriated and transformed these erstwhile purely creole representations? Which traits of these representations have facilitated their appropriation among non-creoles? To what extent does creole identity contradict popular assumptions that conceptualize the African nation as an umbrella covering a number of ethnic groups? How do creoles bridge this dichotomy by connecting their identity with modern concepts of nationhood? To what extent did creoles assume a key role in fostering nationalism and laying the foundation for a postcolonial nationhood?

The final cluster is dedicated to the quality of Bissau-Guinean nationhood—as opposed to statehood—as imagined by the country's citizens: How do Bissau-Guineans conceptualize their nation? How do they define Bissau-Guinean nationhood with respect to that of the neighboring countries? How do Bissau-Guineans differentiate between nationhood and statehood? Which factors have contributed to national cohesion despite cultural and ethnic diversity since independence?

Theoretical Premises

The book follows a constructivist approach toward collective identities. Accordingly, I regard ethnic identities as socially constructed, situational, flexible, malleable, and multilayered. In contrast to essentialist or primordialist approaches, it is "the ethnic *boundary* that defines the group, not the cultural stuff that it encloses" (Barth 1969: 15; original emphasis). This drawing and maintaining of social boundaries defines both membership and the "dichotomization of others as strangers, as members of another ethnic group" (Barth 1969: 15). The concept of "boundary markers" that distinguishes "insiders" from "outsiders" has gained much prominence in recent decades, appearing in studies on ethnicity, nationalism, migration, and diasporas. Research has shown the adaptability and versatility of such markers, thus their social construction. Nonetheless, members of "we-groups" like ethnic groups or nations *believe* that they are bound together by the same or at least similar cultural markers of difference (Elwert 1989: 446; cf. Weber 1978: 1:395). In other words, these commonalities are imagined (Anderson 1999).

Different from this analytical perspective, in everyday life ordinary citizens point to primordial cultural contents (material and immaterial cultural representations such as language, religion, habitus, material culture, etc.) as constituents of group consciousness. Specific ethnic markers are used by groups to construct their identitarian boundaries and generate a sense of ethnic belonging. These ethnic identity markers used from within the group operate in opposition to features of sociocultural distinction imposed by others. Markers from a repertoire of "cultural stuff" can be used deliberately or unconsciously without postulating instrumentality or intentionality but rather suggesting complex negotiation processes between groups and their members.

Nations are socially constructed and imagined in much the same way as ethnic groups (see Hobsbawm and Ranger 1983; Gellner 1998; Anderson 1999). However, in contrast to ethnic groups, nations refer to either an existing state or one that is to be formed, thus implying citizenship (Elwert 1989: 446). The reference to a common state apparatus does not mean, however, that a nation and a state are congruent. Identity entrepreneurs often imagine their ethnic groups or nations as having a historically deep-rooted continuity: they use references to the past selectively, historically charging and reifying them (cf. Assmann 2002: 133).

Crucial for the theme of this book is that ethnicity can entail varying degrees of ethnicization or "groupness." This means that ethnicization processes can result in either strongly ethnicized groups or weakly ethnicized categories of identification. In Brubaker's view, groups are "mutually interacting, mutually recognizing, mutually oriented, effectively communicating, bounded collectivity with a sense of solidarity, corporate identity, and capacity for concerted action" (Brubaker 2004b: 12). In contrast, ethnic categories can be characterized as a collection of individuals that display to varying degrees "a potential basis for group formation or 'groupness'" (Brubaker 2004a: 39). In other words, "whereas social groups define themselves, their name(s), their nature(s) and their boundary(s), social categories are identified, defined and delineated by others" (Jenkins 1994: 201). Increasing levels of groupness, in turn, can lead to the transformation of ethnic categories into ethnic groups (Brubaker 2004a: 40).

Variations in ethnicity can occur according to situation and context. The multiplicity and situationality of ethnicity are particularly evident in processes of creolization. Transethnic identities are formed due to alliances that embrace various other ethnic identities, thus assuming the aspect of an umbrella identity that encompasses various ethnic identities or their segments. Such multiple identities enable individuals to switch between identities, depending on the specific situation and context (Elwert 2002: 39–40). Over the course of time in ethnicization processes, new transethnic meta-identities can replace, to varying degrees, the original collective identities. Diverse origins of group members, however, can continue to be reflected in certain narratives or customary practices (cf. Knörr 2008: 4).

Outline

Thematically, the scope of this monograph includes a study of the processes of creolization and the evolution of creole identities, the nationwide expansion of the representations of creole culture, the significance of creoles for nationhood and nation-building, and the current situation of the nation as well as the state in postcolonial Guinea-Bissau.

I will start by discussing, in both historical and contemporary perspectives, how creoles in Guinea-Bissau have contributed in manifold ways to postcolonial nation- and state-building. More precisely, postcolonial African political leaders—and in Guinea-Bissau creoles figured prominently among those who advocated, prepared, and fought for national independence—of many young African states identified the prevailing cultural and ethnic identity as a challenge that threatened to undermine their efforts to successfully build a nation. Following independence, they took efforts to contribute "top-down" to interethnic integration, and this included setting up new national traditions and supporting movements and events that were supposed to bridge cultural and ethnic differences. However, in many African countries ethnicity has been manipulated by political entrepreneurs for reasons of power, and both colonial and postcolonial Guinea-Bissau was no exception. For instance, since about the 1950s, Cape Verdeans—migrants and their descendants originating from the archipelago off the West African coast—were portrayed as scapegoats both by the Portuguese colonial administration and some postcolonial political leaders. Against this background I will proceed to analyze the formative impact of creoles on nation-building in Guinea-Bissau and which factors have "glued" together the Bissau-Guinean nation in the past decades, despite high degrees of cultural, social, ethnic, political, and religious fragmentations. Against this background I will also explore the relationship between the modern concepts of nation and state while analyzing which factors contribute to national cohesion in contemporary Guinea-Bissau.

Chapter 2 will be dedicated to the analysis of creole identity in Guinea-Bissau. In that chapter I will discuss the key theoretical concepts used to explore the issues at stake. Here, I will examine the concept of cultural creolization. Creolization is here understood from an anthropological perspective. As such, creolization is conceived as a process that entails the intergenerational replacement of diverse original identities by a new, shared creole identity. In the course of this process of ethnicization the people concerned also develop an identification with their new home. As creolization encompasses the (re)negotiation of identitarian boundaries, its analysis brings to the fore tensions and diverse perspectives between in- and outgroups, between analytical and inside views. The conceptualization of creolization as introduced in this chapter implies that this process is not limited to colonial settings, nor is "creole" to be considered as something "incomplete" or "false." Further, "creolization" as it is used within the context of this book targets localized identitarian perspectives—while globally circulating ideas and models always have an effect on culture and identity in micro-settings. I will explain how creole identity in Guinea-Bissau has evolved historically and discuss the factors that have contributed to its shaping. At this juncture, I will analyze the processes underlying creole self-identification and the ascription of creole identity. In the course of this analysis, I will also examine the terms used to describe these processes and the way in which creoles construct their identitarian boundaries. Subsequently, I will proceed to explicate the three different varieties of creole identity that can be found in contemporary Guinea-Bissau.

Chapter 3 will analyze the postcolonial spread of certain formerly creole cultural representations that have contributed to national integration from below. The examples derived from Guinea-Bissau have to be seen in the larger framework of similar processes observable in many parts of the world. In a number of nation-states, cultural representations that used to stem from particular groups have been incorporated by other groups in a process that can be called "transethnicization" or "cultural pidginization." This transfer process is sometimes simplified as one-way "homogenization." However, the integration entails not only the translation, reshaping, and adoption of circulating cultural and identitarian models into "local" repertoires but also the repercussion and resilience of such adopted models or parts of them. Hence in the course of pidginization, homogenization comes along with heterogenization. In contrast to creolization, pidginization does not include the complete substitution of original identities. In a nation-state, transethnic cultural and identitarian features—occasionally initiated and fostered by the state—can thus contribute to interethnic and even national integration, transforming formerly ethnic representations into traditions cultivated across ethnic lines. Due to the heterogenous cultural and ethnic ancestry of creoles, their cultural representations appear to be especially suitable for adoption by other groups. By contributing to an interethnic integration from below, pidginization may consequently serve to counter both popular and academic allegations that most African countries cannot develop "real" nations, given the high degree of prevailing cultural, religious, and ethnic diversity. In what follows, I describe from a bottom-up angle how cultural representations previously exclusive to Guinea-Bissau's creole culture have been used for postcolonial interethnic, national integration. In this regard I will discuss the formation, transformation, and postcolonial expansion of three such cultural features—the creole language Kriol, *manjuandadi* associations, and carnival festivities—in terms of their significance for nationwide interethnic integration after independence. I will thus explain how the creole project has turned into a national project.

Chapter 1

Guinea-Bissau
A Creole Nation?

In many cases the postcolonial African state fostered national unity and a common national culture—sometimes under creole auspices, as was the case in Guinea-Bissau, which sets a good example in this respect. The West African country seems to correspond well to Benedict Anderson's (1999) model of creole nation-building and the making of "Guineans": creoles not only figured well in the victorious liberation movement that fought Portuguese colonial rule, they have also been prominent in postcolonial governments, administration, and among intellectuals. Apart from this successful creole nation-building from above, which has been described and analyzed by various authors, creoles and creole culture have also had a marked influence on national integration across ethnic (and religious) boundaries from below, i.e. from among the ordinary population, resulting in a strong collective imagination as "[Bissau-]Guineans." Most notably, creole representations proved to be well suited to transcend ethnic particularities because they were not associated with specific ethnic groups but integrated cultural elements from different sources instead. Hence, creole groups resembled "small" nations in themselves. The African state thus often played a pivotal role in facilitating or provided the impetus for postcolonial nationhood from below.

Apart from the bottom-up integrative effects of creole popular features, creoles also played an important role in shaping and constructing modern Bissau-Guinean nation- and statehood from above, making it a creole project. This creole engagement and the historical references to events that were framed and marked by creoles have helped to construct both nation

---

Notes for this chapter begin on page 44.

and state in Guinea-Bissau. Speaking about nationhood and nation-building, the state—or, more precisely, the nation-state—must be (almost) inevitably addressed. Nation and state are concepts that are characterized by a complex interdependence, affecting each other reciprocally.

In the following I will start by discussing how postcolonial nation-building was envisioned and achieved, analyzing particularly the role of African middle-class groups in creating and envisioning an independent nation and (nation-)state and how these interrelate. From both diachronic and synchronic perspectives I will investigate which factors have been conducive to successful nation-building and how they have interwoven both bottom-up and top-down approaches and perspectives. The focus will be on links between creoles and creole identity on the one hand and those between creoles and national identity on the other. More precisely, I will examine the political influence exerted by creoles and the way in which prominent creole leaders contributed to the conceptualization of the nation and state prior to independence. With regard to nation- and state-building, I will explore how creole, ethnic, religious, and national identities are interrelated in present-day Guinea-Bissau.

National cohesion is, in fact, quite strong in Guinea-Bissau despite the high degree of ethnic, religious, and cultural heterogeneity prevailing. Evidence suggests that the issue of ethnicity is largely exploited by politicians to serve their own purposes. The question arises as to how inter-ethnic conviviality in people's everyday lives is affected by the politicization of ethnic (and religious) ties. To this end, the case of the creole Cape Verdeans will serve as an example to be discussed. Ethnic heterogeneity, as I will show, is not necessarily an obstacle in the construction of Bissau-Guinean nationhood. Similarly, religious affiliation in Guinea-Bissau is not characterized by exclusivity. Bissau-Guinean metanarratives portray the war of independence as a nation-founding myth and Amílcar Cabral as a national hero and founding father. I will elaborate how, in the long term, struggles for independence, external threats, and the resulting shared suffering played a crucial part in defining national identity, facilitating the integration of various ethnic subidentities under a shared national umbrella identity despite dividing sociocultural factors and political maneuvers.

Envisioning and Building Postcolonial African Nationhood

After World War II, African nations were conceptualized and shaped by politicians standing for independence from European colonial rule. Even though nationalist ideas had already spread in the first half of the twentieth century, the years of World War II signaled a turning point for nationalism all over the African continent. African colonies that had been quite arbitrarily demarcated and seized by European colonial powers only a few decades before turned into arenas of rising nationalism after 1945. The national question was raised by numerically small groups of local elites that drew heavily on the Western concept of independent nationhood (and statehood) (Hobsbawm 1999: 137). Nationalist politicians had to cope with high degrees of cultural, ethnic, and religious diversity prevailing in the colonies, but they were also able to harken back to the (colonial) state's efforts in creating a rudimentary, territory-based feeling of solidarity and belonging among the population, owed to common colonial languages, political arenas, media, and education system, among other things. Examples of such middle-class politicians include Kwame Nkrumah in Ghana, Ahmed Sékou Touré in Guinea, and Patrice Lumumba in Congo-Kinshasa. Some of them, such as Amílcar Cabral in Guinea-Bissau and Cape Verde, Julius Nyerere in Tanzania, Ahmed Sékou Touré, or Kwame Nkrumah, created powerful and ubiquitous ideologies for their independent states-to-be, appealing for national unity despite ethnic and religious plurality.

Many scholars have underlined the important contribution of creoles in the achievement of independence and the construction of postcolonial nation- and statehood in Guinea-Bissau (Chilcote 1972; Rudebeck 1974; Pirio 1983; Galli and Jones 1987; Trajano Filho 1993; 2005; 2006b; Duarte Silva 1997; Wick 2006; Keese 2007; Amado 2011; etc.). Consequently, creoles consider themselves, in some cases, to be the founding fathers of modern nationhood. This view was facilitated by the fact that creole ethnic groups not only perceived themselves as indigenized firstcomers to specific localities but were also generally regarded as a "small" nation on their own, for they united a plurality of ancestral ethnic identities (see also Kohl 2009a, b).

Indeed, tiny creole groups, strongly represented in colonial economies and civil services, were instrumental in playing decisive roles in the process of African nation- and state-building. While Americo-Liberians had dominated state- and nation-building in Liberia since the nineteenth century (Liebenow 1969), important segments of the Afro-Brazilians of Togo (Amos 2001: 302, 308) and the creole population of Guinea-Bissau and Cape Verde (Dhada 1993; Duarte Silva 1997; Lopes 2002; Keese 2007) advocated independence; the Aku in the Gambia, however, seemed to have an ambivalent attitude toward independence (Perfect 1991: 73, 75–78; Hughes and Perfect 2006: 108–9, 115, 131, 133–34, 138–140, 145–46). Conversely, the Krio of Sierra Leone (Wyse 1989: 105) and the Fernandino (or Krío) of Equatorial Guinea (Sundiata 1996: 183) largely opposed independence because they feared that they would be marginalized by other, numerically stronger ethnic groups.

Most African colonies were marked by high degrees of ethnic and cultural diversity. Nationalist movements advocated independence and sought to overcome ethnic divisions "from above." One powerful method to unite heterogeneous societies during the struggle for independence was to "sacralize" (a word referring to nineteenth-century Europe) the nation-to-be (Weichlein 2006: 140–41; Berger 2008: 11). In some countries like Guinea-Bissau, Guinea, and Algeria, nationalist independence movements and the newly independent nation-state attempted to mobilize the population and increase people's commitment to the nation by projecting an ideal of nationhood with religious connotations. Sometimes, as in the case of Guinea-Bissau, the population appropriated these top-down projections, internalizing and popularizing them. Political leaders reverted to languages with religious symbolism in order to produce strong emotional feelings of togetherness (cf. Graf 2004: 119–24). In many African countries, independence was believed to entail significant material and immaterial benefits for the disadvantaged population that had suffered from colonial oppression and exploitation. In other words, nationalists projected the image of a victimized nation by employing a rhetoric with religious undertones (cf. Reuter 2000: 139, 143, 154; Sundhaussen 2000: 70–71, 81–83; Wehler 2001: 55–69; Berger 2008: 11; Sand 2013). By doing this, it became possible to use victimhood in order to achieve national mobilization. The sanctification of the nation in combination with collective distress led to the depiction of this variant of nationalism as "political religion" (Hayes 1926; Vögelin 2007; cf. Weichlein 2006: 137–38; Kennedy 2008: 120–21; Sand 2013: 80–82).

The discursive victimization of the nation was all the more powerful when it was associated with a charismatic personality who represented a nation's rescue and salvation from collective colonial distress. This applied to all national projects that were headed by charismatic leaders such as Amílcar Cabral, a creole, Kwame Nkrumah, Ahmed Sékou Touré, and Samora Machel, among others. The contemporary collective self-victimization of Bissau-Guineans as "underdogs," regardless of ethnic or religious references, in light of a supposed "state failure" (socioeconomic difficulties, political instability, etc.) is one manifestation that preserves national cohesiveness (Kohl and Schroven 2014).

Despite the efforts of nationalist governments to create a new common culture and national identity following independence, ethnicity has nevertheless remained an important issue. Politicians in Africa have repeatedly attempted to exploit ethnicity for power purposes. Frequently, it was the "'tribal' imperative," as Patrick Chabal called it, that has often been "represented as ultima ratio of African politics" (Chabal 1996: 48; emphasis omitted). In many cases, political entrepreneurs have strategically exploited ethnic ties for political and economic ends in postcolonial times—albeit without limiting the citizens' commitment to nationhood. Moral ethnicity (Lonsdale 1996), as an internal dimension, can be specified as a "discursive and political arena within which ethnic identities emerged out of the renegotiation of the bounds of political community and authority" (Berman 1998: 324). Moral ethnicity is embedded in vertical moral-economic patterns of behavior among patrons and clients. In contrast, the diametrically opposed political tribalism, as an external dimension, depicts the ethnic basis of the horizontal competition between different patron-client networks (Lonsdale 1996; Berman 1998: 324–30, 338–39).

The long-term success of nationalist movements' and governments' endeavors to unite the nation is reflected in times of international armed or transnational social conflict. In such circumstances, the citizens' commitment to the nation comes to the fore as people of different origin stand united as one nation against foreigners who are regarded as a common threat to their nation. This phenomenon vaguely resembles what came to be known as "balanced antagonism," as referred to by Edward E. Evans-Pritchard (1940: 125, 134, 161; cf. Meeker 2004). This principle provides for the construction and maintenance of a social boundary and attempts to unite the nation across ethnic and religious boundaries and positioning it against a generalized, collective other.

State- and nation-building are not identical, yet they are often mutually dependent. For instance, while some states "failed" because they did not take into account local knowledge (Scott 1998: 34), Bissau-Guinean *manjuandadi* associations illustrate how the postcolonial state was quite successful in making use of local features, "vernacularizing" (cf. Merry 2006: 39) modernist models of "global north" political mass-movementism in local institutions and meanings. Historically, not every state-building process was connected to nation-building. In cases where nation-building occurred, the process was not continuous.

Thus, analytically, nations and states have to be distinguished (Gellner 1998: 5–6; Barrington 1997: 713; 2006: 4), although these notions are often used synonymously—particularly in English parlance (Wehler 2001: 25; cf. Gromes 2012: 26, 36–37). Hence, the people's disaffection with the present manifestation of the state (governance) does not necessarily call into question the nation's categorical commitment to conviviality in "its" state. A nation (or, respectively, the individuals constituting it) can have the will to live together in one state but can, at the same time, reject the everyday practice, i.e. the concrete functioning and performance of statehood (Abrams 1988: 82).

In European contexts, a shift from the state to the nation-state did not take place before the late eighteenth century (Langewiesche 2000: 27–28).

This also holds for France, where a modern nation-state was created in the aftermath of the French Revolution (Weber 1976). Hence, the French were "created" after the foundation of the French nation-state. In other cases, the nation preceded the state, such as in Germany, Poland, or Italy.

In Africa, developments were different. Here,

> the colonial state imposed the territoriality principle everywhere and demar-
> cated state borders, but it was not a nation-state. The idea of the nation emerged
> only in the anticolonial movements. As a ... result, ... nation-states without
> an organically evolved nation developed in late colonial times. National inde-
> pendence was thus not the result of a consciousness of national identity and
> unity but rather preceded the latter. (Eckert 2006: 95; my own translation; cf.
> Osterhammel 2009: 77)

In other words, effective nation-building had to be pursued after independence, as the project of the nation had largely been confined to small
groups of African politicians and intellectuals, usually benefitting from
European-colonial education. In doing so, the secular, despotic, and bureaucratic colonial state became the father of its postcolonial successor.
Nationalists necessarily had accepted "as the unit of self-determination
the colonial territory" (Young 1988: 33). They reinterpreted the colonial
state as a nation-state, and postcolonial politics eventually adopted the
homogenizing claims of the European concept of the nation (Osterhammel 2009: 76–77). Thus, although the model of nation- and state-building
was borrowed from Europe, it was often realized in ways quite different
from it. Accordingly, many postcolonial African nation-states attempted
to nationally integrate their ethnically and culturally diverse societies,
contributing to the reshaping of identities. This task, in fact, had been
initiated by the colonial state after achieving territorial integration in the
early twentieth century. Hence, colonialism paved the way for this process by influencing, manipulating, and shaping ethnic identities (Ranger
1993: 63). Since the nation was supposed to be composed of an integrated
people from a nationalist perspective, those individuals "who are to be
unified or integrated are required to submit to a particular normative order" (Asad 2006: 496). Apart from integrating techniques, which the state
can apply in the form of disciplinary acts, the postcolonial nation-state has
the ability to weld ethnic options rigidly "on to the state structure and its
formal procedures" (Elwert 2002: 40).

To summarize, creole identity and creoles played significant roles in
postcolonial nation- and state-building processes. In a number of countries,
as members of the middle class, they prominently figured in nationalist
movements calling for independence, thus advocating political activism
and national ideologies that stressed national unity without rejecting eth-

nic diversity. Nationalist movements employed the image of a population victimized under colonialism and combined it with millenarian anticolonialism, thus creating a basis for mass-mobilization and ensuring national cohesion. Already on the eve of decolonization, nationalist movements had started to employ certain cultural features that not only served to connect to the masses but also transcended ethnic diversity. The independent African nation-state managed to create a national culture (see also Knörr 2010a). In doing so it continued to discipline its population in order to form a governable nation, thus resuming a practice that had already been initiated by the colonial state.

Creole Contributions to Nation-Building

At an early stage in the history of Guinea-Bissau, from the sixteenth century onward, the creole population in the *praças* (literally "[market] square," meaning the colonial, nominally Portuguese but creole-dominated commercial trading posts; the term refers nowadays to town centers) had indigenized to a sufficient degree to distinguish themselves from both the colonial rulers and the inhabitants in the countryside; they styled themselves as the de facto masters of the *praças* and, later on, of Guinea-Bissau. Although constituting only a tiny minority of the country's total population, they followed the example of American creoles and advocated independence. What Bissau-Guinean creoles had in common with American creoles is the fact that they were born in the colonies and often opposed colonial rule. However, since Bissau-Guinean creoles are also connected to the European legacy (cf. Anderson 1999: 47–65), they have been influenced by European models of nation- and statehood: as shown before, the general idea and ideology of a people forming a nation and living in a nation-state has been borrowed from Europe. However, the case of Guinea-Bissau differs from European examples like Germany or Italy, where nation-building preceded, at least to some degree, state-building. Instead, in Guinea-Bissau, the nation could only be constructed from both above and below after independence—mainly on the basis of anticolonialism and discourses of shared suffering as well as local values and forms of sociability (such as *manjuandadis* and the carnival).

One of the first demonstrations of creole unity against colonial rule was the dismissal of the colonial administrator and appointment of his immediate replacement by an elected board of creole traders in Cacheu, which occurred as early as 1684–85 (Brooks 2003: 148–50). Long periods of the eighteenth and nineteenth centuries were characterized by the virtual absence of any effective Portuguese rule in the colony and repeated creole rebellions and insurgencies (see Pélissier 1989; Mendy 1994; Soares 2000; Cabral 2002: 171). This may have fueled ambitions among parts of the creole population to aspire to economic and political independence (Cardoso 2002: 13). The colony's creole interim governor, Honório Pereira Barreto, drafted in 1843 a vehement critique of the Portuguese administration's negligent governance and the increasing French influence (Pereira Barreto 1843; cf. Ribeiro 1986; 1993: 289–90; cf. Arassi Taveira 1989). The cession of the Casamance to France in 1888 evoked severe criticism of the colonial authorities from several of the urban creole inhabitants. Numerous Bissau-Guineans, among them many of creole ancestry, stress even today that Kriol continues to be spoken in Ziguinchor, the main city of the Senegalese Casamance that used to be part of Portuguese Guinea. In particular, those creoles and other Bissau-Guineans who are influenced by colonial ideology still emphasize the historical significance of creole presence in the former *praça* of Ziguinchor, ascribing the Senegalese city a special significance with regard to Bissau-Guinean history. In this manner, they construct both creole and Bissau-Guinean identity against the background of the loss of Portuguese Bissau-Guinean territory to (French) Senegal.

From 1911 onward until its militarily enforced dissolution in 1915, the Liga Guineense (Guinean League) actively advocated the social, political, and economic interests of urban middle-class Cape Verdean and Kriston traders (Mendy 1994: 329–43). The year 1912 had marked the end of the alliance between the Portuguese and the Kriston; in 1915 the Kriston became the targets of the Portuguese and their new Muslim allies' pacification campaign. As early as the beginning of the 1890s, Kriston commercial control had started to erode (Havik 2011: 212–23), signaling the political, economic, and cultural sidelining of creoles in the course of Portugal's increasingly successful colonization efforts. Some scholars regard the Liga Guineense as Guinea-Bissau's first (proto-)nationalist movement because of its demand for a nationalized and "lusophonized" commercial setup and its call for administrative transparency and good governance (Cunningham 1980; Pirio 1983; Pélissier 1989: 295–302; Mendy 1994: 329–39; Havik 1995–99: 120–25). In contrast, Wilson Trajano Filho points out that the affiliations of the Liga protagonists were quite ambiguous: their identification with Guinea(-Bissau) was both encompassed and opposed by their Portuguese identity (Trajano Filho 1998: 309–11). In the late second decade of the twentieth century, the Partido Caboverdiano (Cape Verdean Party) opposed Portuguese occupation and aimed at the creation of a constitutional, Liberian-style republic; members of this party included Cape Verdean as well as Kriston residents (Bowman 1986: 476–77). From 1920 onward, Marcus Garvey's Universal Negro Improvement Association

(UNIA) became active in several *praças*. It had a predominantly Pan-African orientation and included many former leaders of the Liga Guineense. The colonial government labeled it an independence movement and therefore banned the organization in 1922 (Cunningham 1980: 41–42; Pirio 1983: 16–17). The so-called Revolução Triunfante (Victorious Revolution) of 1931—a military revolt against the New State regime that caused the temporary dismissal of leading colonial representatives—was supported by leading Cape Verdean and Kriston residents (Montenegro 1993; Matos e Lemos 1995: 308, 311, 313, 316, 326, 341–42).

A new batch of clandestine, illegal nationalist movements emerged after World War II. The emergence of these movements can be also attributed to a general dissatisfaction among the "more developed natives, principally in Bissau" (Silva Cunha 1959: 67; my own translation) with the social situation, as a report found in the late 1950s. Most of these movements were short lived and formed by the fusion and fission of other movements (for an overview, see Chilcote 1972: xxxvi, 603–7; Dhada 1993: passim; Duarte Silva 1997: 28–34; 2010: 81, 86–87, 91–100; Pereira 2003: 80–88, 113–26). Some movements, like some precursors to the later victorious independence movement PAIGC, were directly related to the Liga Guineense (Dhada 1993: 212, 216). "Civilized" Cape Verdean and Kriston clerks and low-level officials (excluding the administrators, who sided with the state) figured prominently in political groups that, since the 1950s, began to agitate against the suppressive character of Portuguese colonialism and the rampant economic, infrastructural, and educational underdevelopment in the country. Recent historical evidences suggest that the agency of the Cape Verdeans—who were popularly identified with the colonial state but were at the same time regarded with suspicion by the Portuguese—has been overestimated (Keese 2007: 502–6, 510–1). Their nationalist engagement "was a result of their education, professional skills, and links to international movements" (Keese 2007: 503); hence, it was a result of their special and privileged status in society, not of their identity. I will return to this question.

By and large, the prevailing competing political currents in the 1950s and 1960s were divided into the following factions: first, pro-Portugal versus pro-independence (i.e., the local branch of the Portuguese, quasi-single-party União Nacional [National Union)] and state-supported creole-led factions such as the Union des Ressortissants de la Guinée Portugaise [URGP, Union of Citizens of Portuguese Guinea], also known as União dos Nacionais da Guiné Portuguesa [UNGP, Union of Nationals of Portuguese Guinea], which favored home rule against independence movements like the PAIGC) (see Braga da Cruz 1988: 155–78; Dhada 1993:

131, 215–18; Havik 1995–96: 129–30; Gonzaga Ferreira 1998; cf. Duarte Silva 2010: 81–122; Amado 2011: 153–95); second, bi-nationalism versus mono-nationalism (i.e., bi-nationalist movements like the PAIGC that aimed at a single state comprising the insular Cape Verde and mainland Guinea-Bissau—because many of the PAIGC leaders were Bissau-Guinean Cape Verdeans and Guinea-Bissau had been an administrative subunit of the colony of Cape Verde until 1879—against groups such as the Frente da Luta pela Independência Nacional da Guiné-Bissau [FLING, Front for the National Independence Struggle of Guinea-Bissau] and its predecessor Movimento de Libertação da Guiné [MLG, Movement for the Liberation of Guinea(Bissau)], which advocated a mono-national state consisting solely of Guinea-Bissau) (for more information on FLING, see Chilcote 1972: 346–49, 603–4; J. C. Mendes 2007; on the PAIGC, see Cabral 1976: 126–29); and third, negotiation versus bellicose struggle (although individual organizations, like the URGP/UNGP, attempted to negotiate with Portuguese dictator António de Oliveira Salazar in order to obtain provincial autonomy, most nationalist movements, like PAIGC and FLING, opted for armed struggle to obtain independence) (Chilcote 1972: 606–7; Dhada 1993: 131, 215–18). These divisions indicate that creoles in Guinea-Bissau (like creole groups elsewhere) were diversified within and did not act as a single political group.

The PAIGC eventually got the upper hand and emerged victorious from the war of independence (1963–74) (see Rudebeck 1974), which can be regarded as a French-style or revolutionary approach to the foundation of a nation-state. The movement owed its success to its charismatic leader Amílcar Cabral, a Guinea-Bissau-born Cape Verdean. Amílcar Cabral stood out because of his effective and strategic political self-marketing and leadership qualities (see Chilcote 1972: xlii–xlv). In contrast to African leaders like Ahmed Sékou Touré, Kwame Nkrumah, or Samora Machel, Amílcar Cabral did not aim at the erasure of ethnic identities in favor of a new national identity, although his approach appears to be contradictory at times. Though Amílcar Cabral was convinced that the era of ethnic groups in Africa was over ("o tempo de tribos em África já passou," or, in English, "the time of tribes in Africa has passed") (Cabral 1976: 143), he did not consider ethnicity as a problem, per se, but believed that it could become one if it was exploited by self-interested, "detribalized" opportunists. He urged Bissau-Guineans to unite: "We, Balanta, Pepel, Mandingo, sons of Cape Verdeans, etc., we can be united, advancing together" (Cabral 1976: 145; my own translation; cf. however Cabral 1976: 128).

By referring to different "natural" ethnic groups, Amílcar Cabral revealed that ethnic heterogeneity did not stand in the way of national unity. He was apparently confident that ethnic feelings would vanish as soon as the new nation-state was established. It appears, therefore, that Amílcar Cabral supported a "unity in diversity" model of the nation: according to Cabral, national culture (patriotism, development, humanism, solidarity, etc.) would then coexist with popular culture, which embraces indigenous cultural traits. According to Cabral, however, the former was not a synthesis of the latter (Cabral 1976: 232–33; cf. Mendy 2006: 14; Wick 2006: 55–59). In other words, Cabral's writings suggest that he actually advocated a process of cultural pidginization, or national transethnicization. His tacit paternalistic and elitist spirit shone through when he demanded nonviolent combat against negative and harmful cultural African practices such as the belief in "magic." Following the modernist zeitgeist, he was convinced that culture had to be developed (Cabral 1976: 140–42; cf. Wick 2006: 54–58). With regard to the new nation that had to be built, Amílcar Cabral was quite ambiguous and imprecise in his writings: in some places, he would mention the "people of Cape Verde and Guinea[-Bissau]," while he would refer some lines later to the "people of Cape Verde" (Cabral 1976; 1977: passim; cf. Pereira 2003: 103–4). Against the prevailing colonial ideology, however, Amílcar Cabral regarded himself and Cape Verdeans as Africans (Mendy 2006: 14–15, 18; Cabral once declared, "Sou um simples Africano," or, "I am a simple African"; see Caldeira 2001). In this manner, he emphasized the equality of the inhabitants of both Guinea-Bissau and Cape Verde.

Similar to Cabral, many Bissau-Guineans, including creoles who had been classified as Portuguese citizens, felt marginalized and alienated by the Portuguese and therefore turned away from European culture, which was by then regarded as the most superior culture within colonial society. These disgruntled groups, therefore, sought to revive their African roots. Within this process of identitarian redefinition, they ended up shaping a "hitherto non-existent national identity" (Cabral 1976: 145; my own translation; cf., however, Cabral 1976: 128).

The early postcolonial nation-state was built from a party (see Lopes 1987b: 69, 72): the victorious PAIGC conferred its own structures, including those developed to administer areas previously liberated from colonial rule, to the territory of the entire state. Hence, a left-wing, autocratic, centralized one-party state was subsequently established (see Forrest 1993). Mass organizations such as the previously mentioned UDEMU (União Democrática das Mulheres da Guiné, Democratic Women's Union of Guinea) and JAAC (Juventude Africana Amílcar Cabral, African Amílcar Cabral Youth) were responsible for mobilizing the population. The transformation of postindependent society was characterized by political surveillance and tight control over the domestic sphere, economic planning that involved a closing off of the economy to the outside world, an expanded state bureaucracy, and the exclusion and elimination of political dissenters (cf. Forrest 1992: 47–55; 1993; Mendy 1996: 36–37). Since media, schools, and mass organizations, especially in urban contexts, were controlled by the state, Bissau-Guineans were strongly influenced by the state ideology, which, in turn, was mostly founded on Amílcar Cabral's ideals. After independence, when the Portuguese officials left the country, their positions in public administration were most often taken over by Cape Verdean and Kriston bureaucrats who had previously been in subordinate positions. While the top elites (military and political leaders) were replaced, there were hardly any changes within the middle strata of the state bureaucracy, at least until the introduction of multiparty democracy in the early 1990s (Lopes 1987b: 69, 85–90; Cardoso 2002: 17–18, 20, 25; Schiefer 2002: 153–59).

The narrative of the struggle for independence was henceforth monopolized by the PAIGC, sidelining previously competing visions of nation- and statehood, as for instance advocated by FLING. The struggle for national liberation consequently became the founding myth of the new state, because it had also welded people together across ethnic boundaries and generated solidarity. Carlos Lopes stated, "The national liberation movement achieved an outstanding mixing of inter-ethnic groups. During the armed struggle the different ethnic groups shared a common cause. They interacted. They believed in the same watchwords. They discovered collective purposes" (Lopes 1987b: 43).

Ever since independence, Bissau-Guineans have proudly referred to the victorious war that liberated Guinea-Bissau, turning the colony into "Portugal's Vietnam" (Duarte Silva 1997: 167). Meanwhile, the ongoing war waged against Portugal even caused the overthrow of the Portuguese dictatorship in April 1974. Thereafter, the war served as a positive example of national unity.

After independence, it became a normative taboo to speak about "tribes," owing to the fear of fostering divisions along the lines of "tribalism." On the contrary, national development was intended to benefit all people, regardless of their ethnic affiliation (Ribeiro 1994/95: 3; cf. Idahosa 2002: 35, 50–51). Against the background of this hegemonic "national-unity-in-ethnic-diversity" discourse, ethnic identities were considered to be of subordinate importance. In the 1970s, for example, a former senior PAIGC politician remembered that ethnicity was relegated to the cultural sphere: "The question of national identity dominated completely the debates or reflections of the Guineans to the extent that the pulsation of ethnicities … remained relegated to a … simply or substantially cultural, not really political, field" (Delfim da Silva 2003: 152; my own translation; cf. also Dumas Teixeira 2008: 76).

The leadership of the PAIGC was dominated by middle-class individuals of urban origin, the colonial local elite (Lopes 1987b: 90)—many of them were creoles. Some of them, like Amílcar Cabral, were influenced by the originally European idea of nation- and statehood. In conjunction with European Marxist anti-imperialism, this ideology promised liberation from colonial domination, subjugation, and exploitation. While constructing a postindependence state, leading party officials reverted to originally creole cultural features, such as Kriol, *manjuandadis,* and carnival, which—through a process of cultural transethnicization, as I will describe—subsequently spread all over Guinea-Bissau. Despite announcing their intention of constructing an entirely new and better society, the creole party leaders did not succeed in shaking off the past in a double sense: on the one hand, they continued to stick to aspects of their creole heritage by employing them for the cultural harmonization of the new nation, and on the other hand, they relied on a social and state order that often paralleled structures cultivated by the fascist colonial state, as evinced by practices such as authoritarian repression, political monopoly, and mass-movementism that were employed by the ruling party. While both the nation and the state were considerably conceptualized and constructed by creoles, it is the state that has been characterized by "crisis and decline: that is, of political, institutional, economic, and even identificatory deterioration" (Vigh 2006: 144) for numerous years. By contrast, Bissau-Guineans are strongly committed to their nation—and to the Bissau-Guinean state ("state-idea," Abrams 1988: 82). Thus, even though they are profoundly dissatisfied with state functioning and performance (concrete state practices, structures, governance, or "state-system," Abrams 1988: 82), they are proud of their nation. In other words, even if the state is not "delivering" as expected by its citizens and has been repeatedly labeled with ahistorical, atheoretical, state-centric, and validity-lacking attributes such as "weak," "failed," and "fragile" (cf. Trajano Filho 2005: 99; 2006b; Huria 2008; Boege et al. 2009: 17; Bethke 2012; cf. Kode 2013) mostly from media, development, and political analysis circles, Bissau-Guineans' identification with the nation is very expressed. This national imagination from below is also very much driven by the disempowered, poor, and disadvantaged majority of the country's population. This majority raises its voice in the "parliaments of the poor," as Henrik Vigh has described them. The term describes a loose social space that is based on friendship, solidarity, and mutual cooperation. The parliaments of the poor are characterized not by political action but by routinized irony, which emphasizes the political and social marginalization of the disadvantaged and excluded participants (Vigh 2006: 146–48). Bissau-Guineans of any age use this social space of the parliaments of the poor, as do people elsewhere, to vent their anger at the socioeconomic challenges, blaming the government for bad governance, incompetence, and corruption. At the same time, they portray themselves as defenseless, powerless, and helpless victims in the face of an ignorant, egoistic, and inscrutable state apparatus that has been eaten away by clientelism and personal interests.

Although the introduction of the multiparty system and the rise of polarizing politicians like Kumba Yalá in the mid-1990s led to attempts by politicians to exploit ethnicity, the interethnic consensus remains dominant among the majority of the Bissau-Guinean population. This is also because the narrative of the (creole-led) successful struggle for independence continues to ensure interethnic unity (cf. Dumas Teixeira 2008: 76).

Apart from these primarily politically motivated contributions to postcolonial nation- and statehood by individuals of creole ancestry, Kriston have also contributed to the construction of postcolonial nationhood in various respects, although on a more symbolic level. Many individuals of Kriston origin think of themselves as a superior category of Bissau-Guinean. Some explicitly mentioned that they were mixed in cultural as well as ethnic terms, often rejecting any particular ethnic connection. They consider themselves superior to other Bissau-Guineans who belong to "ordinary" ethnic identities, partly because of the internalization of European norms and values, partly because of heterogeneous origins. On the basis of their families' extended residence in the *praças* and their heterogeneous ancestry, many individuals of Kriston origin became indigenized to such a degree that they regard themselves as the founders and landlords of the former trading posts and, consequentially, as the precursors to Bissau-Guinean nationhood. It is true that Kriston have had some impact on postcolonial nationhood, for some of their own ethnic markers eventually turned into nationally unifying representations. The process of indigenization, as part of cultural creolization, had resulted in a close attachment between creoles and the trade settlements. Subsequently, these individuals dissociated themselves from their heterogeneous ancestral backgrounds (cf. Knörr 2007: 58–59).

This self-identification is most prominently expressed in Guinea-Bissau by a number of weakly ethnicized creole informants' frequent self-assessment as *guineense*—a term that alludes to their often highly heterogeneous ethnic and geographic origins. In this connection, they occasionally stressed that they had European, Levantine (Lebanese), Cape Verdean, and African ancestors. Because of this heterogeneous ancestry, several of my interviewees stated that they were unable to assign themselves to an "ordinary" ethnic group. Some informants and their families who had been substantially influenced by colonial ideology even explicitly demonstrated their sense of sociocultural superiority as *guineense* by deliberately drawing communal boundaries to differentiate themselves from the inhabitants of the *mato* (bush) who belonged to different ethnic groups.

In any case, these individuals analytically contradict the officially fostered unity in diversity model. This model, which was apparently also favored by Amílcar Cabral, rests on the assumption that nationhood encompasses various ethnic identities, and Bissau-Guineans have often referred to this model in order to explain the interrelation between ethnic and national identities in Guinea-Bissau. The Bissau-Guinean case illustrates, moreover, that ethnic identities are not necessarily subnational identities (cf. Knörr 2007: 59–61), if we imagine the various ethnic groups as branches of a tree trunk that symbolizes the nation. On the contrary, the creole identity is able to transcend these supposedly fixed and clearly delineated boundaries, thus giving rise to an amalgamation of ethnic and national identity. As shown, creoles tend to distance themselves from the other, "ordinary" ethnic identities, while positioning themselves above the latter. When asked about their ethnic identity, *guineenses* either entirely rejected tribalism or were convinced that they could not be classified under an "ordinary" ethnic group. Allusions to their diverse ancestry thus demonstrate how creoles in general—whether overtly or covertly—regard themselves as microcosms of postcolonial nationhood or as a nation "in small." The example of the transethnic Kriston category shows how diverse ethnic identities can be transcended by a shared ethnic marker and how a continuous process of cultural creolization can eventually result in an ethnic identity. This applies not only to the Kriston de Geba, who believe that their present-day identities have emerged from a sea of different ethnic identities that have, in turn, originated from various geographical locations, but also to weakly ethnicized creoles who, while identifying with an "ordinary" ethnic group, often also assert their heterogeneous ethnic ancestry.

With regard to the interrelation between ethnic and national identities, the Bissau-Guinean Cape Verdeans seem to occupy a special position. In contemporary Guinea-Bissau, most Cape Verdeans regard themselves—and are also regarded by third parties—as one of many ethnic groups existing under the umbrella of the Bissau-Guinean nation (e.g. interviews DuN, IM, and FN; MCF; MM). However, some conclude that they were different from other, "ordinary," "native" ethnic groups in Guinea-Bissau in the sense that they possessed heterogeneous origins (interview JJSDS). In contrast to other Bissau-Guinean citizens (including individuals of Kriston origin and non-creoles) who hold foreign passports (mostly Portuguese), those Bissau-Guinean Cape Verdeans who hold Cape Verdean as well as Bissau-Guinean citizenship are sometimes accused of having conflicting loyalties and of exploiting opportunities. Given the political and economic hardships that have been prevailing in Guinea-Bissau for more than three decades, some Cape Verdeans living in Guinea-Bissau yearn for a better life in the islands. In their case, it is possible for them to migrate to Cape Verde by making use of their ancestral origins—an opportunity for which they are envied by others. Some Bissau-Guinean Cape Verdeans feel uneasy about their Bissau-Guinean nationality. Although the majority of them were born in Guinea-Bissau and even though most of them have never been to Cape Verde personally, they tend to idealize their ancestral home country. Pointing to Cape Verde's reportedly higher standards of living, economic performance, and political stability, Bissau-Guinean Cape Verdeans portray Cape Verde as a role model for Guinea-Bissau and express regret at the fact that the PAIGC's original vision of unity between the two countries could not be realized. Indeed, Cape Verde has attracted for many years mainland African labor migrants, among them many Bissau-Guineans (Marcelino 2016). Nevertheless, Bissau-Guinean Cape Verdeans share with other Bissau-Guineans a sense of pride in the country's independence, achieved by means of a victorious armed struggle that saw the participation of a significant number of Bissau-Guinean Cape Verdeans.

As regards Kriston culture, the former *praça* of Geba likewise indicates creole impacts on postcolonial nation-building. In Geba, Catholicism serves as an important ethnic marker among the Kriston. The inhabitants of Geba proudly referred to the big stone church located in Geba's old, abandoned center as the first one ever constructed in Guinea-Bissau. Other Christians, however, believe that Guinea-Bissau's oldest chapel is situated in Cacheu. Although smaller than Geba's contemporary church, Cacheu's chapel dates back at least to the late eighteenth century (cf. Dias Vicente 1993: 101, 106–7, 128). In fact, creoles as well as representatives of other ethnic groups in Guinea-Bissau underline the crucial role of Geba (interviews AuF; FVS) and Cacheu (interviews AJPB) as the locations that housed Guinea-Bissau's first church or chapel, respectively. That way, they evoke a sense of pride in the historical significance and antiquity of these former centers of Christian-creole culture, thus constructing a common, historically rooted Bissau-Guinean "we-sentiment." In doing so, they conceptualize Guinea-Bissau as an autonomous territory and country, rooted in a time when its borders had not yet been demarcated and neither modern state structures nor a modern nation existed.

Diverse and ambiguous religious beliefs have not prevented a strong nation-building in Guinea-Bissau. This is also due to creole culture and its Christian traditions that have played a crucial role for postcolonial nation-building. For centuries, Christianity was the dominant religion in the *praças*, thus constituting the most important reference point for creoles, who continue to regard themselves as the firstcomers and landlords of the former trading posts. The positive correlation between Christian religion and urban life is tangible to this day in the capital. As I have already mentioned, many Bissau-Guineans of creole and even non-creole, non-Christian ancestry proudly allude to Geba's church or Cacheu's chapel, which they consider to be the country's first. Until independence, moreover, Catholicism was openly promoted by the colonial state.

Even today, Christianity in Guinea-Bissau, in fact, encompasses Islam. Hence, Islam and Christianity are not equal players in opposition to each other—on the contrary, the relationship between the two religions is hierarchical. In the words of French anthropologist Louis Dumont, this "hierarchical opposition" can be characterized as the "encompassing of the contrary" (Dumont 1986: 224), a feature that has seemingly emerged from the crucial role played by creole culture in Guinea-Bissau. This is reflected in the creole lingua franca, which was originally spoken exclusively in the trade settlements. The Portuguese and Kriol terms *igreja* (church) and *capela* (chapel) refer not only to Christian churches or chapels, respectively, but also to Muslim mosques. In their conversations with me, both Muslims and Christians often referred to mosques as *"igrejas (muçulmanas)"* (literally, "Muslim churches") or to smaller buildings, as *"capelas (muçulmanas)"* (Muslim chapels). Conversely, during my fieldwork, I never encountered any Bissau-Guinean referring to Christian churches as Christian mosques.

The integrative effects of creole culture and identity are also expressed by the fact that Muslims and Christians live together peacefully at the community level (for prior assessments, see Travassos Valdez 1864: 362 or Marques Geraldes 1887: 476), sometimes even seeking spiritual advice and protection at the same sacred site. This is, for example, the case in the village of Geba, once a major Portuguese trading post and crucible of creole culture and identity. There exists the *Stalero di Geba* (literally, "Shipyard of Geba"), the name relating to Geba's former importance as a river port at the head of navigation, possibly associated with precolonial trade networks (cf. Brooks 1993b: 91). The shrine is located close to the settlement, in a forest surrounding the Geba River (see map 2.2). The site consists of a small stone circle[1] that bears two graves—one of which is reportedly the grave of a Muslim scholar. There is a holy well situated near this site, approximately three hundred-thirty feet (one hundred meters) to the east of the stone circle. People following different religions pray at the site: "You only have to trust in the site's force," I was told (IDC, DDSR, and MS; cf. Kohl 2009b: 83–85).

Despite the fact that Muslims outnumber the Christian population in contemporary Guinea-Bissau—according to current estimates—Christianity continues to occupy the dominant position in terms of language as well as popular perception, thus encompassing Islam. At the same time, Guinea-Bissau's national ideology calls for national unity in ethnic and religious diversity. Yet, this is another indication of the way in which creole culture, which became prominent in the *praças* due to its reference to Christianity, has left its cultural imprint on postindependence Guinea-Bissau.

In addition to this religious feature, the Bissau-Guinean and Cape Verdean creoles—and among them the ancestors of the Kriston de Geba—have served as commercial intermediaries and political gray eminences in Guinea-Bissau's former trade settlements for centuries, thus laying the economic foundation of the colony. In the cultural sphere, creoles have contributed the Kriol language and several other cultural features to the cultural repertoire of postcolonial nationhood. Taking into account these economic, religious, and cultural features, they often proudly refer to Geba—and creoles from other regions as well as many other Bissau-Guineans agree with this description—as the "first capital of Guinea[-Bissau]" (*primeira capital da Guiné*). As the representatives of all other people of Kriston ancestry, the Kriston de Geba were from their viewpoint, so to speak, the first, precursory Bissau-Guinean nationals, long before independence was achieved and the new postindependent nation founded. While Kriston de Geba (like other people of Kriston ancestry) express pride in their ancestors' historical achievements and thereby stress their creole identity, their commitment to the nation is supported by Guinea-Bissau's aforementioned efficient state ideology, which appeals to national integration and unity in the face of ethnic diversity.

The Nation, Ethnic Fragmentations, and the Cape Verdean Issue

Few scholars have held the view that a Bissau-Guinean nation would not exist for long—"we cannot speak of a Guinean nation " (Conceição das Neves Silva 2002: 121; my own translation)—while pointing to the high degree of ethnic and religious heterogeneity that prevails in Guinea-Bissau (cf. Lyon 1980: 165–66; Ostheimer 2001) to explain the supposed lack of national identity. The picture depicted is that of a highly fragmented society that was labeled as a "black Babel" (*Babel Negra*) as early as in the 1930s (Landerset Simões 1935). For years, some minoritarian, not well-informed circles in academia, the media, political analysis, and development cooperation (see, e.g., Conceição das Neves Silva 2002: 121; Voz di Paz 2010; Araoye 2014: 163–64; de Vlaminck 2015) have emphasized the risk of an "ethnic conflict" in Guinea-Bissau, reinforcing the picture of an ethnically divided country unable to achieve national unity.

However, even the Military Conflict of 1998–99 (van der Drift 2000; Rudebeck 2001; Vieira Có 2001; Rodrigues Zeverino 2005) can be regarded as an example of how a heterogeneous population can close ranks together in the face of alien intruders who are collectively perceived as enemies of the nation, thus also illustrating the success of creole-led nation-building.

On 7 June 1998, former general chief of staff Ansumane Mané launched a coup d'état against the democratically elected government headed by state president "Nino" Vieira. Vieira called for military assistance from the governments of Senegal and Guinea-Conakry. Estimates suggest that approximately five hundred Guinean and fifteen hundred Senegalese soldiers were involved in the fighting in Guinea-Bissau (Rodrigues Zeverino 2005: 83; Trajano Filho 2007: 376). For the *junta militar* (military junta) formed by Mané, many independence war veterans and young Balanta men from the countryside fought alongside Casamance rebel fighters from neighboring Senegal who had joined the junta (Vigh 2006: 70). The conflict lasted until 11 May 1999.

The majority of Guinea-Bissau's population sided with the junta because the foreign troops called by Vieira were largely considered to be invaders, and were therefore treated as a threat to independent nationhood. Hostility toward Guinea and Senegal has also been nourished by widespread oral narratives circulating among Bissau-Guineans that both countries planned to divide the supposedly rich Guinea-Bissau between themselves (cf. Henri Labéry in Chilcote 1972: 314; Davidson 1981: 62; Keese 2003: 119). The fact that France openly supported the Vieira faction, in line with their geopolitical interests, not only increased the Bissau-Guineans' resentment against France (cf. Rodrigues Zeverino 2005: 104–5) but also reinforced the citizens' impression that foreign countries posed a threat to Bissau-Guinean independence and nationhood. Vice versa, Bissau-Guinean solidarity across religious and ethnic boundaries was intensified by the fact that Bissau residents who succeeded in fleeing from the combat operations in the war zone met with a high level of interethnic solidarity from their fellow citizens in the countryside.

Another important factor that contributes to interethnic integration in Guinea-Bissau is a collective self-victimization as a nation, stemming from the widespread and generalized dissatisfaction with the state apparatus. Thus, national cohesion is achieved by Bissau-Guineans' collective discursive self-assessment as innocent victims of an incompetent, corrupt, and anonymous state apparatus. In short, Bissau-Guineans tend to portray themselves as a "solidarity community of victims" (Kohl and Schroven 2014). Wilson Trajano Filho has described this way of representing the nation as the "ethos of *koitadesa*," referring to Bissau-Guineans as a nation of "*koitadis*" (Trajano Filho 2002: 154–57). The Kriol term *koitadesa*, derived from Portuguese, means "poverty," "infelicity," and "misery" (cf. Scantam-burlo 2002: 313), thus depicting a mode of life in resignation, deprivation, and suffering (Trajano Filho 2002: 155–56). Both colonial and postcolonial political authoritarianism as well as socioeconomic grievances (such as limited employment opportunities, reduced earning power, lack of infra-structure, and omnipresent corrupt practices) have led Bissau-Guineans to believe that they are "faced by a system in which they feel they cannot succeed, but must participate in and thus perpetuate in order to survive" (Pink 2001: 112). As early as during the liberation struggle, the PAIGC had portrayed the Bissau-Guinean nation-to-be as a suffering collectivity that was contained, exploited, and oppressed by Portuguese colonialism, hoping to mobilize and win the people's support for their strategic as well as utopian goals, that is, national independence, unity, prosperity, and welfare. However, the independent country's dependent rentier economy (see Schiefer 2002) and strategies of extraversion (Bayart 2012: xii) have resulted in a "mentality of dependence" (Acção para o Desenvolvimento 1993: 41; my own translation). This implies that many people "think that their things are of less worth" (Portuguese cultural affairs coordinator quoted in Figeira 2013: 245).

As a consequence of these experiences and developments, people suf-fer not only physically and materially but also mentally due to structures that, the people believe, they are powerless to influence. This explains why Bissau-Guineans nostalgically and melancholically look back in search of a reputedly better past. The fatalist discourse of the Bissau-Guineans is commonly represented by frequent sayings such as *"djitu ka tem"* (there is no last resource), *"n'sufri"* (I suffer) (see also Trajano Filho 2002: 155; Barros and Lima 2012: 111), and *"koitadi"* (poor blighter). The victim-ization—or sacralization—of the nation consists of two components, representing external and internal dimensions respectively. On the one hand, a mechanism that vaguely resembles balanced antagonism pro-vides for the construction and maintenance of a social boundary, at-tempting to unite the nation across ethnic and religious cleavages and positioning it against a generalized, collective other. On the other hand, the exploitation of the feeling of distress tries to ensure that the nation is portrayed as a collectivized victim suffering from socioeconomic crises and hardships.

The Bissau-Guinean *koitadesa* discourse also incorporates the national metanarrative of the successful and glorious war for independence. A crucial aspect in this regard was played by Amílcar Cabral. In various conversations, it occurred to me that Bissau-Guineans were waiting for a redeemer, regarding the charismatic Cabral postmortem as a "mes-senger of truth" (Barros and Lima 2012: 99, 111). From observations and conversations during my fieldwork, I realized that, in retrospect, many Bissau-Guineans regard Amílcar Cabral as a martyr who would have ensured not only the nation's redemption from the burden of colonialism but also its salvation from postcolonial distress—if he had not been assassinated shortly before independence in 1973. He was a charismatic personality who unveiled a utopian strategy to redeem, while his ascribed ethical rigorism conceded him superiority over his peers (cf. Mühlmann 1964: 251–60, 318, 397). As a strong, charismatic leader, he could produce a formidable sense of national cohesion, clearing the way for a narrative that developed into a crucial component of Guinea-Bissau's national history (cf. generally Berger 2008: 9). Hence, many Bissau-Guineans I conversed with held the opinion that only an incorrect and incomplete implementation of Cabral's utopian ideology—aimed at overcoming exploitation and suppression—as well as the renouncing of his ethical rigorism resulted in Guinea-Bissau's political and economic decay after independence.

The widespread popular appreciation of Amílcar Cabral is all the more remarkable because he was a creole of Cape Verdean ancestry, born in the Bissau-Guinean town of Bafatá. He thus belonged to the small but influential creole minority whose members were regarded by many Bissau-Guineans as henchmen of Portuguese colonialism. However, Cabral—as Cape Verdean—was not related to any of the various "ordinary" ethnic groups in the country. The minority status of Bissau-Guinean Cape Verdeans may have fostered Amílcar Cabral's perception as a nonaligned political leader who did not act on the basis of ethnicity and thus would not have favored any one of the "ordinary" ethnic groups.

However, there exist ethnic fragmentations in Guinea-Bissau that can be analyzed based on the concepts of "moral ethnicity" and "political tribalism" (Lonsdale 1996, Berman 1998: 324–30). As discussed, moral ethnicity can be understood as a vertical moral-economic behavior pattern among politico-economic patrons and clients on an ethnic basis, whereas "political tribalism" refers to horizontal competitions between different ethnic patron-client networks (Berman 1998: 324–30, 338–39). Politicians in Guinea-Bissau attempt to exploit ethnic ties in power games, seeking to ensure their own and their respective networks' access to power and resources while eliminating rival politicians and parties. In this attempt, the network leaders are under pressure from their clients. Henrik Vigh has pointed out how clientelist networks in Guinea-Bissau generally depend on access to power and resources. This access is very important in a country that is—in contrast to Europe, for example—marked by the possibility of comparatively rapid upward and downward mobility. This does not mean, however, that social positions are subject to constant change in Guinea-Bissau, where "many cultural and social understandings and practices are relatively enduring" (Vigh 2006: 145). Hence, according to Henrik Vigh, if a

> network is disempowered, as a result of elections, conflict, or war, the result is radical social change that affects the entire network. A small minority within the "declassed" network will most probably have secured themselves a relatively strong economic foundation, yet for most the resources gained will already have been redistributed, through social and political networks, meaning that political changes entail entire networks and societal groups becoming without means, losing positions and possibilities that dramatically affect their everyday existence. (Vigh 2006: 145)

In the process of empowering their networks, ethnopolitical entrepreneurs try to reify and exploit ethnic identities. If they succeed, their attempts result in the political fiction of a unified ethnic group (Brubaker 2004b: 37). In Guinea-Bissau, for example, former president Kumba Yalá was repeatedly accused of manipulating and exploiting ethnic ties in order to garner votes and support. To this end, as part of his populist style, Yalá employed symbols and rhetoric that were well received by Balanta.

The flip side of such a strategy of ethnic mobilization consists of negative ethnic campaigning. During the presidential election process of 2005, for instance, according to numerous Bissau-Guineans I informally talked to, João Bernardo "Nino" Vieira attempted to fuel fears of his Muslim rival candidate Malam Bacai Sanhá's coming to power, warning the people to resist an impending Islamization of Guinea-Bissau. Indeed, Vieira was able to win a clear majority of votes in areas characterized by non-Muslim populations, such as Biombo (as *tchon de Pepel*, or "land of the Pepel ethnic group," often regarded as Vieira's stronghold; *tchon* is derived from the Portuguese *chão*, meaning "land" or "soil") and Bolama (see the results in Vaz and Rotzoll 2005: 540). Beforehand, during the Military Conflict of 1998–99, Vieira was said to have recruited predominantly young men from "his" Pepel ethnic group to form the Aguenta militia (Vigh 2006: 54). Simultaneously, Vieira and his network attempted to represent Malam Bacai Sanhá as a Mandingo even though Sanhá regarded himself a Beafada. This was part of a deliberate strategy to discredit Malam Bacai Sanhá in the eyes of the Fula voters, since many Bissau-Guineans think of Fula as historical slaves to the Mandingo.

Despite these attempts of electoral mobilization on ethnic grounds, the peaceful conviviality of Bissau-Guineans has not (yet?) been affected. This is because, as Marina Termudo argues, politicians in Guinea-Bissau have so far failed to instrumentalize ethnicity, as part of their moral ethnic strategies, to such an extent as to result in political tribalism (Temudo 2008: 260). This means that horizontal competitions of various extensive ethnic networks—which may cause third parties to believe that ethnic groups form a unified monolithic bloc—have not yet come into existence in Guinea-Bissau. Termudo has analyzed the case of the Balanta ethnic group. During the rule of the late state president Kumba Yalá from 2000 to 2003, observers detected a distinct *balantização* (balantization) of Bissau-Guinean politics (cf. Costa Dias 2000; Ostheimer 2001: 6; Nóbrega 2003b: 293; Magalhães Ferreira 2004: 48). So far, however, Yalá and the Partido da Renovação Social (PRS, Party for Social Renewal) have failed to exploit ethnicity as part of a moral ethnic strategy that was intended to result in political tribalism. The interethnic conviviality, mutual relations and exchange, and the Bissau-Guineans' commitment to nationhood still seem to be strong enough to prevent such an instrumentalization at large. Temudo points out that this is also because the Bissau-Guinean political leaders who attempt to establish a patron-client network based on moral ethnicity are, in fact, dependent on their actual clients, thus reversing the patron-client model and its underlying urban-rural power relations. In Guinea-Bissau, politicians who want to win elections and exercise power often depend on local spirits and religious practitioners. This practice empowers the population, in turn, because they and their spirits wield the power to withdraw their support. The ethnic manipulation of Balanta by PRS elites, as Temudo argues, was effective not because of a top-down instrumentalization but due to the spiritual bottom-up attribution of power to politicians who, according to the rural dwellers, were expected to make up for the historically rooted neglect and marginalization of Balanta (Temudo 2008: 256–60).

So far, external observers are actually taken in by the leaders' groupist rhetoric while at the same time overlooking internal discrepancies or other, more complex, and sometimes cumulative (for instance, emotional, economic, value-rational, or affectional) underlying reasons. In the end, "high levels of groupness may be more the result of conflict (especially violent conflict) than its underlying cause" (Brubaker 2004b: 45). In other words, the mere existence of ethnic diversity does not automatically lead to violent conflicts.

As regards Guinea-Bissau, so far there is limited support for ethnic groupist rhetoric, and no political party has presented itself overtly as an "ethnic organization" (Temudo 2008: 260). Further, even though the majority of Balanta voted for Kumba Yalá, it is unlikely that they voted unanimously for him. Moreover, election results suggest that Yalá gained major support from Muslim voters in the runoff election of 2000, even in the stronghold of his rival Malam Bacai Sanhá (Rudebeck 2001: 71; Nóbrega 2003a: 71). In addition, when it came to the 2005 presidential runoff election, Malam Bacai Sanhá and "Nino" Vieira ran neck and neck in the eastern region of Gabú, an area wherein the majority of inhabitants are Fula (see Vaz and Rotzoll 2005: 540), thus proving that Vieira's strategy was least successful. In other words, the application of an ethnic arithmetic is not (yet) feasible in the case of Guinea-Bissau because politicians have not yet managed to create a system that can be termed "political tribalism." One reason for this is that national cohesion and interethnic cooperation are very pronounced in Bissau-Guinean society.

One alleged example for "political tribalism" and the use of "groupist rhethoric" that I would like to present in greater detail here is the creole Cape Verdean community in Guinea-Bissau. By some authors (e.g. Araoye 2014: 163–64) it has been portrayed as a prime case of a deeply rooted ethnic division that has supposedly menaced national integration in Guinea-Bissau. Historically, Cape Verdeans dominated public services and trade in the region from the nineteenth century onward (Havik 2004: 353). From the 1920s to the 1950s, the Portuguese increasingly sent Cape Verdeans to Guinea-Bissau and other Portuguese colonies. This was because they possessed relative education advantages (cf. Pereira 2003: 32, 89) over most other Africans in Portugal's colonies. In colonial Guinea-Bissau, they worked mainly in the public service, trade, and agriculture. As "non-Africans," they were supposed to contribute to Portugal's colonial "civilizing mission" (Forrest 1992: 21; Vale de Almeida 2007: 124). Cape Verdeans used their "civilized" status (both in legal terms and in terms of socially ascribed and self-imagined cultural superiority) "to their advantage in order to integrate themselves into the expanding colonial administration" (Havik 2007a: 64; cf. also Forrest 1992: 22). Because of their privileged, often superior status in twentieth-century colonial society, Cape Verdeans evoked much resentment among Bissau-Guineans (Forrest 1992: 38). Due to intensified racism and racial segregation after 1900, Cape Verdeans' separation from other Bissau-Guineans intensified—a process that continued until the outbreak of the war of independence in the 1960s (Havik 2004: 354).

As early as 1959, a Portuguese report pointed to tensions between Bissau-Guinean Cape Verdeans and the remaining population of the colony: "An exception to the cordiality in the cohabitation is manifested in the distrust and some hidden hostility toward the Cape Verdeans, be it from the Whites or the natives" (Silva Cunha 1959: 67; my own translation). Yet, the report added, "None of these phenomenons, however, has yet any crucial importance that would affect the social situation in the province" (Silva Cunha 1959: 67; my own translation).

Although most Cape Verdean civilians as well as the administrators employed by the colonial state in Guinea-Bissau remained loyal, the Portuguese attempted to exploit anti–Cape Verdean feelings during the war of independence that started in 1963. This was because many Cape Verdean clerks and low-level officials figured among the ranks of the leading independence movement PAIGC (Dhada 1998: 586, 589; Keese 2007: 503, 505–6). The Portuguese launched campaigns to foster and use anti–Cape Verdean feelings for their political purposes, dividing the independence movement and alienating the Bissau-Guinean population from the nationalists' agenda (Chabal 2002: 134; Dhada 1998: 586, 589; Keese 2007: 503, 505–6). The Portuguese propaganda tapped anti–Cape Verdean feelings that were widespread among Guinea-Bissau's indigenous population. Irrespective of Cape Verdeans' emphasis of their sociocultural distinctiveness (see below), this was allegedly also due to the fact that many intermediate colonial administrators were Cape Verdeans, who were therefore often regarded as allies of the colonizers (Forrest 1992: 38; Keese 2007: 502). In pursuing this strategy, the Portuguese reinforced or even coined a negative stereotype of the Cape Verdeans, thus trying to code the ongoing conflict as "ethnic." Beyond the political sphere, however, it was not clear "that there was much resentment against Cape Verdeans in Guinea as a whole.... To say that there was a traditional antagonism between Guineans and Cape Verdeans in Guinea is to fly in the face of the historical evidence. There simply is no record of this issue until the Portuguese propaganda campaign of the late sixties" (Chabal 2002: 138, 139–40).

Many Bissau-Guinean Cape Verdeans tended to distinguish themselves from the autochthonous population because they perceived themselves as more "civilized" than the indigenous population. This distinction existed in varying degrees, for Cape Verdeans both in Guinea-Bissau and in the archipelago have been characterized by heterogeneity, ranging from an intellectual elite to the skilled middle classes to illiterate masses (scholarly literature mainly focuses on the Cape Verdean intellectual elite; for example, see Fernandes 2002; 2006; Brito-Semedo 2006; or Batalha 2007). The distinction thus apparently turned out to be more pronounced among the Bissau-Guinean Cape Verdeans of higher socioeconomic status. Those who held this view of cultural superiority were encouraged by Portuguese colonial ideology as well as by the prevalence of Cape Verdean intellectuals.

> It is certain that there was already great internal resentment over the predominant role of Cape Verdeans within the national liberation movement. Cabral and most of the other top leaders had been culturally and educationally immersed in the Europeanized context of Cape Verde's elite society, and these leaders were viewed as essentially Cape Verdean and European-oriented in their personal behavior and parlance—qualities that made some Guineans very suspicious. (Forrest 1992: 38)

Upon the rise of nationalism in Guinea-Bissau, several divisions among nationalists became apparent. A crucial one concerned the question of whether Guinea-Bissau and Cape Verde should form one state together once independence was achieved or if Guinea-Bissau should go its own way. Here, anti–Cape Verdean feelings played a role, as PAIGC rivals like François Mendy and members of other clandestine parties that opted for a "mono-national" solution criticized the Cape Verdean–dominated PAIGC for its "binationalist" project. François Mendy denounced Amílcar Cabral as a Cape Verdean perpetrator and accused Cape Verdeans of intending to merely replace Portuguese colonialists upon independence. However, the question remains to which degree Bissau-Guineans were opposed to all Cape Verdeans in general settling in the country's territory—taking into account widespread beliefs of cultural superiority among Cape Verdeans that may foster resilience among other Bissau-Guineans. Or were such sentiments merely directed at political protagonists, put forward by parties that did not have many followers inside Guinea-Bissau (Chabal 2002: 138)? And to which extent could accusations of a "Cape Verdean conspiracy" be taken at face value? Are such statements rather expressions of interpersonal animosities and/or cheap political propaganda? Hence, were the rivals of the PAIGC against Cape Verdeans in general or against the "bi-national" project and their social and professional status in society? As a matter of fact, recent historical evidences by Alexander Keese, who analyzed Portuguese archive material from between 1955 and 1965, suggest that the agency of Cape Verdeans—who were popularly identified with the colonial state but were at the same time regarded with suspicion by the Portuguese—in the anticolonial struggle has been overestimated (Keese 2007: 502–6, 510–11). While affirming that anti–Cape Verdean sentiments among various social layers in Bissau-Guinean society existed (Keese 2007: 502), he concluded that Bissau-Guinean Cape Verdeans' nationalist engagement "was a result of their education, professional skills, and links to international movements" (Keese 2007: 503).

Aristides Pereira was a high-ranking PAIGC politician of the first hour and first Cape Verdean state president after independence. Born in the archipelago, he had labor-migrated to Guinea-Bissau where he became involved in political activities. He recalled that after the outbreak of the independence war the anger of Bissau-Guineans against Cape Verdeans was a localized phenomenon among those originating from Bissau, people who were striving for recognition. He concluded that among "the people from the countryside there weren't any problems at all. In the assassination of Cabral one can see that only people from the city, the so-called calcinhas [literally: "shorts," i.e. those urbanites who wore shorts, in contrast to the rural population], were involved" (Aristides Pereira quoted in Lopes 2002: 210; my own translation).

The PAIGC, in turn, whose armed struggle for independence the colonial state attempted to undermine by exploiting and fostering ethnic or "racial" resentments against the allegedly overarching role of Cape Verdeans among its ranks, had to undertake great efforts to restrain and suppress internal divisions among its ranks caused by the anti–Cape Verdean propaganda, as Aristides Pereira remembered. Another party member recalled the "openly hostile ambiance against the Cape Verdeans" in 1972 (Lopes 2002: 209). In that respect the PAIGC members apparently rejected Patrick Chabal's argument that there was little evidence that the "alleged division between Cape Verdeans and Bissau-Guineans was a politically salient issue in the party" (Chabal 2002: 140). Some sources indicate that Amílcar Cabral's assassins—they shot the PAIGC leader in January 1973 in front of the PAIGC headquarters in the Guinean capital Conakry (cf. Amado 2011: 322–37; Soares Sousa 2012: 505–23)—were reportedly discontent party members who had denounced Cabral as a "Cape Verdean." Prior to this incident, tensions between leading Bissau-Guinean and Cape Verdean PAIGC officials had risen at this time, following Aristides Pereira (Pereira 2003: 226–27). At first glance, Cabral's murderer, Inocêncio Kani, reportedly of Manjaco descent and a "fierce Anti-Cape Verdean" who intended, together with other conspirators, to overthrow the "pro-binationalist PAIGC leadership" (Dhada 1993: 46–47; Castanheira 1998: 118), seems to support very well the hypothesis of an assassination on ethnic grounds. However, Inocêncio Kani had previously been dismissed as commander of the movement's small navy for pocketing money from selling of PAIGC's transportation equipment (Dhada 1993: 34, 95; cf. also Amado 2011: 333) and therefore had also been expelled from PAIGC's supreme body Comité Executivo da Luta (Executive Committee of the Struggle) for misconduct in 1971 (Chabal 2002: 134–45; Galli and Jones 1987: 70; Lopes 2002: 202). Yet we do know very little about Kani's motivation to importune and finally kill Cabral. Was it due to his supposed anti–Cape Verdean attitude? Or was it instead because of hatred against political leaders, who he believed had offended his honor when degrading him in order to undermine his lucrative illicit dealings? Possibly, Inocêncio Kani was even lured by Portugal's secret police (Dhada 1993: 48). Patrick Chabal noted that the Cape Verdean issue was no decisive factor for Amílcar Cabral's assassination: "None was known to have expressed concern over the issue prior to his [Kani's] conviction . . . Their [i.e. Kani's and his co-conspirators] declared hostility to the Cape Verdean leadership thus appears as a justification rather than a motive for their action" (Chabal 2002: 140).

This argument is in line with Rogers Brubaker's deliberations on ethnic coding biases. According to him, nowadays we are "no longer blind to ethnicity" but rather "blinded by it," overestimating ethnicity as the root cause for all kinds of conflict and violence (Brubaker 2004a: 93). Guinea-Bissau's first government after independence was headed by Luís

Cabral, Amílcar Cabral's half-brother who was also a Bissau-Guinean Cape Verdean born in Guinea-Bissau. The country's first constitution provided for the equality of both Bissau-Guineans and Cape Verdeans (§20 of the Constitution of 24 September 1973, in Godinho Gomes 2010: 372). (Illegal) opposition parties—the PAIGC was the only legally recognized party—like the União Patriótica Anti-Colonialista da Guiné-Bissau (UPANG, Patriotic Anti-Colonialist Union of Guinea-Bissau) strongly criticized the "Cape Verdean neo-colonialism" and the "dictatorial imposition of the unity of Guinea[-Bissau] and the Cape Verdean islands" in 1976. While Cape Verdeans served in the Bissau-Guinean government, no Bissau-Guineans were entrusted with prominent public functions in the archipelago (Semedo 2011: 106–8; my own translation).

Luís Cabral and his government were ousted in a coup on 14 November 1980 in the so-called Movimento Reajustador (Readjustment Movement). The new head of state, Cabral's former prime minister Vieira, a deserving fighter from among the ranks of the ruling PAIGC and of creole origin (part Kriston de Geba and part either Kriston Pepel or Cape Verdean, according to inconclusive local narratives), claimed that while Bissau-Guineans were not against Cape Verde, Luís Cabral had not worked in the interest of Bissau-Guineans. Another leading party official reportedly condemned Cape Verdean colonialism. The putsch was perceived as racist by some external observers, including scholars (cf. Chabal 1983: 202; Lopes 2002: 641, 642). Even individuals close to the new regime opined that the "return to Africa" started at this point, and the overthrow reputedly laid the foundations for the reemergence of Bissau-Guinean nationalism (Delfim da Silva 2003: 154–55; Duarte Silva 2010: 196; cf. Lopes 1987b: 147). Although a handful of isolated brawls may have reportedly broken out in Bissau directly after the overthrow, there is little support for the assumption that anti–Cape Verdean racism was the reason for the coup (Chabal 1983: 202i; cf. interview IISDS; cf. however REMBDC; SM and IFS). On the contrary, Cape Verdeans were, as scapegoats, held responsible for creating serious scarcities of foodstuffs and political oppression, later corroborated by the uncovering of mass graves (Chabal 1983: 202; Lopes 1987b: 89–90, 133–40; Forrest 1992: 56). A contemporary witness remembered that a light-skinned, non–Cape Verdean friend was attacked in a melee (interviews SM and IFS; cf., however, JJSDS; MM). This was due to the fact that lighter-skinned people, known as *burmelhos*, have often been popularly equated with Cape Verdeans. A closer look at the incidences, however, confirms that the coup was not based on ethnic motivations. In fact, it appears that a plurality of reasons initiated the coup—for instance, the aggravating food crisis, plans for full integration with Cape Verde, and political repression were major motives that may have triggered the coup. The idea that the putsch was directed against Cape Verdeans on ethnic grounds was vehemently disavowed by a former military official who participated in the coup. Himself a Cape Verdean with close ties to the archipelago, he clarified that political and economic motives were paramount among the leaders of the coup. At the time of the interview, my informant was still convinced that the coup was necessary, given the growing political oppression and severe food shortages at the time (interview MM). The argument that the coup had been launched because of a problem with Cape Verdeans proves untenable because the state apparatus and its urban-oriented Cape Verdean bureaucracy (which had mostly taken over subordinate charges from the colonial state) changed little after the incident. "Nino" Vieira knew that he could not run the country without the Cape Verdean educated elite, and it appeared that the interests of this state bureaucracy did not coincide with the single party's rural backbone (cf. McCulloch 1983: 33–34; Chabal 1983: 203, 205). The latter segment, however, has dominated the postcolonial police force, the army, and the lower ranks within the state bureaucracy (Schiefer 2002: 156), most of them loyal to "Nino" Vieira (Duarte Silva 2010: 193). From this perspective, the putsch can be interpreted as an attempt by the rural base to acquire positions and power after Luís Cabral and his entourage had attempted to maximize their influence: "Some leaders, lacking a political clientele, used the strength of ethnic identification to create their own political base" (Lopes 1987b: 147).

By this means, political leaders were able to exploit latent anti–Cape Verdean sentiments among the population for their own power purposes after the overthrow, thus contributing another attempt at reconstructing the nation. Altogether, the "ethnic card" argument turns out to be a red herring that is used by certain politicians to disguise their and their clientele's power-hungry ambitions.

Ten years later, the Cape Verdean issue was back on the political agenda. In the early 1990s, Guinea-Bissau underwent a process of political liberalization. This resulted in the introduction of multiparty democracy, culminating in the first free general elections in 1994—a new political constitution came in effect. In the light of a possible defeat in these elections, leading politicians opted to aggressively defend their sinecures and access to posts and power by playing the ethnic card again. By subjecting their rivals to criticism amounting to character assassination, these individual power players attempted to exclude inter alia Cape Verdeans from high political offices by undermining their popularity and competence (cf. Davidson 2003: 40). Due to these intentions, the new constitution—which was enacted in 1993—stipulated that the grandparents of the state president had to have been born in Guinea-Bissau.[2] Against this background, even state president and party leader Vieira, an illegitimate child, was forced to dispel accusations that his father was not a Cape Verdean, as persisting rumors continued to assert. The constitutional provision was interpreted as the outcome of a debate concerning the exclusion of *burmelhos* from political offices by means of "othering" and "alienation" and was, at that time, tacitly directed against Bissau-Guinean Cape Verdeans and in favor of Bissau-Guineans who were *preto nok* (literally, "very black") (cf. interviews CV; DCDA; FN; IMMN; JH; JH and JFN; MCF). Ulrich Schiefer has noted that the darker Cape Verdeans often remained in office at the time, while there were attempts within the PAIGC to expel lighter-skinned *burmelhos* from the party. After the general elections, the new government— again led by Vieira and the PAIGC—apparently returned to a policy of following the national consensus (cf. Schiefer 2002: 160). The democratic metamorphosis of Guinea-Bissau in the early 1990s offered new opportunities for highly skilled and well-educated individuals, including many citizens of Cape Verdean or Kriston origin. Since the early 1990s, they have left the dominant but scarcely attractive state sector and have since taken up better-salaried positions in civil society (in nongovernmental organizations, short NGOs, and the development cooperation sector), liberal professions (as consultants and agents), or international and supranational organizations (e.g., under the United Nations system). Many former state and party employees have even founded their own local nongovernmental organizations (Gomes Viegas and Koudawo 2000: 12–13; Schiefer 2002: 189). Notably, many of the leading nongovernmental organizations at the time were run by Bissau-Guinean Cape Verdeans and other individuals of colonial "civilized" origin. Hence, the ethnopolitical debate within the political sphere was futile because many Cape Verdeans in high-ranking positions had already secured a better living outside the state apparatus. Thus, despite the exploitation of anti–Cape Verdean sentiments for political purposes, the era of Vieira, himself a creole, was characterized by new income opportunities (not only) for creoles. Nevertheless, creoles were seemingly exposed to new challenges, after the introduction of multiparty democracy in the early 1990s saw the increasing fragmentation of politics, the diversification of clientelist network systems, and the rise of new entrepreneurs and administrators (on these transformations, see Cardoso 2002: 21–23). This signaled a growing competition for creoles, including Cape Verdeans, who had to adapt and forge new alliances. The present idealization of the colonial past by some creoles, in this way, might reflect not only their ambiguous historical role as both precursors to independence and auxiliaries of Portuguese colonialism but also their latent fears of losing ground in contemporary Guinea-Bissau; hence, apart from some complaints of latent discrimination (interviews DuN, IM, and FN;

M; SM and IFS; cf., however, MCF), they often lament the way in which nation-building has occurred in their country since independence.

Since the mid-1990s, the Cape Verdean issue has seemingly lost its political significance. This might be related to the continued emigration of Bissau-Guinean Cape Verdeans. Nevertheless, ethnopolitical entrepreneurs like the late state president Kumba Yalá have continued to attempt exploiting existing reservations against *burmelhos,* demonstrating how local concepts may be adapted to serve as enemy images. During the 2012 presidential election campaign, he denounced the (eventually ousted) prime minister and rival presidential candidate Carlos Gomes Júnior, offspring of a rich, originally Bolama-based Kriston trader family. Deliberately ignoring his ties to "native" ethnic groups, Yalá obviously tried to impress his potential, lower-class electorate: "Everybody knows who Carlos Gomes Júnior is. Me, I am a Balanta, him, he is a Mandingo, and this one there, he is a Fula. . . . But him [Carlos Gomes Júnior], so, who is he? What ethnic group? What region?" (Grands Dossiers 2012; my own translation; quoted in International Crisis Group 2012: 6).

Hence, it seems that not only Cape Verdeans but also Kriston and many other non-creole Bissau-Guineans with a pronounced urban basis and elevated social status may fall in the *burmelho* category often associated exclusively with Cape Verdeans. In this way, anti–Cape Verdean sentiments were politically manipulated in the past in order to ensure power bases for individuals and their entire clientele networks. Despite these attempts, politicians were unable to create a model of negative, exclusive political tribalism directed against Cape Verdeans because, first, the state still depended on their know-how, and, second, many Cape Verdeans emigrated abroad in search of a better living or left the civil service anyway. Although it is true that Cape Verdeans were rather unpopular due to their role as the colonizers' allies, on the one hand, and often continue to be distinguished from other Bissau-Guineans in terms of their social habitus, on the other hand their mere differentness does not automatically become the reason for violent ethnic conflicts.

The case of the Cape Verdeans illustrates how political entrepreneurs rely on strategies of "political tribalism" and "moral ethnicity" (Lonsdale 1996; Berman 1998) to pursue their political and economic goals. Yet, different from other African countries, these (ethno)political entrepreneurs have—at least—not yet managed to exploit sentiments against certain ethnic groups to such an extent that quite discrete, opposing ethnopolitical factions have developed—in processes introduced as "focalization" and "transvaluation" by Stanley Tambiah—that may undermine the country's successful national integration. Conjointly they contribute to a "polarization and dichotomization of issues and partisans": More precisely and in

Tambiah's words, "By focalization I mean the process of progressive denudation of local incidents and disputes of their particulars of context and aggregating them, thereby narrowing their concrete richness. Transvaluation refers to the parallel process of assimilating particulars to a larger, collective, more enduring, and therefore less context-bound, cause or interest" (Tambiah 1990: 750).

Nonetheless, ethnopolitical entrepreneurs will continue challenging Guinea-Bissau's predominantly peaceful interethnic fabric once (pro) claimed by the PAIGC, a concept-ideology substantially based on creole transethnic, national integration.

Notes

1. The question whether this stone circle is of recent date or, in fact, a neolithic site (Brooks 1993b: 66–67) must remain open.
2. Article 63 (2) provides the following: "Citizens of Guinean origin, children of Guinean parents of origin, over 35 years of age, in the full enjoyment of their civil and political rights are eligible for the office of President of the Republic." (Ministério da Administração Interna 1995: 27; my own translation).

Chapter 2

Creole Identity in Guinea-Bissau

To better understand the nature of creole identity in Guinea-Bissau and elsewhere, its evolution and development, it is necessary to discuss theoretical aspects of processes of (cultural) creolization at the onset. Only after these theoretical foundations have been laid will I shed light on the different varieties of creole identity in Guinea-Bissau, from both historical and contemporary perspectives. Currently, three different variants of creole identity can be found at present in Guinea-Bissau, which have been ethnicized to various degrees, ranging from weakly ethnicized to strongly ethnicized identities. The different varieties of creole identity in Guinea-Bissau have in common that they refer to a specific set of ethnic markers, providing for the construction of boundaries to native ethnic groups. These markers comprise the Christian faith, the fluency in either Kriol or Portuguese, the creole families' long-time residence in the *praças*, and their historical role as political, economic, and cultural brokers. I will trace back the development of these variations to historical processes. Following this, I will examine the role of the colonial state in shaping creole identity, both in colonial and postindependence times. Evidence suggests that the colonial regime contributed at least in some degree to the transformation of creole identity in the twentieth century by means of ideology, censuses, legal classifications, and other disciplinary acts. I will accordingly discuss the transformation of creole identity from colonial to postcolonial times. Finally, I will discuss and analyze the forms through which contemporary creole identities are expressed.

Notes for this chapter begin on page 116.

Creating Something New: Cultural Creolization

Historically, the word "creole" and the notions that are etymologically related to it "have meant lots of different things at different times" (Stewart 2007: 5). Originally, "creoles" constituted those inhabitants of the former colonies in the Americas of pure European descent and born in the New World (Anderson 1999: 47). Later on, all the descendants that emerged from mixed immigrant groups (slaves and colonialists) were termed "creoles." Skin color eventually became an important distinctive feature to be designated as a "creole" (Knörr 2008: 3, 6-7). Creole phenotypical connotations have changed over time and from setting to setting (see Dominguez 1977; Gabbert 1992; Constant 1997; Cohen and Toninato 2010: 8; Corrado 2010: 108–9). A couple of ethnic groups have borne the word "creole" (or its local linguistic variants) as part of their ethnonyms since those times. However, it is analytically irrelevant whether a creole ethnic group that has been identified as such from an etic perspective bears the word "creole" (or its variations, such as *krio, crioulo, créole,* or *criollo*) as part of its ethnonym or not (Knörr 2008: 7): in many settings, creole groups do not bear "creole" or its variations as part of their ethnonyms (cf. Sundiata 1972; McGilvray 1982; Chan 1983; Ribeiro 1986: 3; Wyse 1989; Knörr 1995; 2007; 2014; Guran 1999; Britz et al. 1999; Frederiks 2002; Kohl 2009a; Schaumloeffel 2009).

Analytically, historians and social scientists frequently employ the term "creole" to denominate "mixed," "hybrid," "syncretistic," or "detribalized" ethnic identities. In this process, however, scholars deny the uniqueness of creole culture, thus reducing it to an imitation of different cultural elements from an implicit or explicit culturalist or even racist standpoint (Frederiks 2002: 227). By contrast, Jacqueline Knörr interprets cultural creolization not as a kind of cultural mixing but as a process that necessarily involves ethnicization and indigenization (Knörr 2010b: 733–34). According to her, creolization occurred especially, albeit not exclusively, in colonial societies that were characterized on the one hand by culturally and ethnically diverse immigrant groups and on the other by sharp social and racial hierarchies that prevented or restricted free upward or vertical social mobility (e.g. the relation between African slaves and European masters). Creolization is not only restricted to oppressed groups but can also occur among dominant groups (Knörr 2010b: 732). This means that although the evolution of creole languages (and, consequently, creole culture and identity) is largely unpredictable, it depends on a particular "social ecology" or environment, thus of political, social, cultural, and historical patterns as well as a pool of cultural features available to those undergoing a process of creolization (Ansaldo 2009: 11–16, 52).

In the course of creolization processes, old boundaries are dissolved and replaced with new ones. This transformation is accompanied by a recontextualization of both identity and culture. The process of ethnicization entails the emergence of a new common culture and ethnic reference out of a pool of heterogeneous cultural and ethnic ancestries. Cultural creolization, however, does not merely imply ethnicization—it is accompanied by an indigenization of the new identity. This means that the emerging groups in question gradually develop new collective identifications with their new home. In other words, they tend to identify their new setting as their homeland and perceive themselves as founders, owners, and landlords of a certain locality and develop a special relationship with that territory. This principle of precedence "ties firstcomers to latercomers to lastcomers in a chain of hierarchy" (Kopytoff 1987: 53) and provides the firstcomers with a certain legitimacy of authority.

Creole identities may also be accentuated by means of specific social habits and lifestyles that, from an emic perspective, are believed to be superior to those practiced by other ethnic identities. Gradual internal and social stratifications and subcategories emerged within creole groups wherein a certain lifestyle was portrayed as superior and served as a role model for those aiming at social advancement. In cases concerning oppressed groups, individuals and groups that wished to advance in society and/or distinguish themselves from other groups pretended to be "civilized" and therefore adopted certain "superior" sets of social values and norms. In colonial societies, for instance, those who tended to adopt these "superior" habits were often dismissively regarded as performing ridiculous mimicry by socially superior individuals and groups and remained subject to racial constraints (Wyse 1989: 46–50; Ferguson 2002: 553; Knörr 2008: 3; cf. Bernatzik 1933: 1:1). Little by little, people have integrated (without suggesting intentionality) "useful" characteristics into their cultural repertoire while dropping "incompatible" ones (Walker 2005: 192, 195). If a process of cultural creolization comes to an end, the resulting creole identity, or "creoleness" or "creole continuity" as Knörr terms it, may continue to have a highly integrative potential. However, as she explains, it "is not 'creole' that is over but creolization" (Knörr 2010b: 736). This particularity of creole identity is due to the fact that "creole groups emerged in the process of interaction and integration of different ethnic groups" (Knörr 2010b: 736). Knörr argues that creolization processes are not usually aimed at the establishment of such cultural spaces in between, as suggested by Ulf Hannerz and Thomas Hylland Eriksen, but rather at overcoming them (Knörr 2008: 4; cf. Hannerz 1992: 264–25; 1998: 67; Eriksen 1999: 15–16).

In contrast to "ordinary" ethnicity, creoleness "often characterizes comparatively 'young' ethnic groups" (Knörr 2010b: 737) that can, in the long run, transform into "ordinary" ethnic groups if creoleness loses its sociocultural significance and sense. New boundaries and a new sense of home are, in fact, likely to emerge during the processes of ethnicization and indigenization that differentiate creolization from other processes of interaction and mixture (Knörr 2008: 9; 2010b: 733). In that, Knörr suggests the possibility of varying degrees of ethnicization—or "stability" (Eriksen 2007: 173). Thus, creolization can result in the formation of an ethnic group whose boundaries are somewhat consolidated and which are recognized as such by group members and third parties. Alternatively, ethnicization can lead to the formation of weakly ethnicized categories of identification or transethnic identities. What may have started as a (relatively) open category of identification may eventually develop into a (relatively) closed (ethnic) group. After achieving a certain ethnic stability and indigeneity and once a creole group's original heterogeneity and exogenesis fall into oblivion, it may in fact become just another "normal," "established" ethnic group (Eriksen 2007: 174).

Creole identities are commonly stratified into subcategories. Knörr and Eriksen have demonstrated that creole groups, unlike "ordinary" ethnic groups, may remain fairly open for quite a while and maintain flexible boundaries to enable the integration of newcomers. Despite this openness creole identity may be well pronounced to such an extent that "creole culture is perceived as stable and fixed, although it lacks ... an illustrious past" (Eriksen 2007: 174). Nevertheless it may be "more open to new recruits than other ethnic groups" (Eriksen 2007: 174). In this case creole groups often expect the full ethnic and cultural integration of these new entrants. Rather than generating (new) in-between identities, the newcomers' original ethnic identity and their intermediary state of "in-betweenness" are likely—or at least supposed to be—replaced by the identity of the creole group. This sort of integration may be facilitated by the fact that, historically, individuals of the original ethnic groups had already been recruited into the creole group in question. This creole capacity of integration, in turn, may contribute to the forging of historical ties between specific indigenous ethnic groups and new creole groups (Knörr 2010b: 736)—as in the case of Guinea-Bissau, for example (Kohl 2009a).

Due to its specific historical origin, a creole group may revive its integrative potentials should the need arise. Depending on the social framework conditions, creole groups may either stress the ethnic dimension of their own creole identity or emphasize their connectedness with others. In ethnically heterogeneous postcolonial societies, for instance, creoleness may exert an integrative role, providing for both ethnic and transethnic identification. These options—inclusivity or exclusivity—contribute to the ambiguity of creole identities. At the same time, creole groups are often regarded as inferior given their heterogeneous origins and their lack of indigenous historicity (Knörr 2014).

To sum up, creolization involves both ethnicization and indigenization, resulting in the dissolution of old boundaries and the formation of new ones and the recontextualization and replacement of heterogeneous cultural representations by new, common, and authentic cultural features. The resulting creoleness allows for rather flexible identifications that are simultaneously ethnic and transethnic (in regard to both creole and other groups), without ruling out the possibility of the group's eventual transformation into an "ordinary" ethnic group with clearly demarcated boundaries.

Creole Plurality: Varieties of Lusocreole Identity in Guinea-Bissau

In Guinea-Bissau, we can identify at least three different ideal types of creole identity that have been constructing and maintaining their ethnic boundaries. Both ethnic self-identification and ethnic ascription are congruent among Cape Verdeans and Kriston de Geba, indicating the strong ethnicization of their creole identities. In other words, processes of cultural creolization have led to a comparatively high degree of "groupness," reflected by the creole groups' ways of speaking. By contrast, the third variant is creole categories of identification whose sense of groupness or ethnicization is relatively weak. A weak common identity is constructed by references to common ancestry, urban residence,[1] Christian beliefs, and significance in history, among others. Although much intermingling has been going on among creoles in everyday life, for analytical reasons I will study creole identitities, notably Kriston and Cape Verdeans, separately as "ideal types" (Weber 1978).

Firstly, Guinea-Bissau's Cape Verdeans possess an ethnic identity that relates to Cape Verde. This community is composed of various generations that maintain varying degrees of ties and contacts with the islands—some members of the older generations who themselves migrated from the archipelago to Guinea-Bissau in colonial times continue to keep in touch with their families in the archipelago. Therefore, a number of individuals continue to shuttle between the two countries, while a few Cape Verdeans who were residing and doing business in Guinea-Bissau informed me that eventually, after retirement, they wished to relocate to the archipelago. In contrast, many individuals whose families have been residing on the continent for a couple of generations were born in Guinea-Bissau and consequently no longer retain any kind of familial ties with the archipelago.

Historically, Cape Verdean identity evolved through a process of cultural creolization. Shortly after its discovery in 1455, the archipelago saw the arrival of the first slaves from the African continent. Cape Verde rapidly turned into a plantation society and a hub of the slave trade between the African coastline, Europe, and the Americas. Thus, apart from Portuguese officials, clergymen, and traders, there were increasing numbers of slave residents originating from the African continent in Cape Verde. The relationship with mainland Africa, however, was not one-sided: the so-called *lançados* (envoys) were sent as trading agents from Cape Verde to the Guinean coast. These agents developed contacts with the local population, both commercially and socioculturally, and thus acted as cultural brokers. This pattern of close political, military, economic, and cultural connection between coastal Guinea-Bissau and Cape Verde has continued to exist until the twentieth century (Meintel 1984: 31–53; cf. Mark: 2002: 13–32; Nafafé 2007a: 133–54; 2007b).

The roots of Cape Verdean identity can be traced back to the first half of the seventeenth century (Green 2010: 60). Distinct cultural features, such as the creole language or Christian brotherhoods, first emerged during the sixteenth century. Since the 1880s, the Nativistas (Nativists), an intellectual and cultural movement, claimed Portuguese citizenship for the Cape Verdeans. At the same time, however, they glorified Africa and the Africans and described the archipelago as an African motherland. By contrast, the Claridade (Brightness) movement emphasized since the 1930s Cape Verdeans' miscegenation, which was regarded as an indication of the islanders' cultural Portugueseness. This meant that Claridade perceived Cape Verdeans to be closer to Europeans—who were regarded as superior to Africans—reproducing colonial racial ideology (Forrest 1992: 21; Fernandes 2002: 16, 70–80; Brito-Semedo 2006: 195–332; Vale de Almeida 2007: 124).

Historical sources suggest that in littoral Upper Guinea, ethnic boundaries between Cape Verdeans on the one hand and local creoles on the other can be traced back to the seventeenth century (Havik 2007a: 63). At that time, only Cape Verdean immigrants were generically regarded as "creoles" (Havik 2004: 88; 2007a: 52, 60). From the nineteenth century onward, Cape Verdeans dominated public services and trade in what is now known as Guinea-Bissau. There, some of them integrated into extended local (Kriston) families, using their official positions to promote private dealings (Havik 2004: 353). Educated Cape Verdeans were increasingly sent to Guinea-Bissau and other Portuguese colonies from the 1920s to the 1950s. Because of their privileged, often superior status in twentieth-century colonial society, Cape Verdeans evoked much resentment among the Bissau-Guineans (Forrest 1992: 38). Due to intensified racism and racial segregation after the turn of the century, Cape Verdean settlers were increasingly isolated and estranged from Bissau-Guinean creole communities. This distancing continued right until the outbreak of the war of independence in the 1960s (Havik 2004: 354).

A census revealed that there were 1,703 citizens of Cape Verdean origin in Guinea-Bissau in 1950; they accounted for less than 1 percent of the total population. Half of them resided in Bissau, while 12 percent resided in Bolama, the former capital (Junta de Investigações do Ultramar 1959: table 5), making the presence of Cape Verdeans a predominantly urban phenomenon. Despite their tiny numbers, the Cape Verdeans held 70–75 percent of the posts in the colonial bureaucracy in the 1950s, while also increasingly acquiring positions in the trading business (Forrest 1992: 21; Mendy 1994: 307; Havik 2004: 354). Since the late 1950s, Cape Verdeans figured prominently in independence movements—one of them being the charismatic leader of the PAIGC, Amílcar Cabral (Dhada 1993: 5–6; Keese 2007). After independence, Bissau-Guinean Cape Verdeans and other individuals who had held citizenship in colonial times formed a numerically small group of urban elite that dominated politics and state bureaucracy (Schiefer 2002: 155–56, 160).

Secondly, the Kriston de Geba (often referred to simply as "Geba" by both themselves and other Bissau-Guineans) represent another variant of creole identity. They trace their roots back to the early Kriston communities that began to emerge in a number of trading posts in littoral Upper Guinea during the sixteenth century (Teixeira da Mota 1951; Mark 1999; 2002; Silva Horta 2000, 2011; Brooks 2003). Kriston identity emerged at that time as a transethnic category. The Kriston de Geba regard the former *praça* of Geba in central Guinea-Bissau as their ancestral home, although most of them now reside either in nearby Bafatá or in Bissau.

The emergence of Kriston identity is strongly connected to the European-African colonial encounter. Since the mid-fifteenth century, European adventurers, delinquents, and merchants settled down in the littoral area. They acted as commercial middlemen between African, European, and Cape Verdean businessmen. Small and isolated Portuguese trading posts (*praças*), with maritime links between them, turned into exchange hubs for commodities and served as locations for European-African cultural encounters. Apart from Portuguese officials and militaries, Catholic clergymen established themselves in the *praças* to proselytize Africans. Often, however, the *grumetes* (literally "cabin boys") or *cristãos* were cut off from any religious assistance for longer periods of time, prompting the emergence of a "country-style" Christian faith that integrated both Catholic and local religious features (cf. Teixeira da Mota 1954: 2:117). Within these *praças,* due to much interethnic mixture and intermarriages, there emerged new cultural representations and a new common creole identity. Identity among the Kriston communities was ultimately defined by language (a Portuguese-based creole vernacular), the locally integrated version of the Catholic religion, and a distinctive architecture (rectangular houses with verandas) (Mark 1999: 174–79). Varieties of creole identity co-existed with each other: while some *praças,* such as Cacheu or Geba, were dominated by local Kriston, Bissau was hegemonized by Cape Verdeans and Portuguese (Brooks 1993a: 51–52).

Creole identity was plural, fluid, and malleable. Initially, the term *grumete,* which was used synonymously for "Kriston," "generally implied some form of servitude or labour contract with a trader household in a settlement" (Havik 2004: 130, cf. Teixeira da Mota 1954: 2:23–24). Creole culture and identity were closely associated with residence inside or close to a *praça* (Correa e Lança 1890: 48). Transethnicity was paramount, as a British traveler acknowledged: "These Christianised natives, of any tribe, are called Grumetes" (Mills 1929: 113; cf. Sociedade de Geografia de Lisboa 1939: 26). Other observers stated that "grumetes" (thus "Christianized natives," or, *christãos da praça*) were not organized into "tribes" (Rogado Quintino n.d.: 26; Senna Barcellos 1905: 348). Its female equivalent was originally *grumeta. Grumete* was rarely used after 1920 (cf. Havik 2004: 131), acquired an invective connotation, and became reserved to lower-class people (Trajano Filho 1998: 247; cf. Loff de Vasconcelos 1916: 50; cf., however, Couto 1994: 17).

In contrast, the words *tangomão* and *tungumá* denominated outcasts and renegades involved in the riverine trade who had integrated into African society. Starting from the seventeenth century, the female term was used to denote free, baptized women. Both terms were less frequently employed after the early nineteenth century and fell into disuse. In the nineteenth century, the term was initially used to refer to a freeborn woman who acted as a professional trader (Havik 2004: 54–55; on the etymology of *tangomão* and *tungumá,* see Nafafé 2007b). Around 1900, the word *tungumá* was still in use, but it was now used as the female equivalent of *grumete* (Marques de Barros 1897/1899: 272; 1902a: 278; 1902b: 180).

The expression *filhos da terra* (literally, "sons of the land") historically referred to individuals of European-African origin born in the African continent who, like the Cape Verdeans, considered themselves and were generally regarded as Portuguese. At that time, the epithet "Portuguese" was not defined by a person's place of birth or phenotypical characteristics but by sociocultural and professional characteristics (Mark 2002: 13–14; cf. Sousa Monteiro 1853: 230–31; Alkmin 1983). More generally, *filhos da terra* can also refer to first settlers who have established spiritual contracts with a certain piece of land; as such, the notion is at present frequently used particularly in rural settings and not limited to people of creole origin (cf. Lundy 2012).

Profound changes occurred by 1800 with the spread of a narrow and rigid European understanding of identity. Consequently, skin color ("white" slave traders vs. "black" slaves) came to be associated with social status (Mark 1999: 183–86).

Evidence suggests that Catholic religion had become a boundary marker by the early nineteenth century and served to distinguish Kriston (*cristãos da terra*, or "Christians of the land") from groups and individuals nominally professing Islam or local beliefs—yet, social practice has been marked by religious fusion. The Kriston began to draw more rigid boundaries around their group in this century (Mark 1999: 188–89). Simultaneously, society in the *praças* became more stratified into, first, the "dignitaries" (*notáveis*) or residents (comprising Kriston, Cape Verdeans, and the Portuguese); second, soldiers (mainly Cape Verdeans); third, the lower classes, including the baptized servile auxiliaries among the Africans (Kriston known as *grumetes*); and fourth, the slaves (Havik 2004: 53–54).

Another way for specifying creole identity has been provided by toponymical references. As in present-day Guinea-Bissau, people referred to their *tchon* where they were raised or to which they were linked by ethnic ties. To date, all ethnic groups are associated with certain *tchons* or geographical areas within Guinea-Bissau. By contrast, Kriston are indigenized to the *praças*. Identitarian references to Kriston identity often refer to these settlements, Kriston claiming, for example that they or their ancestors originated "from Farim" (*di Farim*) or that they were "sons or daughters of Bissau" (*fidjus di Bissau*).

Creoles refer to toponymical references of former *praças* by stating, for instance, that one is a *Kriston di Bolama* (Christian of Bolama). Nonetheless, if someone says that a certain person or family is *di Cacheu* (from Cacheu), without stating any ethnic affiliation, then it is most likely that the individual is from a creole family. Likewise, if a creole proudly remarks that his or her family originates from Bolama, for instance, then it is quite likely that the family is of Kriston origin. In the case of Kriston de Geba, the transethnic toponymical references have even become part of their ethnonym. In contrast to other creole individuals who continue to refer to themselves in specific situations as Kriston of various former *praças*, the Kriston de Geba identity is strongly ethnicized. This means that their ethnic ascription and self-identification are congruent and their groupness is very pronounced.

I argue that Kriston identity adopted a transethnic character (cf., however, Havik 2004: 129). It was based on the distinction between Kriston who primarily inhabited the *praças* and were (at least formally) Christianized on the one hand and non-Christian populations in the hinterland that followed non-Christian beliefs on the other. Hence, Christianity (and its local practice, cf. Pattee 1974: 61) and the Portuguese-based creole vernacular which were associated with urban settings, became a distinctive marker of creole identity. Aged creole informants (interviews GSD, HA, SG) confirmed that they too were, as Kriston, simultaneously affiliated to "ordinary" ethnic groups. Members of the upper class meanwhile apparently tended to negate any ethnic affiliation. Thus, while identifying with various ethnic groups (such as the Pepel, Manjaco, or Mancanha), creole middle- and lower-class members simultaneously identified themselves as Kriston. The Kriston category, thus, served as a kind of umbrella identity that coexisted with other terms related to creole identity (for instance, *fidju* of a *praça*, or *grumete* for lower-class individuals). This constellation of identities allowed creoles to maintain their ties with the "ordinary" ethnic groups outside the *praça*. While the latter presumably continued to ascribe to Kriston their ancestral native ethnic identity, both their creole fellows and other townspeople regarded them as Kriston. Consequently, Kriston were able to switch between identities, depending on contexts and situations. Yet, the Kriston, or *grumetes* respectively, were proud of their identity and sought to emphasize their difference from the *gentio* (literally "pagans"): "Here in Guinea, it appears to me, nobody confuses a grumete with a pagan" (Marques de Barros 1882: 723; my own translation).

Why did Kriston emphasize religion as the dominant ethnic marker for drawing their identity-determining boundaries? On the basis of historical evidence, I believe that the accentuation of certain ethnic markers was by no means accidental. The emphasis of ethnic markers can be interpreted as a response to the challenges imposed by socially embedded power structures. While it is true that the social boundaries of the past dissolved over time, while culture and identity were simultaneously reconceptualized in order to provide the Bissau-Guineans a new orientation in life, a people's self-identification as "Christians" implied a social advancement in the colonial social hierarchy. Based on this identity, individuals hoped to be socially recognized and to attain a position on par with that of the Europeans, who ranked at the top of the colonial hierarchy and were convinced of their cultural superiority and civilizing mission. Conversely, the local people met ethnocentric European expectations if they converted to Christianity and adopted European habits. In other words, the cultural adoption of models emanating from Europe was, at least to some extent, imposed on Africans—who in turn adapted to European expectations based on manifold different reasons (i.e. emotional, economic, value-rational, and affectional).

The identity policy that was enacted by the colonial state since the 1920s and intensified migration of non-creoles into towns, especially Bissau, over a number of decades, accompanied and accelerated the semantic change in the meaning of the term "Kriston." When speaking Kriol, descendants of these migrants refer to their place of birth in the same way as creoles do. Migrants and their descendants, however, continue to strongly identify themselves with their (ancestral) homes in the countryside—that is, their *tchon*—and do not relate to creole heritage, history, and ancestry. Although these migrants often regard themselves as townsfolk, they are not the firstcomers to the former *praças*. Since both ethnicization and indigenization are strictly required for creolization processes, I refer to these migrants as "urbanized newcomers." Simultaneously, since the 1960s or 1970s, at least, Christianity ceased to be the predominant feature of the few former *praças*. A person who was a Kriston (that is, a Catholic) did not necessarily have to be a creole, because the meaning of the former word had widened over the years. This was mainly due to the fact that the Catholic religion had begun to spread beyond the few former *praças*. Given the relentless missionary efforts on behalf of the Church, the inhabitants of the countryside also converted to Christianity. This way, they also became nominal Christians, but they were not creoles. Accordingly, Christianity gradually stopped being an almost exclusive marker of urban residence, that is, a marker that solely characterized European, Cape Verdean, and Kriston residents. Hence, from this perspective, the term "Kriston" partly lost its semantic status as an ethnic reference to creole identity. Merely due to specific semantic contexts, it was henceforth possible to relate the category Kriston to the creole identity by adding toponymical references (such as *Kriston di Bolama*), alluding to familial genealogies and ancestral residence in the former *praças*.

Thirdly, one variant of creole identity consists of different categories of identifications that are situated between being weakly ethnicized and being opposed to ethnic categorization. A weak, loosely connected identity is chiefly based on common ancestry, residence in the former *praças*, language and religion, and significance in history. Individuals of this variant are characterized by the fact that either they or their ancestors had been classified as citizens (as against subjects) in colonial times. While this creole identity in some cases is transethnic—in the sense that it overlies "ordinary" ethnic identities—in other cases, individuals explicitly reject being categorized as a member of an indigenous ethnic group. While many creoles of this variety trace their origin to Kriston ancestors, most are also able to refer to more recent non-creole African, European, Cape

Verdean, and Lebanese (*sirianos,* Syrians, that arrived since about 1910; Havik 2011: 216) ancestors.

Before I present contemporary ethnographic evidence on the three varieties, let me elaborate on colonial and postcolonial creole identity policies and transformations.

Counting and Classifying Creoles

Despite the existence of creoles, neither the colonial and postcolonial censuses nor the official documents of Guinea-Bissau have contained a "creole" category. What are the reasons for this omission, and how have creoles been classified in censuses? How did this practice influence, if at all, the development of creole identity? To answer these questions, let us take a look at postindependence and colonial classification practices.

The last population census in Guinea-Bissau was carried out in 2009. This census did not specifically offer creole categories, such as "Cape Verdean," "Kriston," and so on. Respondents could instead choose between several "indigenous" ethnic groups (*etnias*) (see figures 2.1–2.3) (Instituto Nacional de Estatística e Censos 1996: vol. 1, table 3.5). As per this census, Guinea-Bissau's total residential population comprised 1,442,227 (Instituto

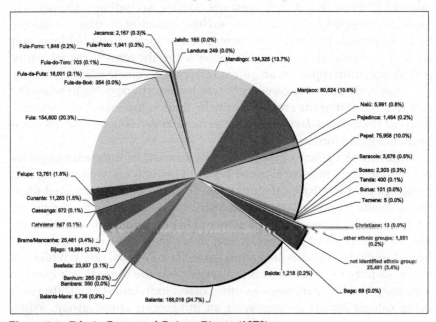

Figure 2.1. Ethnic Groups of Guinea-Bissau (1979)
Source: Departamento Central do Recenseamento (1982: 121)

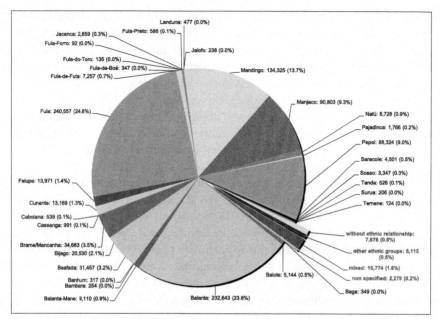

Figure 2.2. Ethnic Groups of Guinea-Bissau (1991)
Source: Instituto Nacional de Estatística e Censos (1996: vol. 1, table 3.5)

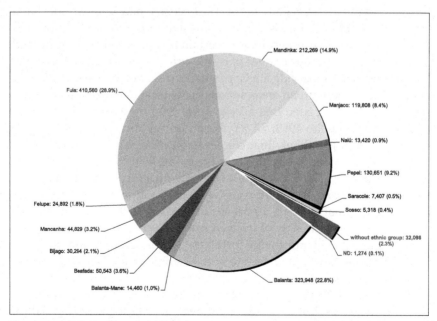

Figure 2.3. Ethnic Groups of Guinea-Bissau (2009)
Source: Instituto Nacional de Estatística (2009: 25)

Nacional de Estatística 2009: 25) compared to 979,203 individuals in 1996 (Instituto Nacional de Estatística e Censos 1996: vol. 1, table 3.1) and 760,143 in 1979 (Departamento Central do Recenseamento 1982: 121; note the contradictory figures). As in censuses conducted elsewhere, the census regulations did not permit multiple answers—a fact that limited the options of respondents who were of heterogeneous ancestry. The category of "ethnic group" was defined on essentialist, "objective" assumptions, encompassing common language, behavioral manners, shared religious institutions, clothing, and alimentary habits as well as common "cultural practices" (music, literature, arts, etc.) (Instituto Nacional de Estatística 2009: 17).

If respondents were not able or willing to identify with one of these thirty-two (1979, 1996) or thirteen (2009) ethnic groups, respectively, two residual options were offered in 2009: without ethnic group affiliation (*sem etnia*) or "*ND*" (i.e. *não definido/a,* nondefined). Similarly, the census of 1991 (figure 2.2) provided the opportunity to enroll in four residual categories, which consisted of *sem relacionamento a uma etnia* (without ethnic relationship), *outras etnias* (other ethnic groups), *mixto* (mixed), and *não especificado* (nonspecified). Presumably in many cases, creoles chose one of these residual categories. The census of 1979 (figure 2.1) contained three residuum categories: *etnia não identificada* (nonidentified ethnic group), *cristãos,* and *otros tribos* (other tribes).

Trajano Filho, with regard to the 1979 census, had pointed out that a large number of individuals who had enlisted in the *etnia não identificada* category were primarily residents of certain neighborhoods of Bissau and other former *praças,* thus cradles of creole culture and identity. According to him, the census data indicated a positive correlation between the length of presence in these urban areas as well as the level of education and literacy. Therefore, he argued that a large number of these respondents were creoles (Trajano Filho 1998: 77–78). Based on my own research, I argue, however, that it is unlikely that creoles had *exclusively* enlisted in the residual categories offered by the census (cf. implicitly Trajano Filho 1998: 75–81; Kasper 1995: 257, 307). While creoles with a highly ethnicized identity (Cape Verdeans and Kriston de Geba) might indeed have enrolled in one of the residual clusters, this does not necessarily apply to all individuals who belong to weakly ethnicized categories of creole identifications because they also identify with "ordinary" ethnic groups, and, in many cases, they may have opted for one of the "ethnic group" clusters instead of any of the residual clusters. Similar observations hold true for the most recent census of 2009—some creoles may be indeed "hidden" in the residuum categories, but evidence is ambivalent: a little more than half of those individuals counted in this way resided in Bissau. Almost 70 percent of those identified as *sem etnia* did not speak any local African language, yet a majority used Kriol as first language, followed by comparatively high percentages of command of Portuguese, French, and English (Instituto Nacional de Estatística 2009: 70, 72–73). The percentage of Muslims is particularly high among those *sem etnia* (Instituto Nacional de Estatística 2009: 31). These combined findings suggest that these categories may also, apart from creoles, include Senegalese, Guinean, Mauritanian, Lebanese, and European residents who hold Bissau-Guinean citizenship as well as Bissau-Guineans who identify with an ethnic group that was not on the census menu. Thus, also for this reason it is difficult—if not impossible—to specify the exact numbers of creoles in Guinea-Bissau.

Most categories used in postcolonial censuses date back to colonial times. The colonial state acted as an initiator of censuses and imposed legally binding ethnic classifications that became embedded in the state's ideologically framed and racially biased colonial policies. According to Michel Foucault (1995), the state sought to discipline and classify individuals in order to allocate each one of them a definite place in society. Nonetheless, it remains difficult to assess to which extent colonialism was able to shape ethnic identities. It can be expected that colonialism has left a lasting impression on ethnic identity construction, even though evidence is controversial, as I discuss later. Direct and indirect colonial impact in a sociocultural, political, and economic environment strongly influenced by European presence and interaction may explain, though, why Kriston identity could ethnicize to such a great extent in the case of Kriston de Geba while it did not in other cases. In view of the Bissau-Guinean Cape Verdeans, colonial policies also seem to be at least in part responsible for distancing them from Kriston.

By introducing both the census system and legal classifications based on demographics, the colonial state not only was able to distinguish between citizens and subjects (Kertzer and Arel 2002: 3, 8) but also attempted to impose its "totalizing classificatory grid" (Anderson 1999: 184) over the population in order to "make them governable" (Kertzer and Arel 2002: 9; cf. Eckert 2002: 25). In order to achieve this aim, the state had to classify the population under various heads. The colonial authorities developed official lists of ethnic groups living in the respective colonial territories and issued identity cards that indicated the "tribe" to which its holder belonged. In their turn, these classifications helped the individuals concerned to objectify and reify their own cultural and collective identity (cf. Kertzer and Arel 2002: 2, 5–6, 11–12, 31–32). Although references to ethnic identity were often removed from identity cards and many other official documents after independence, the classifications have nevertheless made a lasting impression on people's perception. However, the colonial state was never as omnipresent and overpowering as it was wished by agents of colonial rule and asserted by some historians. For that reason, the thesis of a purely instrumentalist imposition of state governance (and, thereby, also of identities) by means of measurements and classifications has been rejected by some historians (Cooper 2005: 143). Whereas census takings were anonymous and cursory, identity cards and other official documents imposed identity in a more forcefully sustainable way (Brubaker 2004a: 67–68). The effective territorial colonial seizure of Guinea-Bissau after 1900 was accompanied by an ambiguous, tightening, regulating grip of the colonial state and its administrative body (cf. Pélissier 1989; Bowman 1980: 161, 263–64). Colonial rule in Guinea-Bissau nonetheless remained characterized by a lack of hegemony and limited domination, hence by ambivalence (cf. Cooper 2005: 50; Stoler and Cooper 1997). Those subjected maintained open spaces, while colonizers even depended to a certain degree on those coopted (cf. Cooper 2005: 25–26). In other words, even when participating in processes of colonization, at least some Africans were always able to maintain agency or "autonomy of action" (Bayart 2012 xiv–xv; cf. Kohl 2016).

Unfortunately, we do not know much about the performative, "political" interplay between census takers and colonial officials responsible for assigning "tribal affiliations" in official documents on the one hand and respondents or citizens/subjects on the other. It remains unclear to what extent the former influence or "negotiate" the outcomes and how their counterparts reacted. It is evident and owed to the "transitory nature" of lived identity that "formal" "identity fabricated through census forms" differs (Goldberg 1997: 32). It can be assumed, though, that census results in terms of ethnic affiliation would be much different if the ethnic indication did not have to be in line with the preselected "ethnic code" list (Departamento Central de Recenseamento 1979: 7) but if respondents were able to freely "choose" their identity when interviewed, as other census examples demonstrate (Nagel 1995). All these complex issues must be borne in mind when talking about census takings and identitarian, legally binding classifications.

Early censuses in Guinea-Bissau were conducted in 1882 (Ministério das Obras Públicas, Commércio e Indústria 1884: 722; cf. Dias Vicente 1992: 103) and in 1893 (Instrucções para o Recenseamento Geral da População da Guiné Portugueza), supposedly only in the *praças*, but no data appear to be known. In addition to the *raça* ("race"), the *tribu* ("tribe") was supposed to be indicated. However, estimated data for the years 1888–89 were published (Correa e Lança 1890: 48).

Systematic attempts to record and classify colonial Guinea-Bissau's population started with the establishment of a statistical service in 1896 (Circular). However, obviously, for more than fifteen years no population counts were realized, as no data from a census announced for 1900 are known (at least without scholars being aware of it), possibly because it was never carried out (Instrucções para se Realisar o Recenseamento Geral da População da Província da Guiné). This census did not contain provisions to classify the population according to ethnic groups. This was a deviation from prevailing practices in colonial Guinea-Bissau at the time that recorded the respondents' "race" and "(skin) color" (cf. Estatística).

This example highlights the gap between colonial ambition and reality and the obsession with regulations and statistics (see Starr 1987: 52). In the beginning, the population in the *praças* was classified according to phenotypical markers (e.g. Instituto Nacional de Estatística 1900: 681). These phenotypical classifications served as social constructs—they were statistical markers as well as political instruments (Nobles 2002: 47–48, 58). Initially, there was apparently neither an attempt to classify the population according to ethnic affiliation (self-identification and/or ascription) nor the inclusion of a creole category. The first countrywide census conducted dates back to 1911 (Annex No. 1; Annex No. 2; Annex No. 3; Annex No. 4). Its fragmentary character reflects weak state penetration. Among other details, the census collected information on the population's ethnic and religious affiliations. Interestingly, the "Christians" in the countryside were regarded as an ethnic group, while "Europeans" and "Cape Verdeans" were grouped together. We also come across the category of *grumete*. This might indicate the colonial officials' uneasiness regarding how to classify creoles.

Around the same time, the colonial state started to legally classify the population. First attempts of a legal distinction between "civilized" citizens and the "indigenous" subjects date back as far as 1899 (Regulamento do Trabalho dos Indígenas; Regulamento do Trabalho das Indígenas das colónias portuguesas; Regulamento das Circunscrições Civis da Província da Guiné; Lei Orgânica de Administração Civil das Províncias Ultramarinas). However, concise definitions to distinguish the "native" subjects from the "civilized" citizens only emerged in 1917 (Carta Orgânica da Província da Guiné: §§307–8), signaling the restriction of flexible, malleable, and situational identities. The colonial state attempted to divide the population by forcibly separating individuals into certain legally binding categories. By offering the creoles—who had been recognized as citizens—further incentives for social advancement in colonial society, the state attempted to discipline and assimilate them. In this way, the government sought to perpetuate its rule. Despite some progress, the colonial state by 1920 still had not developed sufficient classificatory information to allocate every individual a legally unambiguous, binding identity (e.g., through a mention of the person's ethnic affiliation on identity cards), which might have provided the state a clear position in an increasingly hierarchically organized colonial society (i.e., for planning and allocating specific residential areas, etc.).

However, the censuses and classification efforts apparently stimulated a process that led to a crucial semantic change. In the past, the term "civilized" (*civilizado*) may had been loosely used to designate Christianized local dwellers residing primarily in the *praças*—that is, creoles. Creoles used this identity to construct a boundary between their group and the "uncivilized," "pagan" rural population. Seemingly, it became more and more difficult to equate "civilized" people with "creole" or "black" people. On the contrary, the categorization laid the foundation for associating "black" with inferiority and a "lack of civilization." It is important to note that the new legal regulations neither mentioned nor integrated creoles into their conceptualization. By contrast, the newly introduced legal categories differed from conventional classifications, such as the earlier notion of *civilizado*, which had largely equated creoles (as Christians and speakers of Portuguese or Kriol) with Europeans. A radical rupture from the past signified the rise of the autocratic New State regime in 1926, which lasted until 1974. Assimilation was made the focus of attention. Propagandistic endeavors were amplified after 1945, when Portugal's imperial concept was replaced by an ideology of national unity: the "colonies" that were re-named "provinces" were—at least officially—equated with the metropolis to justify Portugal's ongoing presence in Africa and Asia (Alexandre 1997: 83–84; cf. Moreira 1951). Originally developed by Brazilian sociologist Gilberto Freyre, the new ideology was accompanied by a new pseudoscientific doctrine that came to be known as *luso-tropicalismo* (lusotropicalism). This doctrine attributed the Portuguese with an exceptional ability to acclimatize to the tropes and socioculturally fraternize with the colonized people, thus depicting the Portuguese way of colonizing as superior. The doctrine of lusotropicalism ignored the fact that cultural reciprocity had never existed in Portugal's colonies—instead, these colonies had undergone hierarchical concurrence via assimilation, leading to the paralysis and eventual elimination of cultural miscegenation. The New State regime even invited Freyre to visit Portugal's colonies, (mis)using him in a propaganda campaign to defend Portuguese colonialism (Castelo 1999: 35–43). In fact, Portugal continued to pursue a Eurocentric and racially motivated colonial policy wherein Europeans and Cape Verdeans were believed to be superior to the native population.

The lusotropicalist propaganda in colonial Guinea-Bissau referred to the creole society of bygone times, depicting Honório Pereira Barreto, creole governor of the colony in the mid-nineteenth century, as a positive example of Portugal's civilizing mission and commitment to Portuguese values and nationhood (see Sarmento Rodrigues 1947: x–xi; Ponte 1953: 4, 16, 19; York 1959: 1–2). Lusotropicalist ideology, in this way, projected a distorted view of a deceptively peaceful and harmonious colonial society, which had never existed in reality.

On a pragmatic level, the New State regime effected the total seizure of the colony's territory along with an increasing bureaucratic state penetration and law enforcement. The state perfected its systems of classification and control of the population. The colony's inhabitants were definitely divided into citizens and subjects after 1927 ("Indigenato," or "Native Statute") (Estatuto Politico, Civil e Criminal dos Indígenas de Angola e Moçambique; Decreto 13.698; Portaria 39; cf. Diploma Legislativo 535). The assimilationist conditions to qualify for citizenship were minutely defined, down to the smallest detail. An intermediary, qualifying legal category called *assimilado* (assimilated) existed from 1930 to 1946 (Diploma Legislativo 535; Diploma Legislativo 1,364).

Both historical references and my own ethnographic data suggest, however, that the situation in real life differed considerably from the legal and political claims. This was evident in the way in which these legal classifications were decided—they were at least partly arbitrary (Mendy 1994: 309–12). Indeed, social practice must have been quite different from what legislators pretended. This may be illustrated by two ethnographic vignettes from the field. Traveling to Farim in northern Guinea-Bissau in 2006, I was addressed by a man in his mid-sixties who came along one of the streets. We started a conversation and it turned out that he was of Mandingo origin. What struck me was the fact that he bore, quite untypical for Mandingo, a Portuguese given name. He explained that he was a child to "indigenous" peasants. In Farim, a Portuguese trader became aware of him when he was a boy, the trader's attention obviously being drawn to the boy's intelligence and outstanding talent. With the consent of his parents, the Portuguese took the young boy from Farim to Bissau in order to promote his capacities. In Bissau, he was awarded citizenship and therefore could attend grammar school and join a local football club. Although a Muslim by birth, he was obliged as *civilizado* to adopt a Christian-Portuguese name, which he maintained after independence, though he added a Mandingo one (interview AFQ). This episode underlines how advancing in colonial Guinea-Bissau also depended very much on personalized relationships—underlining the heterogeneous interests of colonizers—and this made the colonial system, at least to a certain extent, more permeable.

Another informant remembered his father's experiences becoming a civilizado. According to him, "civilization" therefore had to be virtually staged, reducing colonial civilizing attempts to absurdity. Groups were summoned to a residential house in one of Bissau's neighborhoods where they, one after another, had to pass a test to prove that they maintained a cultivated, "civilized" European style of living in presence of a colonial official. Precisely, one applicant after another had to display a command of European-style table manners, demonstrating how to sit at a table and, dressed in European fashion, to prove their knowledge of using cutlery and crockery "correctly" (interview AGF). This "exam situation" exemplifies colonial ambiguity and hypocrisy, manifesting the discrepancy between social reality and ideological-legal desirability.

In total it can be noted that a social order that earnestly strove to prevent the social advancement of subjects and the fact that the "civilized" stratum never accounted for more than 3 percent of the country's total population, in fact, belied the assimilationist state ideology.

From the 1920s, merely being a follower of Christianity would not suffice for any individual to be legally recognized as a "civilized" citizen. Yet, individuals from metropolitan Portugal or the colonies where the Native Statute did not apply were granted citizenship automatically (Ferraz de Matos 2006: 63). Foreigners who also were automatically awarded the status of *civilizado* could be affiliated with non-Christian religions. Under the law, all legally "civilized" individuals (except foreigners) became Portuguese citizens. Africans who had qualified for the "civilized" status were regarded as assimilated, and, consequently, they were—at least de jure—equitably acknowledged as Portuguese citizens, independent of their phenotypical markers. This implied that the African *civilizados* would, legally, "lose" their ethnic affiliation from their identity cards and other legal documents, because they were regarded as Portuguese. In fact, this assimilationist procedure was directed against interculturalism, for it assumed the supremacy of pristine European culture (cf. Gomes 2001). The Native Statute and the resultant legal separation of "civilized" citizens from the indigenous subjects was formally abrogated in 1961, without apparently implying a substantial change (interview AB; Decreto-Lei 43,893; Bender 1978: 155; Ribeiro 1994/95: 10).

The colonial government also enacted laws with implications for non-citizens. Unlike the citizens, who held an identity card, the indigenous subjects had been obliged to carry a *guia* (pass) since 1921 (Portaria 495). This document served to control their freedom of movement. From 1925 onward, the indigenous stratum also had to carry a *caderneta indígena* (indigenous pass) that was issued for those who wanted to travel abroad. This identification paper also required the mention of their ethnic affiliation (*tribu*) (Portaria 177). Likewise, the improved *caderneta,* which served both as an identity card and as a certificate of employment for the indigenous population, contained a section for indicating the holder's "*raça ou tribu a que pertence"* (race or tribe to which she/he belongs) (Regulamento de Transito, Fixação e Deslocação dos Indígenas). Thus, whereas the identity cards of the citizens did not state any ethnic affiliation, those of the subjects mandated the mention of their respective ethnic affiliation. Only after independence, in accordance with the new, integrationist state ideology, this practice was discontinued.

The colonial endeavors were paralleled by later censuses. With regard to the "civilized" stratum, censuses usually recorded the respondents' *raça* and nationality (whether Portuguese; originating from that very colony, other colonies, or the mother country; or a foreigner), but not their ethnic affiliation. Contrariwise, the census of the indigenous stratum contained the ethnic affiliation of the respondents (1926 census: Censo da População Civilizada da Guiné; 1928 census: Carvalho 1929: 168; Duarte 1946: 72; Teixeira da Mota 1954: 2:61; Junta de Investigacoes do Ultramar 1959: 11; Província da Guiné n.d.: 16; 1940 census: Portaria 136; Junta de Investigações do Ultramar 1959: 11; Província da Guiné n.d.: 16; Serviços de Estatística n.d.: 17; 1950 census: Junta de Investigações do Ultramar 1959: 11; Província da Guiné 1961: 49; Província da Guiné n.d.; 1960 census: Província da Guiné 1978: 2, 4; Instituto Nacional de Estatística n.d.: 12; Carreira 1961a).

What were the implications of the Native Statute's introduction and its corresponding classification in censuses on creole identity?

First and foremost, the legal separation of "civilized" citizens from the "indigenous" subjects distributed the creoles into both the categories. While some creoles were henceforth classified as citizens, others belonged de jure to the indigenous stratum—the latter primarily included the majority of the Kriston de Geba. This indicates that, unlike the suppositions of certain authors, the *civilizados* were not the same as creoles (see Ribeiro 1994/95: 11). In this regard, colonial Guinea-Bissau was not different from Angola, for example, where identical (or similar) measures were taken. There, the introduction of the Native Statute and corresponding regulations has been interpreted as the "last stone in the tomb of the creole group" (Bittencourt 2000: 668), dividing, similar to the Bissau-Guinean case, Angola's creole population and adversely affecting its further social advancement and the preservation of social prestige and assets (Bittencourt 2000: 668–69).

In Guinea-Bissau, the "sustainability" of this colonial policy was limited, however. Even though many former *civilizado* families have maintained a certain habitus of social distinction from "uncivilized" (in a popular, inclusive, hence not legal sense) families, younger generations have embodied according attitudes only to a limited extent. Furthermore, the "civilized" stratum contained a significant number of individuals who were not creoles. In fact, the stratum was heterogeneously composed of metropolitan Portuguese, people originating from the colony itself (including creoles and non-creoles), those originating from other Portuguese colonies, and foreigners. A closer look at colonial demographic statistics reveals that Portugal's assimilationist and ethnocentric aim to "protect" and "civilize" the majoritarian indigenous population proved to be only lip service. Comparing the census data of 1926, 1940, and 1950—even though phenotypical assessments may be neither "objective" nor free from both deliberate and unintentional manipulation—individuals classified as "white" and "mixed" were increasingly outnumbering those who were counted as "black." This was obviously due to constant immigration from Portugal, and especially from Cape Verde. A major number of these citizens worked in the public administration (Mendy 1994: 306–8). At the same time, the number of "natives" among the "civilized" population diminished between 1926 and 1950 (Censo da População Civilizada da Guiné: 461; Junta de Investigações do Ultramar 1959: table 5). These numbers suggest a positive correlation between the indicators "black" and "native." Therefore, we can assume that the decline in the number of "black" inhabitants—in terms of both numerical and percentage basis—occurred at the cost of the long-established and somewhat culturally different Bissau-Guinean Kriston, who were increasingly outnumbered and thus marginalized constituents of the "civilized" stratum. In contrast to Cape Verdeans, who are creoles themselves, the majority of the Kriston were very likely to be classified as "black" instead of "mixed." It appears that unlike in the previous centuries, Cape Verdeans integrated to a far less extent into Kriston communities after the strengthening of the colonial rule: the "Kriston were no longer treated as legitimate go-betweens but rather depicted as Africanized actors who stood in the way of colonial modernization. Cape Verdean creoles however, used their 'civilized' status to their advantage in order to integrate themselves into the expanding colonial administration" (Havik 2007a: 64; cf. Forrest 1992: 22).

Apart from this, there were other social factors that influenced the development of creole identity. The "civilized" stratum, which never did constitute a monolithic elitist block, was subject to a gradual standardization in terms of sociocultural values. This policy was in accordance with colonial ideological considerations that regarded "white" European and Christian values and norms as paramount. These norms were regarded as teleological endpoints of social development from an evolutionist point of view. Hence, they became culturally desirable and legally essential prerequisites for gaining recognition as a citizen. Individuals who intended to advance socially, therefore, had to adopt a European lifestyle—at least "on stage"—in order to meet the prevailing sociocultural and thus legal requirements within Portugal's colonial state and society that distributed rewards to individuals and groups upon the fulfillment of specific legal and social stipulations, thus determining the social status of individuals and groups in society—it will be henceforth called "social status reward power system" (Skinner and Harrell-Bond 1977).

From this, it follows that a number of Bissau-Guinean creole lower-class citizens—like many of their "indigenous" counterparts—may have privately led a lifestyle that integrated African traditions, which were socially and legally seen as undesirable and therefore disapproved of by the Eurocentric colonial state. These individuals may have hidden behind a false front in public life, mirroring only the socially desirable behavioral patterns. Some other groups, conversely—and especially the local Bissau-Guinean upper-class creole citizens—seemed to have completely embraced European sociocultural parameters and tended to draw a deliberate boundary between themselves and the lower-class creole and non-creole citizens, on the one hand, as well as the indigenous subjects on the other. These upper-class creoles, in this way, were in the same situation as the Cape Verdeans or the Lebanese who likewise oriented themselves according to European norms and values in order to elevate their social status and differentiate themselves from the lower class and "black" individuals. For example, particularly elderly upper- and middle-class creole citizens and Cape Verdeans largely used to shun Kriston traditions (such as *manjuandadis*) because these traditions were regarded as frivolous lower- and middle-class representations and believed to be hardly consistent with dignified European culture (interviews DN; ECDC; JJSDS; LFDA; MCVE; MuJ; SaM). In other words, in order to distinguish themselves from other practitioners of the disreputable African practices, they used to draw various kinds of sociocultural boundaries between themselves and the lower classes. Accordingly, as a couple of my informants (interviews AJPB; DCDA; JH) told me, those who adopted "civilized customs" were called *brancos* (whites), independent of their phenotypical appearance (see also Teixeira da Mota 1954: 2:25; Carreira and Rogado Quintino 1964: 243). Thus, Kriston were not a homogeneous category but tended to show a pronounced internal social stratification. The logic of the colonial social status reward power system opened up the possibilities of increasing ambivalence, manipulation, transformation, and splitting of the creole identity.

Those creoles who had been categorized as indigenous subjects by the colonial state did not have a separate category in which they could count themselves in censuses and legal documents. Instead, they had to opt for one of the default "ordinary" ethnic clusters, which did not provide for any creole category. The last colonial census that offered the choice of a *cristão* category was conducted in 1940, the category only resurfacing one time in the 1979 census (Província da Guiné n.d.: 18; Departamento Central do Recenseamento 1982: 121),

The Portuguese practice of not recognizing ethnic identities among African citizens was due to the colonizer's assimilationist ideology and color-blind rhetoric. This was in stark contrast to the systematic methodology followed by the British, as their census categories were comparatively flexible. However, due to the assimilationist policies practiced by Portugal in its colonies, Africans who held citizenship were regarded as Portuguese and were therefore not allowed to indicate an ethnic group. Conversely, British census authorities required both subjects and citizens to state their ethnic affiliation—this indicates that the British appear to have been open to accepting and responding to new societal and identitarian realities. Consequently, Sierra Leonean creoles had been classified as such in official documents ever since 1908 instead of being classified under their original, ethnically diverse identities. Nonetheless, the British were sure that notions such as "creole" or its related terms served as a collective term for "detribalized, Europeanized Africans" of different origins who had developed an identitarian, cohesive feeling of togetherness (Skinner and Harrell-Bond 1977: 307–8, 314). Similar conclusions can be drawn from the British practice of population classification in the Gambia where censuses also registered creoles as a separate ethnic group (Hughes and Perfect 2006: 11–14, 20–21). Thus, whereas in both Sierra Leone and the Gambia creoles were counted and regarded as a distinct group, those in colonial Guinea-Bissau were not. They either had to legally "lose" their ethnic identity when qualifying for citizenship or "choose" to be assigned an "ordinary" ethnic identity (since there was no recognition of a separate creole identity), in which case they were categorized as subjects.

We can infer that the legal distinction between citizens and subjects and its practical implications in everyday situations was internalized by the population across generations and thereby turned into a social reality. This profound identitarian transformation is represented by the fact that older terminologies that had previously been used to designate creoles (e.g., *grumete, tangomão*) began to disappear from official documents and censuses after the 1930s. Similarly, terms like *Kriston* or *cristão* appeared to have lost much of their exclusive association with creoles by the 1960s, by which time even non-creole rural inhabitants were increasingly embracing Christianity (cf. Teixeira da Mota 1954: 2:24–25; Pattee 1974: 61). This change in parlance was obviously due to the legal classification of creole subjects in one of the officially recognized "ordinary" ethnic categories, while creole citizens were legally regarded as Portuguese nationals. The general perception and self-perception of Kriston presumably changed as a result of these developments brought about by colonialism.

Why did Portuguese authorities hesitate to recognize the existence of creole identities? The reason might be that creole identity, which could almost exclusively be found in the handful of *praças*, must have appeared as a distorted, unnatural, or false identity to the colonial administrators. As in contemporary Bissau-Guinean censuses, only those ethnic groups that could be regarded as "autochthonous" seem to have found their way into the colonial census makers' deliberations. This attitude is best expressed by the Austrian ethnographer Hugo Adolf Bernatzik. His contemporary, derogative comments on Kriston might well have been a typical refrain, reflecting the spirit of the time among the colony's tiny European elite:

> The city is inhabited by Europeans and half-civilized Negros who proudly call themselves "Christons". Often it is the vermin of the black race which foregather here and flaunt in a peculiar way European dresses of the eighties. . . . Without sufficient opportunity to earn money but still accustomed to the needs of civilization, these Negros, who lack the moral grounds of tribal belonging, become larcenous . . . but they are also dissatisfied with the result of their efforts to match the whites. . . . However, only in the towns it is this way. (Bernatzik 1933: 1:1–2; my own translation)

Only those parts of the population that resided in the countryside in their ancestral "tribes" were considered to be "genuine," whereas the urban local population was believed to be "detribalized" and culturally corrupted. Consequently, it can be assumed that creoles, who resided primarily in urban settings, were regarded as an impure in-between group, neither entirely African nor European, which unjustifiably attempted to abnegate its "true" ethnic roots. Therefore, creole subjects were not officially registered as such in the legal and census categories. Normatively, if creoles wished to be recognized as Portuguese citizens, they had to adopt a European lifestyle, after which they were regarded as having assimilated into the European culture. After lusotropicalism became the official ideology of Portuguese colonialism in the 1950s (Castelo 1999: 87–101; Vale de Almeida 2008: 7), the colonial state's focus may have shifted. This is because lusotropicalism advocated a high potential of assimilation into Portuguese culture, and the official recognition of the existence of creole identity would have disproved the state's ideology of assimilation and incorporation.

In this way, we can conclude that both the new legal categories introduced by the Portuguese colonial state in the early twentieth century and the immanent sociocultural incentives offered under the colonial state's social-status-based reward power system constituted a new social reality. Although colonialism in Guinea-Bissau was characterized by ambiguity, weakness, and an obsession with legislation, classification, and count-

ing—albeit sometimes with limited and ambivalent impact on social practice—the colonial authorities as well as census takers may have unfolded
an effect on the (re)setting of boundaries. In so doing, they may have contributed to some extent to the enduring transformation and shaping of
creole identity in Guinea-Bissau. The outcome of colonial divide-and-rule
policies was the social marginalization of Kriston and a reduction of their
political influence.

Identity Challenges at the Time of Independence

During the transition from colonial to postcolonial times, creole identity
underwent considerable changes. Focusing on the analysis of intrafamilial
and intergenerational changes in creole identity, I will describe and analyze these changes in this section. The transformations in creole identity
were apparently influenced by changes in state ideology and policy, notably the replacement of the Eurocentric lusotropicalist ideology of assimilation by an Afrocentric ideology that advocated national unity in diversity.
Indeed, confronted with colonial racism and repression, Amílcar Cabral
supported the idea of an "African" identity (Wick 2006: 50). "Africaniza-
tion," however, did not remain limited to Guinea-Bissau, Cabral, and other
Portuguese African colonies but also affected many other, newly independent African countries, such as Ghana, Guinea, or Tanzania (see Schramm
2000; Askew 2002), for example. At the same time, in the 1960s and 1970s,
developments like the civil rights movement in the United States and a
valorization and recognition of Afro-American culture and consciousness,
for instance, may have also had some effect on people in Guinea-Bissau,
particularly among upper and middle classes.

An interesting example of how identity changed in that time is provided by a long-established creole family that traces back its ancestry to
the late eighteenth century (interviews AJPB). Once native to the former
praça of Cacheu, most of the family's lineage members are currently residing in Bissau. By interviewing different generations of the same family,
I was able to trace different identitarian self-images across generations.
The head of the family, who was born in the early 1920s, belonged to the
middle class. He worked for a construction company during colonial
times; however, he later pursued a career in the public service, while also
doing business, until his retirement. When I asked him about his ethnic
identity, he replied that he was unsure: "That's a difficult question," he
sighed, while admitting that he did not know his *raça* (cf. also interview
CNDR). He based his assessment on the grounds that nobody actually
knew one's great-grandparents. Therefore, people could never be sure

about their ethnic group. When I asked the question to his son, who was born in the 1950s, he likewise confirmed that he did not know his ethnic affiliation. In contrast to these family members, the son's nephew—who was born in the early 1980s—clearly related to an ethnic group. Referring to his patrilineage, he indicated that he was a Manjaco, just like his father, his father's brother, and his father's father, who was the head of the family (interview AJPB). In this context it is important to mention that the area around Cacheu is known as *tchon di Manjaco*. Even if we argue that these individual representations resulted from on-stage inquiries, which may be subject to social desirability, they nevertheless provide an indication of the intergenerational change in identitarian self-images and, to some extent, telling about the longevity of colonial assimilationist ambitions.

As suggested by these findings, the emergence of creole categories of identification date back to the colonial period. The legal introduction and subsequent implementation of the Native Statute, which resulted in the differentiation between "civilized" citizens and indigenous subjects, in fact, at least influences this development to some degree. Because creoles of the "civilized" stratum were legally recognized as Portuguese citizens, they therefore had to comply with European, Catholic moral and value concepts—at least on the surface.

The extent to which the citizen stratum was subject to this colonial Eurocentric approach is illustrated by the following example that stresses the success of assimilationist policies and family traditions. During an interview with an upper-class woman in her sixties (interview ANE), we discussed the implicit pressure that the colonial social-status-based reward power system imposed on the citizens. My informant's Portuguese father had immigrated to the colony in the early 1920s. Little by little, he established one of colonial Guinea-Bissau's largest commercial enterprises. Since he was initially involved in trading activities in the colony's eastern regions, he became acquainted with an influential Fula clan and eventually married a young woman from this clan. Although my informant was able to speak Fula, her well-educated children were not because they were raised under the Catholic faith, spoke Portuguese and Kriol at home, and had adopted Christian names. Nevertheless, they retained strong familial relations with their Fula relatives and voiced the wish to learn Fula.

The long-term internalization of colonial ideology and social desirability was reflected in the behavior of one of my informants—a very old Kriston woman. This woman, who was almost eighty years old, had been a teacher by profession, belonged to the lower middle class, and had been classified as a citizen under the Portuguese rule. I had a conversation with her at her new home in the Tchada neighborhood, close to the capital's city center. She explained that she still performed traditional Pepel ceremonies; she had inherited this tradition from her mother, who was a Kriston Pepel from the matrilineal side, while her mother's father was of Cape Verdean origin. She stressed that she and her family had always lived in the *praça*. Although my informant performed these ceremonies, she nevertheless regarded herself as a "civilized" person. In my presence, she stressed the fact that she regularly attended mass as a devout Catholic. When she showed me the interior of her house, she claimed that she and her late husband had received good upbringing. She substantiated this statement by revealing that in her household, food was always served on the table, as in Europe—this is how she phrased it (interview MCVE). This example highlights the extent to which the values and norms that were considered desirable in colonial times are still internalized by the older generation. This is also reflected in references to urbanity, Christian faith, and European table manners, which serve to exclude the people from the countryside, who do not share these colonially fostered "civilized" manners.

Like other autocratic political systems, the New State attempted to win over the "civilized" youth by using soft coercive methods. As in Portugal, children and adolescents in colonial Guinea-Bissau were supposed to enroll themselves in the state-run mass organization Mocidade Portuguesa (Portuguese Youth), a body also marked by covert racism (cf. interview AS). As a former member recalled, during the 1960s, participation in this organization was facilitated by the fact that the organization offered uniforms, shoes, belts, socks, and shirts at a reasonable price. This particularly attracted families with low incomes. Apart from this, my informant opined, young persons were also drawn into the organization due to peer pressure, which acted as another source of coercion. Furthermore, many of them were attracted by the prospect of wearing uniforms and participating in camps. The New State and its ally, the Catholic Church, used subtle methods to influence young persons in schools to transmit their values. My informant remembered that as a young boy in the 1960s, he attended a school in Bissau as the son of a family that had been granted Portuguese citizenship. The school was run by the Church. Many of his Muslim classmates formally converted to Catholicism, although they clandestinely continued to follow Islam. One incentive for conversion was the cinema that operated within the Catholic school: tickets were available only to those who attended mass (interviews JH).

Despite these colonial attempts to exert pressure by means of the social-status-based reward power system, it remains doubtful whether Portugal was able to realize its civilizing mission without encountering resistance. Apart from a political radicalization that finally resulted in the outbreak of the war of independence in 1961, Bissau-Guineans used to hide their traditional African beliefs from the colonial authorities and the Church. The following vignette underlines the internal conflicts and lived ambiguities that Africans as "colonized subjects" underwent during colonialism. This is well reflected in the concise title of Frantz Fanon's monograph "Black Skin, White Masks." According to Fanon, colonial rule forced Africans to comply with certain colonially imposed norms on the one hand but also created a desire of being "like the white man" (Fanon 2008: 178) on the other because of his alleged superiority. An aged woman in her seventies, descendent of a Kriston Pepel family that had been classified as "civilized," still possessed a ceremonial object that she had inherited from her Pepel mother. This object was a metallic dish fixed on a pillar, which was placed in the backyard of her residence in Bissau's Chão de Pepel neighborhood. The object was supposed to provide protection against evil forces and spirits. In our discussion on the object's raison d'être, my informant confirmed that it had been in the backyard since colonial times. Moreover, she explained to me, with a smirk, that in the days gone by—as well as today—the Catholic clergy were not to be told about the existence of such objects, because they condemned such practices (interviews TL).

These examples reveal that at least some of the "civilized" Bissau-Guineans, in particular the middle and upper classes, had indeed embraced European and Christian sociocultural values and norms, for they were a necessary, socially desirable prerequisite for existing and progressing as a citizen within the New State's social status reward power system under Portugal. These individuals had accepted the new legal realities and political constellations that had been created by the colonial state and therefore presumably regarded themselves as "Portuguese" citizens. In this manner, the twentieth century saw a change in creole identity, which occurred at the expense of previous creole identifications.

Since the 1950s the new generation of Bissau-Guineans was no longer able to conceal its disaffection with the social, cultural, and political conditions and lack of personal opportunities for development in the colony. The war of independence and the formal abrogation of the Native Statute in 1961 might have affected the new generation's view of ethnic identity. These developments may have contributed to the emergence of present-day creole categories. Evidence suggests that many young Bissau-Guinean *civilizados* successively turned away from Portuguese culture. Instead, they apparently began to increasingly identify themselves as Africans and therefore showed a renewed interest in African culture. This development was accompanied and supported by the influx of large numbers of people from the countryside after independence. Many of these former liberation fighters assumed official positions in the postcolonial government and the civil services. Bissau-Guineans were also influenced by the independence movement's propaganda. This is exemplified by an account provided by an informant of heterogeneous ancestry whose parents belonged to the "civilized" stratum. Now in his fifties, my informant recalled his schooldays in the late 1960s, when he attended a secondary school reserved for citizens' children. According to him, white classmates were given preferential treatment; moreover, they were also provided material privileges. From this vantage point, his generation became acutely aware of the injustices perpetrated by the discriminating presence of the *tugas* (Portuguese) in the country. He and his other classmates used to clandestinely listen to the independence movement's Rádio Libertação (Liberation Radio) at night. The radio station aimed at the mobilization of Guinea-Bissau's population for the independence struggle. On another occasion, the same well-read informant remarked that he and his peers wore an afro hairstyle (locally called the "big boy" at that time), just like Afro-Americans, during their adolescence in the early and mid-1970s (interviews JH; cf. CR). This attempt at being fashionable can be interpreted as the younger generation's search for alternative role models in the late colonial period, directed against the prevailing Portuguese socio-cultural and political values and norms. Similarly, as several of my informants (interviews CR; DCDA) remembered, in the 1950s and 1960s, adolescents began to explore the world of African music by listening to vinyl records, which had become increasingly available in the local shops (see Kohl 2007). Consequently, people were progressively increasing their contact with African cultural elements without hiding them from the allegedly superior European culture.

At the same time, adolescents also appeared to be increasingly attracted to local African culture—owed to a multilayeredness of motivations, such as protest against colonial "civilizing" ideology, a shift toward Pan-African ideas as propagated by Cabral and other African political leaders, and an expression of a generational conflict, the younger generations seeking to define themselves in contrast to the preceding ones. This attraction is exemplified by their renewed interest in an initiation rite known as *fanadu*, a notion that actually describes a wide continuum of practices. This Kriol term stands for both the sociocultural *rite de passage* (rite of passage) between age grades or age sets, which can last for up to three months, and the actual medical intervention or circumcision. Usually, male adolescents attend these ceremonies under supervision of their elders; the rituals are conducted in secluded areas in the countryside. Many Bissau-Guineans, and particularly those from the middle and upper social classes living in urban settings for the last few decades, preferred to consult medical doctors who performed circumcisions under sanitary conditions. However, interviews with informants suggest that it became fashionable among the children of citizenship holders to undergo what they called a "traditional" *fanadu* with peers in the bush. At that time, local citizens mainly underwent circumcision in a hospital or under the care of a medical doctor—similar to children of families that today consider themselves more "modern," "advanced," and "urbanized" (cf. interviews ET; ER and JF; FE; HOS; JDSC; MuJ). One of my informants of Kriston ancestry narrated that he underwent a *fanadu* in the bush in 1970, against his family's tradition. He did so simply because he wanted to join his peers—he wanted to be one of them (interview ICDA). This desire was obviously shared by another informant who was in his forties when I interviewed him. This informant was descended from a long-established upper-class creole family. Both his father and grandfather had been involved in Bissau-Guinean nationalist movements. He recounted that his father, who was a devout Catholic, had strictly warned him against participating in what he called the "traditional" *fanadu*. When my informant, much against his father's wishes, attempted to put his plan into action by joining his peers in the *fanadu* barrack in the bush, his father "freed" him from participating in the ritual by drawing out a sporting gun (interviews CR).

These examples suggest that a growing number of Bissau-Guinean *civilizados*, especially adolescents, were attracted to African culture, which led to a transformation in their attitudes and identity. Their former identification as "Portuguese" was therefore disputed by the emphasis on African roots. Consequently, some individuals who sought to rediscover and reify their identity began to relate themselves to "ordinary" ethnic identities—a trend that continued even after independence, as I will show. Those Bissau-Guineans who continued to regard themselves as Portuguese citizens presumably switched over to the *guineense* identity after independence in 1974. In this manner, they were able to renegotiate their boundaries in accordance with the policy of the independence movement that ruled at the time and that advocated the "national unity in ethnic diversity" approach.

How things changed, and how Bissau-Guineans turned to African cultural representations as the country achieved its independence, was exemplified by a Bissau-Guinean Cape Verdean middle-class informant in his sixties. In the early 1960s he became aligned with the clandestine independence movement while he was employed in the colonial public service. Subsequently, he left Guinea-Bissau in order to join the PAIGC in Conakry, from where he was sent abroad to a foreign university for higher education. Before he had left the country in the 1960s, his parents—who had been born in Cape Verde—would have never allowed him, as an adolescent, to participate in a *fanadu* ritual in the bush. Therefore, he was shocked to discover upon his return to Guinea-Bissau in 1974 that *tocachors* were suddenly being celebrated in the capital's Chão de Pepel neighborhood, which had predominately been populated by middle-class citizens in colonial times. The *tocachor* ceremony is mainly organized among the non-Muslims in Guinea-Bissau on the occasion of someone's passing. After a certain period of time after the death, people close to the deceased person ritually slaughter goats, pigs, and cows, and the attendees often throw a raucous party at which a great deal of alcohol is generally consumed. According to my informant, this kind of celebration was unthinkable under the Portuguese rule ten years earlier. He explained that even the Pepel or Balanta who held Portuguese citizenship would never have dared to organize such ceremonies in the neighborhood during the 1950s. While the *tocachor* had only been celebrated "out there"—that is, beyond the *praça* city center gates—until independence, such ceremonies have become big festivities after 1974 (interview ER and JF).

The trend indicating an increased attraction to African cultural features is also reflected by the legal change of names that has taken place in the years following independence. In the past, colonial legislation required that in order to be recognized as a citizen, a person had to possess a Christian name; this regulation also partly applied to individuals who were classified as indigenous subjects (Portaria 39; Portaria 10). After independence, the Ministry of Justice approved, according to the law gazette (Boletim Oficial da Guiné-Bissau), the Portuguesation of at least (I do not claim to provide the complete figure) seven African surnames and/or given names. At the same time, thirty-six Portuguese surnames and/or given names were changed into local African or Muslim ones. In twenty-six other cases, no clear trend was to be found. What is most intriguing about this name change is the fact that most of the names were modified immediately after independence—that is, from 1975 onward until about 1979.

Summarizing, we can infer that a large number of people who had been previously classified as "civilized" citizens started to accept and openly emphasize their African roots in the late colonial period. This was most probably caused by their growing disaffection for the prevailing colonial social, cultural, and political marginalization—this disaffection was subsequently stirred up by the independence movement's propaganda at the beginning of the war of independence. While the identity of weakly ethnicized creoles who today identify with a native ethnic group gradually began decreolizing ("decreolized creoles")—that is, the former transethnic Kriston identity de-ethnicized to a large extent in order to accentuate the original ethnic identities—the "creolized ethnic" groups followed a different path by disclaiming any ethnic roots as they continued to adhere to the rigorous colonial identitarian reference system established by the New State in the 1920s. Following the colonial ideology, this system sought to suppress African cultural representations and identity and attempted to "civilize" the tiny number of local citizenship holders by imposing European and Christian values and norms on them. After independence, many of these former "civilized" individuals continued to emphasize their group's boundaries by referring to their urban residence and indigenization, Christian religion, and ethnic detachment. This historical framework led to the emergence of new ethnic categories that were characterized not only by plurality and incongruence but also an ethnic self-image and ethnic ascription. These developments, however, resulted less from the colonial state's direct, top-down interference. Given the particular weakness of Portuguese colonial rule, it was indirect impacts, rather—such as social, economic, and political transformations—that influenced ethnic identities.

Cape Verde in Their Hearts: Bissau-Guinean Cape Verdeans

When talking about creoles in Guinea-Bissau, attention is almost always exclusively drawn to Cape Verdeans. Who are these Bissau-Guinean Cape Verdeans and what about their ethnic identity and interethnic cohabitation in contemporary Guinea-Bissau? In discussing these issues, long-term effects of a racially biased colonial ideology and policy have to be considered. It is necessary to take a look at the ways Bissau-Guinean Cape Verdeans distance themselves from both Kriston and "ordinary" ethnic groups. Boundary drawing and its maintenance among Cape Verdeans is predominantly based on the accentuation of a specific social lifestyle, which serves as an ethnic marker for them.

Due to the postcolonial census policy, which does not provide for a "Cape Verdean" ethnic category as they were usually registered as Portuguese citizens, it is difficult to determine the exact number of Bissau-Guinean citizens identifying themselves as Cape Verdeans who are currently living in the country. My own observations during fieldwork suggest that the vast majority of individuals who regard themselves as Cape Verdeans are currently residing in Bissau. Although many of them have chosen to leave the country after independence, we can surmise that their total population does not exceed two thousand to twenty-five hundred individuals. The social, economic, and political turbulences that have shaken Guinea-Bissau since its independence have also prompted many of Guinea-Bissau's Cape Verdeans to strategically use their ties to (re)migrate to their ancestral homeland or to Portugal in search of better living conditions. In this section I will discuss the identity construction and interethnic boundary maintenance performed by these Cape Verdeans.

The fluid and manifold identities that are so common among Cape Verd-
ians in the archipelago itself are not so significant among present-day generations of Guinea-Bissau's Cape Verdeans, according to my ethnographic
findings. Instead, just like other migrant populations in similar settings,
most Cape Verdeans—and especially those who were born in Guinea-
Bissau and whose families have been residing in the country for generations—not only consider themselves but are also perceived by others as
one ethnic group that has been fully integrated into the Bissau-Guinean
nation. Although Guinea-Bissau's Cape Verdeans are aware of the fact that
their Cape Verdean identity has ethnicized against heterogeneous ethnic
backgrounds in the archipelago, virtually none of them, in fact, is able to
trace their familial lineage back to specific ancestors or ethnic groups, with
the rare exception of very few families that proudly attribute their lineage
to historically relevant characters and/or lineage founders.

How does identitarian alterity manifest itself in everyday life and how
do Bissau-Guinean Cape Verdeans define their boundaries against other
ethnic groups? Numerous Cape Verdeans are part of Guinea-Bissau's middle and upper classes (participating in its politics, bureaucracy, civil society, intelligentsia, and economy); however, they constitute a very small
proportion of the country's total population. This does not imply, though,
that all Cape Verdeans in Guinea-Bissau live in comfort. However, since
they can often profit from their colonial privileges—just like other creoles
and non-creoles who had formerly belonged to the "civilized" stratum—
these Cape Verdeans have tended to follow rent-seeking strategies after
independence: they have been renting out their own flats or houses to solvent foreigners or international organizations and have thus managed to
cement their advanced social position. This process of perpetuating their
social position has been sustained by a widespread orientation toward
education and upward mobility. After the end of the one-party state in the
early 1990s, many former leading civil servants—including a remarkably
large number of Cape Verdeans and other creoles—decided to leave their
jobs and instead work for or establish their own nongovernmental organizations, which promised better revenues (cf. Schiefer 2002: 128–29).

My findings indicate that Guinea-Bissau's Cape Verdean middle and
upper classes, in particular, have cultivated a lifestyle based on European
role models (cf. also Forrest 1992: 38). In stark contrast, Cape Verdeans
who belong to lower social classes have not been able to retain this self-
image. My Cape Verdean informants repeatedly claimed that they would
never have their meals, lunch and dinner, in the conventional local way—
the table etiquette practiced among lower- and middle-class Bissau-
Guineans consists of placing a bowl (usually containing boiled rice, which
is garnished with cooked or grilled fish) on the ground, while family

members and friends who are invited to the meal sit around the served dish. Following this, they all help themselves to the food, collectively taking it out of the bowl by hand and rarely using forks or spoons. These local table manners are quite often also practiced by the country's upper social classes—except on special occasions. Some Cape Verdeans, especially the older generations who had grown up in colonial times, proudly stated that they would take their food in the European style, which implies sitting at a table and serving the food onto individual plates (e.g. interviews JJSDS; LFDA). These European table manners are consistent with the ideology-based norms of social desirability that became legal prerequisites during colonial times. Although this self-image may correspond to reality in many cases, it is also true that a number of Guinea-Bissau Cape Verdeans—especially those who belong to the lower social classes and whose families have been residing in the country for a couple of generations—tend to have their meals country style.

Cape Verdeans seem to take a similar stand with regard to the local tradition of initiation, the *fanadu*. Most Bissau-Guinean Cape Verdeans that I talked to stated that they were against organizing *fanadu* ceremonies for their adolescents. Most of the interviewees overtly rejected this kind of *rite de passage,* claiming that a *fanadu* was an African tradition from the bush, which they would not cultivate. Instead, they stated that their boys would undergo a medical intervention, while Communion and Confirmation ceremonies in the church were their chosen cultural *rite de passage* (interviews LFDA; cf. DTN; EHN; JDSC; cf. JN). Even if these claims cannot be verified, they demonstrate how Cape Verdeans attempt to normatively distance themselves from other Bissau-Guineans. Just like the issue of table etiquette, Cape Verdeans' attitude toward initiation can be regarded as an expression of social superiority that had been shaped by colonialism.

The same can be said regarding the issue of Cape Verdean boundary maintenance in relation to the religious sphere. Bissau-Guinean Cape Verdeans have often accused other Bissau-Guineans of believing in witchcraft and magic. Some Cape Verdeans even portray the other Bissau-Guineans as being entirely guided and dominated by "superstition." While superficially adhering to the Christian faith, many Cape Verdeans argue, other Bissau-Guineans often practice witchcraft and magic and consult *djambacoss, balobeiros* (healers, magicians), or *mouros* (Muslim savants and healers) behind closed doors (interviews JJSDS; LFDA). Interestingly, this incriminatory critique is not only directed at Bissau-Guineans from the countryside but also applied to the descendants of local Kriston. Compared to the latter, Guinea-Bissau's Cape Verdeans regard themselves (in both Guinea-Bissau and the islands) as "rational" and loyal followers of Christianity, who do not have anything to do with "superstition" (cf. interview IM). This self-image construct, however, ignores the fact that a belief in witchcraft and magic has been also been part of the social reality in Cape Verde (Silva 1998). In their turn, the other Bissau-Guineans reject the Cape Verdeans' stance on superstition while accusing the latter of hypocrisy. Several of my informants (interviews FVS; cf. DuN) advanced the opinion that Cape Verdeans, in fact, intended to mislead others by stressing their own "true" religious convictions, while they were, at the same time, known to frequent fortune-tellers (known as *cartomantes*). In fact, this rumor contains more than a grain of truth: in mid-2006, I attended a small street party that had been organized by some of my neighbors and their friends, including several people of Cape Verdean ancestry. While enjoying a Cape Verdean–style *feijoada* (a stew of beans with beef and pork meat), we continued to chat cheerfully. After consuming a good deal of Portuguese red wine, the same Cape Verdeans who had previously argued against superstition admitted, in my presence, that they were afraid of the *futseiros* (from Portuguese *feiticeiros*, sorcerers)—beings that were dreaded by the majority of the country's inhabitants (interview EHN and JJSDS).

These observations can be interpreted in terms of an identitarian dispute between Cape Verdeans and the other Bissau-Guineans. Many Cape Verdeans draw a normative, idealized image of themselves, portraying themselves as "real" Christians who stand against the vast majority of Bissau-Guineans who, in their eyes, are only pretending to be Christians or Muslims. Non–Cape Verdeans, in their turn, attempt to turn the tables on the Cape Verdeans, because they do not accept the image imposed on them by the latter. By doing so, the former seek to clarify that many of the Cape Verdeans do not differ fundamentally from other Bissau-Guineans, since they also consult fortune-tellers and believe in supernatural beings. In other words, as in many other cases, there is a gap between these people's practices in daily life and their normative self-image. Narratives of ethnic self- and other-perception can be regarded as a dialogue in which identities are mutually contested and negotiated. Yet, this case illustrates how a pronounced normative self-image is used by many Cape Verdeans to delineate and maintain a strong, very emphasized boundary toward other groups. Another aspect associated with the religious sphere is represented by the *tocachor* ceremony. Cape Verdeans will participate in such events from the periphery if the ceremony is dedicated to a relative, friend, colleague, or neighbor, but they would never organize a *tocachor* on their own, as my Cape Verdean informants agreed in unison.

In contrast, Cape Verdeans are by no means the only people who reject the *tocachor* ceremonies. Based on my fieldwork, I realized that such a rejection is closely related to other indicators such as social class and geographic origin. To cite a concrete example, a *tocachor* was scheduled after the head of a close-knit family had expired. The ceremony took place over a period of three days in the deceased person's place of birth—a small village in the southern region of Tombali. The whole family took part in the *tocachor*, including one of the daughters of the deceased. She had grown up in Bissau and had received part of her education in Portugal; she held a job in the public service and was married to a Bissau-Guinean Cape Verdean, himself a lower-level employee. Though her husband did not like the idea of the ceremony at all, his wife's family, and especially those living in the village, expected him to slaughter a cow—he somehow coped with the task, albeit reluctantly. In the meantime, his wife kept complaining, off the record, about the constraints imposed by the *tocachor* procedures, the difficult living conditions in the village, and the villagers' belief in witchcraft and ancestral spirits. Both the husband and, to a lesser extent, his wife felt distinctly uncomfortable about the ceremony as well as the environment in which it was being performed—both of which were unknown and strange to them. From their perspective, the villagers as well as the ceremony seemed to be expressions of "provinciality" and "superstition" (interview DuN and IM).

Guinea-Bissau's Cape Verdeans used to keep away from Kriston cultural representations. It seemed as if following such traditions conflicted with their self-image as a European rather than an African ethnic group. Hence, they generally avoided participating in *manjuandadi* association activities run by Kriston because they were well known for their frolicking and wild partying. My informant, a Cape Verdean woman in her eighties, explained that her parents, who had migrated from Cape Verde to Guinea-Bissau after the turn of the century, had warned her and prohibited her from joining *manjuandadis* because their members were supposed to have bad and rough manners (that is, the habit of rampant boozing, singing, and partying) (interviews LFDA; cf. DN; LLDC).

All in all, Bissau-Guinean Cape Verdeans continue to be either overtly or tacitly convinced of their cultural superiority. Many acted on the assumption that they were more "civilized" than the non–Cape Verdeans. This conviction was based on diverse elements of their social habitus that served to underline their pretended cultural supremacy. This self-image has been essentially molded by colonial ideology and has been successfully perpetuated against the background of the social, economic, and political problems that Guinea-Bissau has been facing since independence. In view of this, Guinea-Bissau's Cape Verdeans tended to construct a politically stable and prosperous Cape Verde as a positive countermodel to the crises-ridden Guinea-Bissau, even though most of them have never visited the archipelago. Conversely, Cape Verde's recent success has also been noticed by many non–Cape Verdean Bissau-Guineans and has turned into an attractive emigration destination for many mainland Africans (Marcelino 2016).

The Cape Verdeans' self-distinction, as specified above, is mirrored by the way in which they are perceived by other Bissau-Guineans. Their abovementioned sociocultural distinction is recognized by their fellow citizens. My personal impression of the interethnic relations between Bissau-Guinean Cape Verdeans and non–Cape Verdeans was that they were, at the most, characterized by implicit resentment toward each other, though not by overt animosities or hostilities, mainly due to the Cape Verdeans' historical role as the New State's preferred bureaucratic middlemen and their different lifestyles. In fact, several informants (e.g. interviews DuN, IM, and FN; FN; JH; JJSDS), some of them even born after independence, praised the first postindependence government led by the Guinea-Bissau-born Cape Verdean Luís Cabral, which was staffed by a majority of Cape Verdeans, describing it as more efficient and less corrupt than most of the subsequent administrations.

Many Bissau-Guineans generally refer to Cape Verdeans as *burmelhos*—a word that literally means "red" and, juxtaposed with terms like *branco* (white), *branku fandang* (very white), *preto* (black), and *preto nok* (very black), is used in everyday life by Bissau-Guineans to loosely denote people's variation in skin color (cf. Schiefer 2002: 160; Havik 2004: 53–57). (Frequently heard expressions such as *branco pelele* and *preto mbau*, however, appear to be of recent origin and are usually playfully used by children.) The term *burmelho* is often used synonymously with "Cape Verdean," thus implying that all of them are of a lighter skin color than Africans. Analytically speaking, this correlation is untenable because a large number of Bissau-Guineans of Cape Verdean descent are dark, whereas other individuals without any link to the archipelago, conversely, may have lighter skin. This semantic confusion occasionally leads to misunderstandings in labeling people. In any case, the application of the term *burmelho* to Bissau-Guinean Cape Verdeans places them semantically in between "white" and "black" people and thus symbolically reproduces colonial racial ideology. Interestingly, on a more pragmatic level, Cape Verdeans in Bissau were frequently associated with either Bissau Velho or the larger colonial city centers constructed after the 1940s, known as *praças* (see map 2.1), by non–Cape Verdean individuals whom I met during my field research. Although the Cape Verdean population, indeed, continues to be concentrated in these central neighborhoods, colonial settlement patterns (in terms of both ownership and tenancy) have changed since independence (see Kasper 1995: 87–120, 153, 156). At present, Cape Verdeans also reside in neighborhoods that are far away from Bissau's former colonial center.

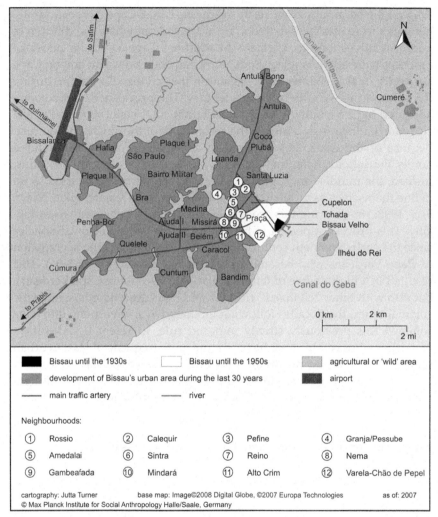

Map 2.1. Greater Bissau

One decisive dimension that ensures identitarian boundary maintenance among Guinea-Bissau's Cape Verdeans was their familial and household structure. Most of them live in domestic groups that comprise only the nuclear family (grandparents, parents, and children). This pattern was also frequently found among other Bissau-Guineans who belonged to the upper social classes, while the majority of lower- and middle-class urban domestic groups lived as extended families (also known as *gãs*, "localities of living"). Moreover, I received the impression that foster children (*meninus di kriason*) seemed to be less numerous among Cape Verdeans.

This might be an apparent result of the fact that Cape Verdean family networks were often less rooted in rural areas, from where the children of poorer relatives tend to originate. In addition, Cape Verdeans' marriage practices were also changing. Endogamy had been prevalent among Cape Verdeans, or at least intermarriage within the "civilized" stratum, during the colonial times in the twentieth century. The prevalence of endogamy appeared to be a result of the social and political transformations that occurred in Guinea-Bissau during the second half of the nineteenth century. Because of the challenges imposed by colonialism on creole extended family household units, they gradually ceased to be autonomous units. Instead, the middle- and upper-class creoles, in particular, started to redefine themselves as a "territory-based elite group" (Trajano Filho 2006b: 9; cf. 1998: 185). During this process, exogamy largely gave way to endogamy. This process appeared to have been reinforced by colonial policies since the early twentieth century, which led to the increasing segregation of Cape Verdeans who became endogamous (Havik 2004: 353–54). This resulted in a high degree of familial relationships among Cape Verdeans, but also with other "civilized" citizens, and their descendants. Unlike the colonial times, the decades following independence have seemed to have softened this previously strictly imposed rule. In recent decades, love marriages across ethnic lines have become more frequent, at least in urban settings, which is also due to the slow but successive social advancement of individuals whose ancestors had previously been classified as indigenous subjects and/or who originated from the countryside.

Memories of a Glorious Past: The Kriston de Geba

The Kriston de Geba are a small group that alludes to Geba, the important former trading post that lent its name to this creole group. The examination of the formation and shaping of Kriston de Geba identity will allow conclusions regarding their integration into Bissau-Guinean society. A brief demographic description of the former *praça* of Geba, where I conducted some of my fieldwork, will foster the understanding of the making-up of Kriston de Geba identity and its relationship to other identities. In this respect I will discuss the reasons for the strong ethnicization of the Kriston de Geba, including an elaboration on their heterogeneous origins and on references to history and locality that contribute to identity construction. The role of the *juiz do povo* (people's judge), who strategically projects himself as a leader of the Kriston de Geba, remains contested and can be interpreted as illuminating the continuous process of increasing the ethnicization of Kriston de Geba identity. Given the absence of exact census data, the total number of Kriston de Geba currently living in Guinea-Bissau can only be estimated to around three thousand to four thousand, at the most.

The Praça of Geba

In the east was located Geba, wistful village,
where each step is facing a ruin, once the cradle of heroic
Catholicism that sought to fence with all the beliefs that
were bustling in the plain, nowadays surrounded by Muslims.
Geba has the mystical and concentrated
appearance of a convent whose slabs are
still echoing the slow steps of the missionaries,
auxiliaries of our colonizing action. Each house
is a chapel, surmounted by the Cross of Christ.
(Duarte 1934: 35, my own translation)

The Kriston de Geba refer to Geba (see map 2.2), which is situated approximately 75 miles (120 kilometers) to the east of Bissau, close to the tidal limit in the middle reaches of the Geba River. According to historical sources, the *praça* was founded in the sixteenth century (Donelha 1977: 162–63; cf., however, Carreira 1984: 48). From the plentiful availability of travelogues, official reports, and correspondence across centuries (Lemos Coelho 1953a: 49–50; 1953b: 159, 172–74; Mollien 1820: 214–25; Chelmicki and Varnhagen 1841: 1:135; Pereira Barreto 1843: 17; Lopes de Lima 1844: pt. 2, 108–9; Bertrand-Bocandé 1849a: 288–89, 319; 1849b: 65, 69; Travassos Valdez 1864: 364–65; Marques Geraldes 1887: 471–90; Cultru 1913: 245–56; Portuense 1974: 71, etc.), we can form a good idea of the former sociocultural, political, and economic circumstances in Geba. A Kriston community has existed in Geba since the seventeenth century. Until the mid- to late nineteenth century, Geba was a commercially vibrant hotspot and the easternmost Portuguese trading post, quite convenient for traffic (slaves and commodities); it has since lost its former importance and fallen into political, economic, and demographic insignificance (Havik 2007b; Kohl 2009b).

After Geba's decline, most Kriston left the locality, and their descendants today live in either Bafatá or Bissau (especially in the Amedalai and Sintra neighborhoods), while only a tiny handful of creoles continue to live in Geba. This process continues: as Geba has little to offer the younger generation, adolescents move to Bafatá or Bissau, where they attend secondary schools and then look for income and employment. Those who stay behind are adults who mainly live on cash crop and subsistence farming.

Visitors who know about Geba's past importance will be disappointed to discover that the former *praça* currently resembles a small *tabanka* (village), like many others. Geographically isolated Geba is poorly connected to the outside world, especially during the rainy season when the narrow and potholed dirt roads become almost impassable.

One thousand feet (three hundred meters) to the north of Geba is located Aldeia (di Mandinka) (village [of the Mandingo]) or Geba di Riba (Upper Geba), which is exclusively populated by Mandingo.

The northern part of Geba (see map 2.2), called "Mouricunda" (roughly translated as "Muslim quarter") by the Kriston, is predominantly inhabited by Mandingo these days. The minorities groups in 2006–7 included Fula, Sarakolé, and Balanta. Since the majority of the inhabitants are Muslim, the mosque is situated in this part of the village. The village's two small retail shops were also located here; one of them was run unsuccessfully by a Mauritanian who left some years before my return in early 2013.

The former city center—or the *praça*—is located further south. The *praça* today is composed of a mixed population, in both ethnic and religious terms, including Kriston de Geba, Mandingo, and Mansonka in 2006–7.

The southern quarter of the settlement is primarily inhabited by Kriston de Geba. Vast parts of the area known as Rodja (literally "rock"), dominated by a massive catholic church located on top of the hill, are now depopulated, as indicated by the numerous flat adobe mounds of collapsed clay houses. The Bessamar port marks the quarter's southeastern end.

The southwestern quarter of Santa Cruz, close to the Geba River and once located to the south and southwest of the cemetery, is now entirely uninhabited. My aged informants remembered that the last houses in this area were abandoned in the 1940s (interviews AF; AVHS).

Kriston de Geba Identity

Although the Kriston de Geba identity is, like Cape Verdean identity, strongly ethnicized, there are minor differences between the two. In the case of the Kriston de Geba, references to their heterogeneous ancestral origins are considered far more important than in the case of Cape Verdeans. The narrative strategies employed by contemporary Kriston de Geba allude to their non-Kriston ancestors who, according to my informants' accounts, were overwhelmingly composed of Beafada (interviews AF; AVHS; CF, JF, and LVHS; FGDL; PJV). This underlines the status of Kriston de Geba as a comparatively young group in which heterogeneity forms an important part of self-perception (interviews FVS).

The Kriston de Geba that I talked to repeatedly referred to the plurality of their group's ethnic origins. One informant claimed, for example, that they were actually quite similar to Cape Verdeans, who had also emerged

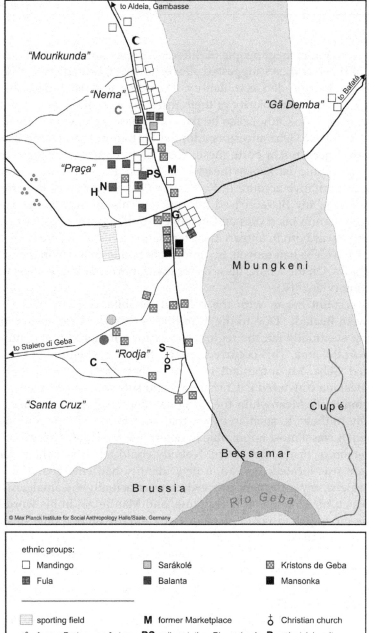

Map 2.2. Geba

from a conglomerate of people of different origins (interviews AF; AVHS; FGDL; PJV; cf. DM). As suggested above, however, Beafada play a salient role in the Kriston de Geba identity. According to Kriston de Geba collective memory, the majority of their ancestors were Beafada before they were converted to Catholicism by the Portuguese. Following these narratives, Kriston de Geba ancestors adopted Portuguese names and learned to speak either Kriol or Portuguese. Thus, both religion and language are significant ethnic markers in the case of Kriston de Geba ethnic identity.

An authoritative account of Kriston de Geba history was imparted to me by one of my Bissau-based informants. This informant was a well-educated man in his sixties and belonged to the upper middle class. Although he was born in a town in eastern Guinea-Bissau where his grandfather from Geba had moved, my informant had been living in the capital for decades. On the whole, his account was confirmed by other Kriston de Geba (interview PJV).

His account began with the original inhabitants of the Geba area, who were Beafada. Due to the Mandingo's westward expansion, these Beafada eventually left the region, except for a minority that continued to live in the area. This occurred around the time when the Portuguese founded Geba. My informant recounted that, breaking with the past, these Beafada converted to Christianity and subsequently formed a Kriston community. Meanwhile, their original identity and ethnonym ceased to apply to them, to such an extent that after five or six generations, he claimed, it was almost impossible to determine the ethnic background of any person or his/her ancestors. Nobody could tell where their *tabanka* of origin was located. Instead, a new identity had emerged. The Kriston de Geba, my informant proceeded, were actually the amalgamation of three cultures: Beafada, Portuguese, and Mandingo. In his words, an "ethnic mixing" had taken place in Geba—firstly among only Beafada, Portuguese, and Mandingo, but thereafter also including other Europeans, Cape Verdeans, and African ethnic groups (such as Fula, Manjaco, and Jacanca). Because of this amalgamation, my informant emphasized, the Kriston de Geba were not a *tribu* (tribe) like other ethnic groups (cf. also Kasper 1995: 257).

Kriston de Geba thus conceptualize the identities of "ordinary" ethnic groups as "normal" ones. These are contrasted with their own identity, which they regard as somewhat special, due to ancestral heterogeneity. From an analytical perspective, the Kriston de Geba are a creole group that, having passed through a creole continuity integrating different ethnic and cultural elements and entailing increasing ethnicization, now appears to be on the verge of transforming into an "ordinary" ethnic group that continues to refer to its heterogeneous origins.

The specific ethnic self-perception of the Kriston de Geba has also come to the fore in narratives of ethnic conversion and ethnicization in cultural creolization processes. An aged, Geba-based informant claimed that they, as Kriston de Geba, were Kriston who did not have any *raça* (ethnic group, ethnic identity). He contrasted this present situation with that of the past. In his opinion, the distant ancestors of the Kriston de Geba, the Beafada, did possess an ethnic identity. He was convinced that all people who converted to Christianity could become Kriston. However, he clarified that unlike the Kriston de Geba, such people would retain their original *raça*. For instance, he explained, Balanta and Mandingo may convert to Christianity, but they would retain their ethnic affiliation (AVHS; cf. DM; CF, JF, LVHS).

It is true that in the past, Christianity was one of the main transethnic markers of creole identity that provided, along with the Kriol and Portuguese languages and the professionalization of trade, for a distinctive common lifestyle among the earlier Kriston communities in the *praças*. Over the course of time, however, Christianity was transformed from a mere religious category into, firstly, a transethnic marker among the early Kriston communities and, secondly and subsequently, an ethnic marker among the strongly ethnicized Kriston de Geba. The reference to Christianity does not mean, however, that Kriston de Geba follow Catholic traditions regularly and exclusively. Nor is this link with the past a recent phenomenon: it was already noted in the mid-nineteenth century that the Christian population of Geba believed in the "errors of the religion of their neighbors, the Mandingo peoples, which is a very deformed Islam" (Travassos Valdez 1864: 365; my own translation). Thus, although ties with neighboring groups continue to be strong, Kriston de Geba still refer to their adherence to Christianity as a strategy in order to distance themselves from a social surrounding that is dominated by Islam. I observed, nevertheless, that Kriston de Geba do not differ much from the Muslims and other believers in their local religious beliefs. Most of them believe in supernatural beings while practicing ceremonies and frequenting specialists and shrines associated with local religious beliefs; some even consult Muslim *mouros*.

Even leading Kriston de Geba have been repeatedly accused of believing in superstition in the past. For example, there were rumors in the late nineteenth century that the *juiz do povo* of the *grumetes* of Geba was suspected of wearing amulets that reportedly contained little chits of paper (containing verses from the Koran, perhaps, which is a widespread tradition in parts of Guinea-Bissau) that served to protect the bearer (Marques Geraldes 1887: 476). The contemporary *juiz do povo*, who claims to represent all Kriston de Geba and resides in Bissau, converted to Islam a couple of years before his nomination as leader. Even though he explicitly professes Islam, he continued to be accepted as their leader, but there were some who contested his authority and others, notably in Bissau, who had not even heard of him. If this example set a precedent, Catholicism may eventually become a less important marker for boundary maintenance among Kriston de Geba, thus signifying an increased ethnicization.

Increasing ethnicization is linked to the disengagement of Kriston de Geba identity from the locality of Geba. In the past, the Kriston de Geba identity had been bound to these people's shared ancestral place of origin, as evidenced by their ethnonym's toponymical reference. Although the Kriston de Geba remain emotionally attached to their ancestral hometown, the majority of them have lived outside Geba for generations, without ever having set foot in the former *praça*. This means that the Kriston de Geba identity has become independent of its eponymous locality, which can be interpreted as a sign of increasing ethnicization.

Their heterogeneous ethnic ancestry is part of Kriston de Geba collective memory. One of the oldest dwellers in Geba claimed, for instance, that one of his female ancestors in the distant past was a Fula slave. When a Kriston married her, my informant added, the former slave converted to Catholicism (interviews AVHS). Similar to this informant, many Kriston de Geba trace back their lineage to specific individuals from different ethnic origins, thus indicating dynamic and open boundaries as well as capacities of cultural incorporation in a creole continuity.

After the New State regime had effectively seized Guinea-Bissau's territory in the 1930s, the relationship between the Kriston de Geba and the colonial state seemed to have become quite ambiguous. Like other inhabitants of the colony, the Kriston de Geba were affected by the colonial policies of legally binding ethnic classification. At the same time, the continuous political and economic decline of Geba transformed the previously important *praça* into a simple *tabanka*. Fostered by these parallel processes, Kriston de Geba began to turn to African culture.

As *grumetes*, the Kriston de Geba had for centuries served as brokers for European and Cape Verdean traders and officials and the non-Christian African population of the continent's interior until the beginning of the twentieth century. As middlemen, they were not "fully in one world or the other" (Merry 2006: 48), thus caught between two stools, but were rather able to integrate and valorize different cultural traits. The Kriston de Geba have put emphasis on this aspect of history, as well as on religion and language as central ethnic markers, which allowed for their alignment (through marriages as well as commercial partnerships) not only with Kriston from other *praças* but also Europeans and Cape Verdeans within the early colonial state's social-status-based reward power system. In doing so, the Kriston de Geba simultaneously pronounced their alterity against the population in the hinterland, which comprised people who spoke local languages and followed Islam or local religions. As indicated above, this strategy was possible because the Europeans and Cape Verdeans, apart from sharing their religion and language with the Kriston, also tended to regard Christianity as a marker of superiority and "civilization." Thus, adherence to Christianity brought along a politico-juridical as well as a sociocultural ascription of superiority by the Europeans and Cape Verdeans. Therefore, religion, like the creole language, not only helped Kriston de Geba to distance themselves from the non-Christian majority that populated the area around Geba but also tacitly stressed their sociocultural preeminence.

However, the implementation of the Native Statute in the late 1920s signified a turning point for Kriston de Geba identity. Unlike the Cape Verdeans and other Kriston that lived in bigger agglomerations such as Bissau or Bolama, most of the Kriston de Geba, under the Native Statute, were categorized as "Beafada" or "Fula" by the colonial officials, who thus contested their Kriston identity. This procedure was applied to not only the punctual population censuses but also the people's official identification papers. Accordingly, being entered as "Beafada" and "Fula" in the *caderneta* or *guia indígena* upset the Kriston de Geba, as my elderly informants remembered, since they did not perceive themselves as belonging to those ethnic groups (interviews AF; AVHS; FM). In particular, my interviewees protested that they were not Muslims (the Fula and Beafada were equated with Muslims) but Christians (Kriston), and, as such, they regarded themselves, in contrast to the others, as "civilized" in a popular sense. The transformation of Christianity from a religious category into an ethnic marker is obvious in this process of identitarian negotiation. The legal declaration of Kriston de Geba as Beafada or Fula was followed by the exclusion of the majority of the Kriston de Geba from citizenship. Hence, we can presume that the legal categorization of the Kriston de Geba as indigenous subjects contributed to the ethnicization of their identity.

Their colonial, legal declaration as "noncivilized" subjects did not only symbolically challenge their self-conception as Kriston de Geba. Historical sources signal a trend reversal: from about the late nineteenth century on, the Kriston de Geba were increasingly cold-shouldered by the colonial state and its allies. As early as 1869, a decree had officially declared all *grumetes* as *gentio,* the Kriston sinking to the level of non-Christianized, and "uncivilized" subjects (Soares 2000: 151). Designated in colonial depreciative terminology as "*grumetes*" (Marques Geraldes 1887), "*cristãos nativos*" (native Christians) (Carreira and Rogado Quintino 1964: 376, cf. 375, 383), "chamadas *cristãos de Geba*" (so-called Christians of Geba) (Munno quoted in Pinto Rema 1982: 629; original emphasis), or "*Christãos no nome*" (Christians in name only, referring to all "grumetes of the praças" or "*christãos pretos*" [black Christians], respectively) (Lopes de Lima 1844: pt. 1, 78, pt. 2, 108), they did not differ from "natives" in the eyes of the Church and the colonial administration. Thus, even their "true" Christian faith became increasingly contested. Presumably, the fact that the majority of the Kriston de Geba were regarded, at least by the colonial administration, as "uncivilized" natives that "followed, in all their habits and customs, like the Mohammedans, the Mohammedan religion" (Costa Pessoa quoted in Teixeira da Silva 1889: 46; my own translation), they were consequently lumped together with other, non-Christian, notably Muslim "natives." This may have caused an identitarian dilemma for the Kriston de Geba, who repudiated this approach. In addition, the economy of Geba had been affected by a sharp decline since the late nineteenth century, which might have evoked nostalgic feelings among the Kriston de Geba. Eventually, they might have augmented their efforts to emphasize their identitarian distance from their non-Christian neighbors by highlighting their different religion as "Christians of Geba." Through this, they may have been able to implicitly stress their historical role as emissaries of European civilization.

Historical allusions to the present ethnonym date back to the 1950s and 1960s (Munno quoted in Pinto Rema 1982: 629; Carreira and Rogado Quintino 1964: 375, 383; Mendes 1966: 542–44), suggesting that creolization had already resulted in a strongly ethnicized identity by that time. Despite the continued existence of Kriston de Geba as subjects under the Native Statute, the colonial state paid them particular attention. Apart from their traditional leader, who continued to be recognized as a contact person by the colonial authorities, they reportedly received certain privileges from the state, as a number of Kriston de Geba in Bafatá asserted. For example, my informants' accounts indicate that they were not assigned to forced labor services, because unlike the Muslim Mandingo (also called *gentio*), Kriston de Geba were considered "civilized" by colonial officials (interviews AF, AVHS). If this was the case, this practice would be another indicator of the ambiguous and personalized character of colonial domination. These representations may not be entirely true, however, in light of the fact that some aged Kriston de Geba from Geba itself remembered their fear of the Portuguese, in general. Although we cannot entirely rule out the possibility that the self-depictions might reflect an attempt at identitarian distinction, such narratives may shed light on the discrepancy between a normative, ideological colonial pretence and the on-site reality with regard to the disparate treatment of indigenous subjects by subordinate local colonial officials.

Heterogeneous Origins as Strategy

What are the strategies that are employed by Kriston de Geba to link themselves to other local ethnic groups and their cultural traditions? Beafada figure prominently in the narratives among the Kriston de Geba. However, the association with Beafada is not merely limited to oral accounts referring to a remote, mystical past. On the contrary, present-day Kriston de Geba continue to follow a number of cultural features and beliefs inherited from their Beafada ancestors even though certain salient customs, such as the ability to communicate in the Beafada language, are now discontinued. These references thus highlight the openness of boundaries and the natural disposition to integrate cultural forms that is a characteristic of creole continuities. While, indeed, "there have been significant cross-linkages (such as intermarriages) among virtually all ethnic groups" (Forrest 1992: 118–20), and before colonization ethnic groups were characterized by openness and their identities by flexibility and malleability, creole groups like the Kriston de Geba are, nonetheless, different. Heterogeneity is an essential component of their group identity that is remembered constantly when talking about the past and genealogies. Borrowing, adopting, and reconfiguring cultural representations of various origins in order to integrate them into their own cultural repertoire is something very explicit (cf. Walker 2005; Knörr 2010). By contrast, individuals of other, "ordinary" ethnic groups usually rather tend to portray their groups as primordial, culturally coherent, and "pristine."

An elder in Geba told me that the ancient affinity between Kriston de Geba and Beafada is also reflected in a myth that harks back to a remote past, around the time when Geba was newly founded (interview AVHS). According to the legend, blood was said to fill a clay pot in Geba as soon as an animal was slaughtered in the Quinará peninsula, located approximately twenty-five miles (forty kilometers) to the southwest of Geba and presumed to be the homeland of the Beafada ethnic group. This occurrence came to an end after the Beafada converted to Islam. Interestingly, this legend resembles a narrative that linked a Pepel shrine on an island next to Bissau's Pijiguiti port to Quinará (Brooks 1993b: 86). This does not only underline the connection of the Kriston de Geba with both the Beafada and the Pepel but also highlights the influence that the Beafada exercised over both the Kriston de Geba and the Pepel, the Christianized segments of both the Beafada and Pepel being part of the *grumete* or Kriston stratum. The kinship system among the Kriston de Geba acknowledges their historical connection with the Beafada, at least in part. The emblematic names used to designate lineages among the Kriston de Geba bear a striking resemblance to those used by the Beafada. For instance, while the three matrilineal *djorsons* (lineages) are known as *malobal, massumo,* and *mabadjo* among the Kriston de Geba, they are termed *málobal, mássene,* and *mabadje,* respectively, among Beafada (Rogado Quintino 1969: 884; cf. Giesing and Vydrine 2007: 376). Unlike Beafada, however, the Kriston de Geba that I interviewed were not familiar with any totems associated with the abovementioned lineages (interviews AF; AVHS). According to colonial ethnography (Rogado Quintino 1969: 884), each Beafada lineage was ascribed a specific totem. Among the Kriston de Geba, the lineage is transferred along the matrilineal line, unless the mother originates from another ethnic group. In such exceptional cases, the children are said to belong to their father's lineage. It appears that the younger Kriston de Geba generations are not very knowledgeable about belonging to a certain lineage. In particular, those adolescents and young adults who grew up in Bissau usually do not know their lineage. This might stem from the fact that lineages seem to be of little practical relevance among Kriston de Geba, except in very few ceremonial acts.

One of the ceremonies that Kriston de Geba perform as a strategy for highlighting their origins as well as their relationship with local groups and traditions is called *cabeça di cama* (literally "head bed"). The Kriston de Geba who performed the ceremony in my presence ascribed it to their Beafada ancestors (interviews AVHS; LVHS and NVHS). In the *cabeça di cama* ceremony, the matrilineal affiliation reportedly inherited from Beafada culture is of prime importance. On a Saturday in December 2006, my informant's elder sister arrived in Geba. She complained that she had been ill for quite a while. Her father's mother, who had died approximately fifteen years prior, had appeared to her in a dream and requested her to perform a sacrifice to her *irã* (ancestor's soul, ghost, or spirit). Then, the grandmother explained, her health would soon improve. Consequently, the family invited other members for the ceremony. After the participants (including the family members, friends, neighbors, and me) assembled for the ceremony in the morning, my informant slaughtered two chickens. As he and his father explained to me, the ceremony could only be performed by male family members. A second prerequisite was that the lineage of the performer of the ceremony and the deceased person had to be congruent. For this reason, only my informant—who bore his mother's lineage— could perform the ceremony. In contrast, his father—the grandmother's son-in-law—was excluded from performing the ceremony because he belonged to a different matrilineage. Subsequently, a meal was prepared, served in a bowl, and consumed by the participants, along with a toast of *agua dente* (distilled beverage). Finally, a candle, the remaining chicken, and a plate (heaped with, among other things, stones and a halved calabash containing some of the distilled beverage) were served to the *irã* at a certain place in the house where the grandmother had once passed the night.

The attribution of this ceremony to Beafada ancestors can be interpreted as an attempt by the Kriston de Geba to highlight their origins, portraying themselves as an indigenized local group that has much in common with the neighboring "ordinary" ethnic groups. At the same time, however, the fact that a number of Kriston de Geba based in Bissau asserted that they did not believe in *irãs* can be conceived as a strategy to distance themselves not only from non-Christian ethnic groups but also their Beafada ancestors. In this way, the Kriston de Geba try to maintain their boundaries with respect to other ethnic groups while simultaneously portraying themselves as one of these very groups.

The Kriston de Geba lineage system suggests that there are further components of their culture that likewise harken back to their Beafada ancestors. For example, Kriston de Geba families are structured along patriarchal and patrilocal lines. This means that Muslim women who married a Kriston de Geba husband in former times had to convert to Christianity. My aged informants concurred that depending on his wealth, a man was allowed to have more than one wife (interviews AF, AVHS). Since polygyny was not accepted by the clergy, such weddings were celebrated only in the "country style," that is, without the blessing of the Church. I noticed that the Kriston de Geba community was characterized by an above average number of matrilateral cross-cousin marriages, which I observed in a number of cases in Geba and Bafatá (interviews AF; FM). Moreover, in at least one particular case I was able to record a patrilateral parallel-cousin marriage. My aged informants confirmed that endogamy, and most notably cousin marriages, had been frequent in the past. Apart from this practice, the older generations of Kriston de Geba used to follow a rule of descent that resembled an agnatic/patrilineal seniority system. Under this practice, family assets were not passed on to the husband's children but to his next eldest brother instead, that is, to the senior-most member of the family. Unlike the agnatic/patrilineal seniority system, though, this rule mandated that after the death of the last brother, the assets would be inherited by the youngest brother's eldest son, not the eldest brother's sons. This principle of inheritance also implied that a brother was obliged to assume responsibility for his deceased elder brother's wife. To cite an example, a Geba-based woman in her sixties—originally a Fula—had been married, along with a couple of other women, to a rich Kriston de Geba trader. After the trader's death, his next eldest brother had assumed responsibility for the family, and ever since then, had been taking care of her and her children. He explained to me that unlike the traditional view (which sanctioned levirate marriages), he did not perceive himself as her husband—he was simply taking care of her (interview AF).

The heterogeneous origins of Kriston de Geba are reflected by their Atlantic heritage. Christianity and Portuguese first came to Geba and the other former *praças* from Europe and Cape Verde. In littoral Africa, Catholicism was appropriated by the emerging Kriston communities and subsequently customized into a distinct new cultural tradition. The Portuguese language underwent the same process, and through interactions between Cape Verde and mainland Africa, notably linguistic Mandingo influence (Rougé 1986: 45; Peck 1988: 331–36), it was customized as Kriol by creoles. Geba's Atlantic orientation, therefore, is not restricted to its erstwhile significant economic ties that connected Africa's interior with Cape Verde, Europe, and the Caribbean—the linguistic traits of Geba mirror this orientation (cf. Martinus 1996: 12–15, 119–45, 197; Jacobs 2009). Geba, situated on the crossroads between the Mandingo empire and the Atlantic world, is consequently popularly (among Bissau-Guineans of various ethnic backgrounds) as well as scientifically regarded as one of those places in the subregion where Kriol was first spoken. At the turn of the last century, Geba had still retained its own dialect (Marques de Barros 1897/99: 297–98; Rougé 1986: 37; Pinto Bull 1989: 78–79; Couto 1994: 32, 51; Kihm 1994: 5). Although I was not able to detect any linguistic differences during my fieldwork, many Kriston de Geba in Geba and abroad proudly insisted that they continued to possess a more extensive and slightly different vocabulary from other Kriol speakers. According to my informants, they consider Kriol as an integral part of their identity; that is, they employ this creole language as an ethnic marker and regard it as their mother tongue. From an analytical perspective, this view ignores the fact that Kriston de Geba who grew up in multiethnic neighborhoods in Geba or Bafatá, which are dominated by Mandingo and Fula, are also able to speak Mandingo or Fula. Since Kriston de Geba learned these languages in their childhood, Mandingo and Fula can be regarded as their mother tongues as well.

Apart from economic and linguistic ties, Geba maintained strong religious links with Cape Verde and Europe for centuries, and clergymen trained there also served in Geba (Pinto Rema 1982). The Catholic faith shared by Cape Verdeans, Europeans, and Kriston provided a common ground for these communities and enabled Cape Verdeans and European government officials, soldiers, or traders to easily integrate and marry into the Kriston de Geba community. Such ties were central to many accounts that I gathered during my field research, narrated both by Kriston de Geba

and by other creoles whose ancestors had resided in Geba. These connections constitute, to this day, an essential element of Kriston de Geba family
histories, thus reflecting the identitarian relevance of Geba's Atlantic orientation. For example, a Bafatá-born Kriston de Geba in his mid-twenties
(interview UM) bore a typical Cape Verdean surname. When asked about
the relevance of his last name, he related that one of his forefathers originated from Cape Verde. He assumed that both these communities must
have mingled, on the basis of their shared religion, that way stressing the
importance of common Portuguese Atlantic and colonial legacies. Another case gives implicit testimony to the facilitating potential of shared
religion and language for identitarian integration. During one of my stays
in Geba, I met a Kriston de Geba woman who was well advanced in years
(interview JC). Illiterate and unable to remember when she was born, she
narrated that her father's father had moved from Cape Verde to Geba. A
soldier by profession, he had been employed by the Portuguese to fight
against insurgents. When I asked her about her ethnic self-perception, she
expressed her uncertainty, ultimately replying that she actually considered herself Cape Verdean, given that her grandfather was Cape Verdean.
She was convinced that she could not deny these roots. Shortly thereafter,
she further qualified her previous comment, stating that all her female ancestors were Kriston de Geba. Therefore, she was actually *djagassi* (mixed),
even though others regarded her as Kriston de Geba.

Narratives as Constituents of Spatial Identity

The locality of Geba seems to be of major significance for identity construction and boundary maintenance among the Kriston de Geba. Moreover, the reference to the locality is crucial for a better understanding of
the process of cultural creolization undergone by this creole group. The
Kriston de Geba were indigenized at this locality, and they continue to
regard themselves as the historical "owners" of the former *praça*. This special relationship is not only indicated by their ethnonym but also by a
number of oral narratives, some of them containing references to certain
sites, which serve as proud expressions of Geba's former outstanding historical relevance. At the same time, other ethnic groups that inhabit Geba
benefit from Geba's bygone significance, once dominated by creole actors,
by acknowledging their pride in residing in the village.

   In the previous sections, I have already explained the significance of
Christianity. Yet, religion, couched in an accompanying narrative and
manifested in the form of a landmark building, is also employed by Kriston de Geba to construct their identity. In our conversations, Kriston de
Geba frequently referred to the big stone church located in Geba's aban-

doned center. Many Kriston de Geba claim that this church was Guinea-Bissau's first church—even though "first" is used metaphorically, because the present massive stone church was constructed only in the 1930s by Kriston, using money collected from the wealthy and successful local creole traders (cf. Pinto Rema 1971: 740–14; 1982: 491). Nevertheless, many Kriston de Geba, as well as a considerable number of other Bissau-Guineans, stressed Geba's crucial role as *the* location that had housed Guinea-Bissau's first church.

The tradition of resistance and rebelliousness that is reportedly prevalent among the Kriston de Geba forms yet another historical narrative topos (cf. Pélissier 1989; Mendy 1994; Soares 2000; Cabral 2002: 171). This narrative is not only shared by Kriston de Geba but also by other Bissau-Guineans. The tradition of resistance harks back to the late nineteenth century, when the area around Geba had been a focal point during the long-lasting Forria wars (Bowman 1997). It was this very turmoil that finally led to Geba's descent into political and economic insignificance. Before that, however, it became a platform for creole resistance against Portuguese presence. Due to a few economic and political reasons, Geba's creole inhabitants rebelled against the Portuguese. Geba's *juiz do povo* formed an alliance with the leader of the Fula insurgents, Mussa Môló, after Geba was besieged by Fula warriors. As a result, the Portuguese lost influence and control over Geba and its hinterland. Eventually, however, the Portuguese managed to recapture Geba and made peace with its inhabitants (Marques Geraldes 1887: 475–76, 479–80; Bowman 1997: 82–84). Oral narratives add that the *juiz do povo* was subsequently removed from office by the Portuguese and later died in Angolan exile (interviews AVHS).

The prevailing historical narrative does not dwell on the details of these events, which are known from written historical sources. Those parameters that are still part of the collective memory are rather selective and inconsistent. While Kriston de Geba identity alludes to an earlier tradition of creole brokerage with the Portuguese on the one hand, the above narrative conversely portrays the Kriston de Geba as resistant to colonial rule on the other. The narrative of resistance in the nineteenth century is connected with the more recent war of independence, lasting from 1963 to 1974. The elder generation among Geba's inhabitants, mainly comprising those who were born in the 1930s and 1940s, was directly affected by this war of independence with Portugal. As in other villages throughout Guinea-Bissau, the liberation movement had established clandestine structures in Geba. Even more importantly, the charismatic leader of this movement and developer of an integrationist state ideology, Amílcar Cabral, was born in Bafatá, which is only 12 miles (20 kilometers) from Geba. Cabral's father Juvenal had been a teacher at Geba's school (Cabral 2002). Therefore, Geba's elderly inhabitants were familiar with the Cabral family. Kriston de Geba elders in Geba knew Amílcar Cabral personally, as they proudly informed me on a number of occasions. The elders (interviews AF; AVHS; FM) nostalgically narrated to me stories about clandestine meetings, concealment of a popular independence movement member, and arms smuggling on behalf of the PAIGC. Some of the elders, among them the clandestine local representative of the independence movement, were even arrested by the Portuguese and held in a concentration camp in Cape Verde (interviews AF). I learned that a number of well-known freedom fighters and postwar politicians either originated from Geba or had ancestral ties to the former trading post—including Guinea-Bissau's late long-time state president João Bernardo "Nino" Vieira. These narratives of anticolonial resistance evidently exhibit a crucial topos for the present-day identity construction of Kriston de Geba. In this way, collective memory harmonizes events from different historical periods of time and thereby contributes to the manifestation of the Kriston de Geba identity against the background of the locality of Geba.

Another anecdote even more deeply rooted in history refers to Geba's former role as one of Portugal's most crucial entrepôts along the Upper Guinea coast, situated at the crossroads of all the trading routes that connected Africa's interior with the West African coastal line, Cape Verde, Europe, and the New World. It connects to the Kriston's traditional role as commercial intermediaries. These former economic ties are described through the narrative of the purportedly oldest mango tree of the "Sierra Leone" subspecies, which is situated in Geba's former, now largely abandoned town center (interviews AVHS; CRL). The mighty tree is situated near a residential plot that has been owned by the creole Vaz family for a very long period of time (see map 2.2). Until today, the Vaz family is regarded as one of the most prestigious creole families not only in Geba but also in Bissau. Historically, the origins of the surname Vaz in the region can be traced back to the seventeenth and eighteenth centuries (Brooks 2003: 133, 149–50, 159, 192, 196, 231–22), although it is by now impossible to verify a direct relationship between the Vaz of Geba (who may have been descendants of the historical Vaz) and those of the remote past. In the past, a number of *juízes de povo* in Geba came from this family. Different versions credit the planting of the tree to either the Vaz family, in general, or a certain Boré Vaz, who, according to historical sources, was the *juiz do povo* in the 1880s (Marques Geraldes 1887: 474–75, 479–80). According to my informants' accounts, the Vaz family or Boré Vaz, respectively, exchanged local goods from Geba for necklaces of a special type and cola nuts in Sierra Leone. Like the other traders, I was told, they/he used to trade regularly along the Upper Guinea coast. One day, either Boré Vaz or some member of his family brought along some mango seeds or seedlings from Sierra Leone. Consequently, the first tree was planted close to the Vaz residence, while another one was planted elsewhere in Geba, near a now-ruined building owned by the Cabral family (no relation to Amílcar Cabral) (interviews AF, AVHS).

Geba, as a whole, can be generally interpreted as a site of memory, displaying both physical and amorphous characteristics. Pierre Nora (1989: 7; original emphasis) has termed such places as *"lieux de mémoire"* "where memory crystallizes and secretes itself." These sites represent "the embodiment of memory . . . where a sense of historical continuity persists. There are *lieux de mémoire*, sites of memory, because there are no longer *milieux de mémoire*, real environments of memory." In other words, the collective memory of Kriston de Geba is crystallized at these identity-defining sites that escape collective oblivion. These *lieux de mémoire* need not be restricted to geographical sites, in the strict sense of the word, but can also correspond to mythical figures, events, archives, or books.

Without doubt, not only do the previously mentioned narratives help shape identity but their topoi also allow us to draw conclusions regarding the historical emergence and early development of creole identity. Emerging from the legend of the mango tree, a narrative topos among Kriston de Geba and Mandingo inhabitants of Geba regarded Boré Vaz to be the settlement's *dono di tchon* (literally, "owner of the land"). Alluding to this belief, the Kriston de Geba argued that the Vaz family was the first to settle in Geba. A few people, however, were of the opinion that the Kriston de Geba collectively represent the *donos di tchon* of the *praça*, that is, Geba's center. Despite these varying beliefs, there is consensus among the present-day population that either the Kriston de Geba or one of their representatives is the original *dono di tchon*. The Kriston of Geba seek to legitimize their presence in Geba by highlighting their status as firstcomers (interviews AF; AVHS)—a view that is also shared by the Mandingo who constitute the majority of Geba's population (interviews SiM and SN).

It remains to be considered whether these migrations actually occurred or if they merely constitute a topos for the Kriston de Geba to confirm their present status by a reference to a mythical past. In the latter case, the local residents may have simply redefined and reconceptualized their identity after their encounter with European and Cape Verdean culture. If we admit the occurrence of the migrations, though, the narrative accords with the concept of the African internal frontier: ethnic groups emerged out of continuing and overlapping processes of migrations. Groups of people left their ancestral homeland or village in order to found a new compound in an uninhabited frontier setting. The small, new immigrant community subsequently became the basis for a village or even a polity.

One reason why individuals migrate and settle elsewhere in unpopulated spaces is that they are expelled from their own village under accusation of practicing witchcraft. Such individuals, who are forced to leave their settlement along with their relatives, subsequently form the nucleus of a new village or a greater polity (Kopytoff 1987: 4–7). Such newcomers may have also laid the foundation for the subsequent formation of creole identity in Geba.

The Kriston de Geba in general and the Vaz family in particular are regarded as prestigious and legitimate firstcomers in Geba, who symbolically "own" the territory. Therefore, even present-day Kriston de Geba feel a pronounced relationship, a natural attachment to the locality of Geba, which translates into a certain degree of authority. Their status as firstcomers and landlords implies that they are tacitly situated at the apex of Geba's social hierarchy. Consistent with Igor Kopytoff's (1987: 49–51, 53–57) approach, the lower layers of Geba's occupant hierarchy comprise various newcomer or latecomer groups. These include Mandingo and Fula, who are believed to have settled in Geba after it had already gained recognition as primarily a creole trading post. The earliest occupants of Geba's population, thus, constituted the nucleus of the Kriston community, and it was only afterward that Geba and its growing population began to attract increasing numbers of migrants. As firstcomers, the Kriston are said to have introduced a "progressive" and "civilized" social order in contrast to both the prior and the current non-Christian modes of living.

The position of Kriston de Geba as firstcomers to the former *praça* is confirmed by another narrative that I heard from many individuals who did not identify themselves as Kriston de Geba but originated either from Geba itself, from its neighboring villages, or from Bafatá or Bissau. Kriston de Geba, however, widely reject this narrative, because this *fama* (literally "rumor") projects them in a poor light. It pertains to the founding years of Geba and parallels Kopytoff's hypothesis that many firstcomers to unpopulated spaces have previously broken with their original groups over ritualistic matters, such as accusations of witchcraft. The excluded individuals were therefore united by links of solidarity; they would also be different from their new neighbors (Kopytoff 1987: 18–19, 24). Exactly the same pattern is depicted in the narrative according to which Geba is described as a haunted place. When I explained that I intended to visit Geba, some people became alarmed and warned me that something bad or evil might happen to me there. This view was shared by a couple of Mandingo, of different ages, that I met in Bafatá. Some of them even maintained close kinship ties with Geba. Many Bissau-Guineans (e.g. interview JV) are convinced that Geba houses the worst *futseiros* in the whole of Guinea-Bissau. *Futseiros* are believed to be evil turned *pauteiros*, seers, if they feasted on human souls. Eventually, as *futseiros*, they would attempt to hunt, harm, and kill other human beings. It is difficult for "normal" individuals to discover the identity of these beings. However, the Kriston de Geba are by some thought to be such *futseiros*. According to the popular rumor, the Kriston de Geba were originally castaways who migrated to the place where Geba was eventually founded. Upon their arrival at this site, the ancestors of the present-day Kriston de Geba founded a new colony, after which the Portuguese proselytized and converted them to Christianity. More importantly, many Bissau-Guineans actually recognize the peculiarity of the Kriston de Geba by reproducing the narrative: their ancestors had split from their "native" groups, transformed into a creolized groups, and integrated into the transatlantic world. Their former parent groups henceforth regarded the Kriston de Geba as different from themselves, yet the groups continued to maintain a network of kin and spiritual relations—as it is expressed in the clay pot myth mentioned earlier that emphasizes ancient Kriston de Geba–Beafada alliances.

The Juiz do Povo

The nomination of a new *juiz do povo* in 2002 can be interpreted as an attempt to represent the Kriston de Geba as an "ordinary" Bissau-Guinean ethnic group, indicating the increasing ethnicization of their identity. Historically, the *juiz do povo* was exclusively associated with lower-class Kriston (or *grumete*) communities that inhabited the *praças*. By the early twentieth century, the *juiz do povo* office was obviously discontinued in Bissau and other trading posts (cf. Cabral 2002: 197)—however, this position survived among the Kriston de Geba, recently culminating in a factional attempt to revive the traditional office. While the majority of the Kriston de Geba agree that the *juiz do povo* is the ancestral representative of their ethnic group, there are controversies regarding the legitimacy of the current Bafatá-based *juiz do povo*. Appointed to the position in 2002, the *juiz do povo* claims to represent *all* Kriston de Geba in Guinea-Bissau. Even though he seemed to be maintaining good personal relations with the then president of the Region of Bafatá in 2006–7, the official regional representative of the central government and follower of then state president "Nino" Vieira, he continued to act independently of Geba's informal *comité de tabanka* (village committee) (cf. Andreini and Lambert 1978: 39–40; Mendy and Lobban 2013: 102) and state bodies in Bafatá region.

To some extent, the desire for a *juiz do povo* can be interpreted as an indicator of the increasing ethnicization of Kriston de Geba identity—despite the dissensions regarding the person currently in charge of the office. To better understand this function in both past and present perspectives, it is necessary to provide a brief historical review of the office before casting a glance at the recent modalities of reinstalling a new *juiz do povo*.

Historical accounts suggest that a *juiz do povo*—a term originating from seventeenth-century Portugal—represented the Kriston (or *grumete*) communities in the *praças* as early as the mid-eighteenth century. The *juiz do povo* was traditionally chosen from among the Kriston elders (interviews AF; AVHS); his office not only epitomized creole self-governance but was also directed against Portuguese influence. At times, however, the *juiz do povo* was responsible for sounding out the creole population on behalf of the Portuguese authorities (Havik 2004: 135–37). Presumably with increased colonial domination, the *juízes do povo* came under the sanction of and were paid by the Portuguese authorities (Lopes de Lima 1844: pt. 1, 55; Teixeira da Silva 1889: 102).

With respect to Geba, historical accounts trace back the office to at least the early nineteenth century (Senna Barcellos 1905: 345–48; Pélissier 1989: 105; Monteiro and Rocha 2004: 191). Report submitted by Portuguese military officials contain more detailed information on the role of the *juiz do povo*. Based on these reports, the *juiz do povo* seemed to be a *primus inter pares* who arranged matters for the Portuguese authorities in cooperation with the Kriston elders, such as regulating the policing of markets and boats, distributing work, and case law. Elders, under the leadership of the *juiz do povo*, represented each of Geba's neighborhoods. The "principal grumetes" used to assemble for meetings in the *rua grande* (main road), which were chaired by the *juiz do povo*. All *grumetes*—thus, the Kriston de Geba—and traders were supposed to obey this board's decisions (Lopes de Lima 1844: pt. 1, 55–56; Marques Geraldes 1887: 475–76, 479; cf. Pélissier 1989: 169).

Oral narratives among Kriston de Geba elders in Geba offered an insight into the office of the *juiz do povo*. In retrospect, the elders opined that the charge used to rotate among the respected personalities of influential Kriston de Geba families (such as Soares, Vaz, Gomes, and Fernandes) (interviews AF, AVHS; NR). Regarding the choice of a *juiz do povo*, the elders surmised that he was selected in a division of the assembly by the elders from among the elders. Although my informants were unable to prove this surmise, colonial sources (Lopes de Lima 1844: pt. 1, 55–56) confirm their description in respect of the mid- to late nineteenth century. One informant added later that the appointment of the *juiz do povo* had to eventually be confirmed by the colonial authorities in Bafatá, which in their turn, nominated the candidate officially (interviews AVHS). This proceeding is likewise affirmed by historical accounts (Sousa Monteiro 1853: 231; Marques Geraldes 1887: 471; cf. Soares 2000: 134–35). This two-stage procedure was apparently applied after the colonial state had started to extend its area of influence by attempting to control and influence traditional leaders of the people. The last appointment following this *modus operandi* reportedly took place in 1969. Supposedly, this last *juiz do povo* of Geba was not formally elected—instead, he was appointed because he was already a commonly accepted and respected leader (interviews AF; AuF, JB, ACMV, MLF, and SMB). Since his death, however, his younger brother, Manuel Vaz, has laid claim to the office. However, both Negado Fernandes and the Kriston de Geba elders in Geba rejected his claims, considering him unsuitable for this office because of his short temper and volatile nature. As per my own observations, Manuel Vaz, in fact, led a secluded life as a small-scale peasant and appeared to be little or not at all involved in the decision-making processes among Geba's elders (interviews AVHS; FM). In former times, Kriston elders in Geba argued, the *juiz do povo* could be removed from office by the people. They stated that Geba's *juiz do povo* used to work under the supervision of the local Fula chief of Ganado, who resided in the nearby administrative center of Gamamudo (cf. Braga Dias 1974: 148, 153–54). According to the elders, whenever the colonial administrators planned to visit the area, they would announce their visits via the *régulo* (chief), who was responsible for informing the *juiz do povo*. While the *régulo* represented the Mandingo, the *juiz do povo* was responsible for affairs that concerned the Kriston de Geba (interviews AF; AVHS). Similarly, Negado Fernandes claimed that no administrator dared to take any decision regarding Geba without previously having consulted the *juiz do povo*. In his view, the *régulo* of the Ganado chiefdom was merely responsible for the Muslims and did not represent the Kriston de Geba in colonial times. Instead, it was the *juiz do povo*'s responsibility to preside over the Kriston de Geba and collect taxes from them, just as a chief would do among his people (interviews AF; AuF, JB, ACMV, MLF, and SMB).

This may be a sign of an increasing embedding of the *juiz do povo* into the colonial power framework. Since the colonially appointed Muslim chief or village headman was presumably less accepted among the Kriston de Geba, the role of the *juiz do povo* may have changed. As an intermediary between Geba's Christian population and the colonial authorities, the *juiz do povo* may have become a more and more subordinated position under colonial rule, supposedly reducing the formerly powerful status to that of an institution responsible for ensuring the smooth imposition of colonial directives among the Kriston de Geba. Even worse, the *juiz do povo* was finally subordinated to the chief of Ganado in the late colonial period, which reflected the continuing marginalization and loss of importance of the Kriston de Geba. Conversely, along with the devaluation of the office, the Kriston de Geba seem to have been even less involved in the nomination process of the *juiz do povo*.

Following Geba's decline since the late nineteenth century, Bafatá has become home to a populous Kriston de Geba community. Bafatá took over Geba's former hegemonic position and became the administrative and trading center of the region. Consequently, the Portuguese authorities installed an additional *juiz do povo* for the Kriston de Geba who resided in Bafatá. The first Bafatá-based *juiz do povo* was reportedly nominated in 1922. As in Geba, the office holders did not necessarily die in office—they usually remained in office for a certain, fixed period of time. Thus, well before the first *juiz do povo's* successor died in the early 1980s, a new person had been nominated by the colonial state. As one of the Kriston de Geba elders in Geba recounted, after the death of the third *juiz do povo* in office, the position remained vacant for many years (interviews AVHS). Just as in Geba, one person claimed the charge after independence, but he was rejected by the Kriston de Geba due to his lack of dignity and serenity.

By then, however, the general framework had been fundamentally altered. The official mandate of the *juízes do povo* that had been legitimized by colonial intervention expired after independence, given the socialist state's complete repudiation of traditional leaders. Subsequent constitutions contained no provisions for the legal approval of traditional leaders (Ministério de Administração Interna 1995: 13–44; Godinho Gomes 2010: 369–80; cf. Fraunlob 2004: 83; Kohl 2017).

The first time I encountered the acting Bafatá-based *juiz do povo* was in mid-December 2006. A friend of mine, a Mandingo born in Geba who also maintained close links with Bafatá, introduced me to Negado Fernandes. Like us, the *juiz do povo* had participated in a *manjuandadi* festival in Bolama, where he had extolled Geba as one of the cradles of creole culture. He came across as a pleasant, charismatic person, due to his tall, slim figure and his friendly, open, and engaging character. Negado Fernandes, who was in his mid-forties, was wearing spectacles and an old suit when he presented himself as the *juiz do povo*. During my conversation with him, he evinced keen interest in my research project and was quite receptive to the details I provided regarding my study.

Later on, I learned that Negado Fernandes was born on a *ponta* (a farm cultivating cash crops) to which his parents—both Kriston de Geba—had relocated. In 2006–7 he continued to live on a *ponta* near Bambadinca, approximately nineteen miles (thirty kilometers) to the southwest of Bafatá, where he grew cashews and ran a small retail shop. At times, he also temporarily resided in Bissau and Bafatá, where he owned houses.

Some weeks after our conversation, in early February 2007 I traveled to Bafatá and met Negado Fernandes at his house in Bafatá's Tunturnin neighborhood. His residence did not differ from other houses in the quarter and was built of clay in the popular rectangular style. He did not possess any trappings of belonging to a royal household or its corresponding insignia that might otherwise be ascribed to traditional leaders. Although he was born Christian, he converted to Islam and openly regards himself as a Muslim. Fernandes asserted that in the past, the *juiz do povo* of Geba would have also been a leader of the local Muslim population. This comment, however, conflicted with the subsequent statements that he made on this issue. He continued that he represented, as acting *juiz do povo*, all the Kriston de Geba in Guinea-Bissau. Apart from Kriston de Geba, he also claimed to represent other ethnic groups that had relocated from Geba and its suburb, Aldeia, to Bafatá. Subsequently, we talked about his election to this position, which had taken place on 15 December 2002. Negado Fernandes had fought the election with only one rival candidate, a Kriston de Geba elder who was born in Bafatá and who still lived there. During our conversation, he proudly presented a photograph of himself wrapped in a traditional *panos* (a traditional fabric that is usually woven of black and white yarn, symbolizing the wearer's dignity and honor—it is worn on prominent occasions such as weddings, burials, and so on; see Carreira 1983; Pink 1999) while being enthroned in the backyard of a residence adjacent to Bafatá's main road (interview AuF, JB, ACMV, MLF, and SMB).

The following day in the late afternoon I again met Negado Fernandes in front of his house, where I had gone to converse with him some more. On this occasion, he had invited a number of fellow participants for our discussion, among them the defeated rival candidate and his friend—a Fula who had converted to Christianity and was working for a nongovernmental organization (interviews AuF, JB, ACMV, MLF, and SMB). Negado Fernandes and the other attendees argued that the elections held in 2002 were the first ones to appoint a new *juiz do povo* since 1969. Before the elections, they informed me, his friend had proposed to appoint a new *juiz do povo*. Subsequently, the present circle of attendees had nominated two suitable candidates. Negado Fernandes emphasized that through this election, he had been indirectly appointed by all the Kriston de Geba residing within the borders of Guinea-Bissau. The attendees asserted that all Kriston de Geba aged eighteen years and above were permitted to cast their vote. It appeared that these attendant informants and their friends had been solely responsible for organizing the nomination process. According to them, about three thousand eligible voters across the country had appointed approximately fifty electors in their respective local reunions. They added that the electors for Bissau had been selected in assemblies, given the great number of Kriston de Geba living there. These electors, in their turn, voted Negado Fernandes to the office of *juiz do povo*, through what was presumably a free mandate. Negado Fernandes reasoned that the election would effectively locate the seat of Kriston leadership at Bafatá, as against Geba, which was characterized by confusion in terms of leadership. Regarding the duties and responsibilities of a *juiz do povo*, Negado Fernandes promised to engage in mediation between various parties and to look for consensus. In doing so, he would at times collaborate with the local chiefs. The new *juiz do povo* vowed to cultivate a good relationship with the Bafatá-based Fula *régulo*. In contrast to chiefs who levied taxes or asked for payments in terms of assets (such as livestock) for their intermediation, he would refuse such payments, for they had the odor of corruption. Apart from this, Negado Fernandes, by his own statement, participated in the organization of the *manjuandadis* run by Kriston de Geba.

However, aside from the above representations, Negado Fernandes's position as *juiz do povo* was quite widely contested in the rest of Guinea-Bissau. As I was able to observe, the Kriston elders of Geba questioned Negado Fernandes's nomination as well as appointment (interviews AF; AVHS). They raised many points of dissension. First, they criticized Negado Fernandes for never having visited Geba, while casting doubts over whether the *juiz do povo* could ever claim to represent the Kriston de Geba of Geba. Second, they found fault with the fact that his election had taken place in Bafatá instead of in Geba, because many Kriston de Geba who resided outside Geba would neither know Negado Fernandes nor be informed about his office (interviews AVHS; cf. FGDL; cf., however, DDC). Third, the elders expressed their doubts regarding whether Negado Fernandes was qualified for the office. They pointed out that, ultimately, he had tended to side with the Muslim community rather than his own Christian people. Fourth, the elders asserted that since Negado Fernandes was born in the *tchon di Fula,* far away from Geba, he was actually an outsider who should have no say in matters concerning Geba. Last but not least, they complained that since Negado Fernandes did not enjoy great popularity across the country, they rejected any claim made by him to represent Kriston de Geba—whether residing in Geba or elsewhere in the whole of Guinea-Bissau.

From an analytical perspective, the appointment of a new *juiz do povo* in 2002 constituted a fundamental break with colonial procedures. Although the old title of a *juiz do povo* was maintained, or rather revitalized, its implications and the way in which the office bearer was appointed was markedly different from the past. The colonial state, as a legitimizing institution, has disappeared, while the independent state has, in its turn, never transferred or delegated any of its duties to the *juiz do povo.* Negado Fernandes shared a good relationship with the then president of the Region of Bafatá at an interpersonal level without the existence of a formal political mandate. Certainly, one may say in the case of Negado Fernandes that he aimed to fill a legal vacuum resulting from the Bissau-Guinean state's limited capacity for settling conflicts and enforcing the law. Although this would be consistent with the *juiz do povo*'s own claims, his self-portrayal as a democratically elected mediator had little to do with reality at the time of my fieldwork, for to my knowledge the *juiz do povo* was not involved in any kind of mediation. From my point of view, his claim to act as a mediator followed the ubiquitous mainstream ideal of propagating Western democratic values and human rights. Furthermore, Negado Fernandes and his entourage may have possibly pursued only their own egoistic or prestige-seeking objectives instead of community-oriented goals and therefore exploited their positions. Of course, similar attempts elsewhere to "revive" traditional leadership have contained a pronounced stress on "tradition," which serves to disguise and enforce political and economic claims (cf. Bräuchler and Widlok 2007: 7, 9). The fact that Negado Fernandes's personal aptitude and legitimacy as *juiz do povo* were challenged may be suggestive of this circumstance.

Indeed, Negado Fernandes successfully advocated his cause. When I met him again in March 2013 I was surprised to see him well-nourished and well-dressed, and topped by a typical Mandingo-headdress, bearing little resemblance with the person I had met six years before. This was also helped by the fact that he now owned a white Mercedes-Benz A-Class model, with one of his young relatives as chauffeur. He and his wife now lived in a nice, neither too big nor luxurious rented house in Bissau's Plubá neighborhood, incomparable to the small building in the capital's Nema-Gambeafada area where I had met him in 2006–7. He explained that he had been advisor to the late state president Malam Bacai Sanhá, himself a Muslim Beafada and PAIGC veteran, and that he had organized the election campaign of then presidential candidate Baciro Djá in 2012. I learned that Negado Fernandes had tried to buy a sewing mill not far away from Bafatá. He confirmed that he had advocated the (re)acceptance of chieftaincies by the state for the past few years. Proudly, he showed me some pictures of chiefs in Ghana whose legal recognition and public appraisal he found a desirable objective. With pride he also he presented me another photograph that showed him, wearing what should presumably represent a "traditional" dress, at the seat of the president of the Region of Bafatá in the presence of some ministers of the acting, so-called "transitional government" in power from May 2012. Clearly visible was the "transitional" prime minister Rui de Barros, who awarded him the Order of Merit—issued for "Augusto Fernandes, Juiz do Povo"—of the Ministry for Territorial and Local Government, the government body that was also responsible for the not yet officially (re)recognized chieftaincies (interviews AuF).

Hence, his installment as *juiz do povo* more than a decade prior was more than a simple "revitalization of tradition," as Negado Fernandes appeared to have an agenda for social and political advancement. As such, he can also be regarded as a political, cultural, and economic entrepreneur—a kind, unostentatious, and nondisruptive one.

Regardless of such reservations, I would like to highlight one matter that is strongly connected to the ethnicization of the Kriston de Geba identity. For this purpose, we need to review the criticism put forth by the Kriston de Geba elders in Geba. The *juiz do povo* office is currently occupied by a spokesman representing the revitalization of traditional leadership. However, as the Geba elders declared, Negado Fernandes has very superficial ties with the ancestral hometown of the Kriston de Geba. The precise content and meaning of tradition has thus been contested between the two factions—Negado Fernandes and those who support him and the electoral process on one side and the Kriston elders of Geba as well as other Kriston de Geba who rejected him and his decision-making powers on the other. As in other cases, the spokespersons within this process of revitalization were individuals who claim to act on behalf of *all* the Kriston de Geba, even though they have never lived and were not even born in the ethnic group's ancestral home and thus possess only a limited amount of legitimate "traditional" knowledge—at least in the view of the elderly generation in Geba. Despite these reservations, Negado Fernandes claimed to represent the "true" tradition in his role as the *juiz do povo* (cf. Bräuchler and Widlok 2007: 12–13).

Both factions not only invoked the authenticity of their respective tradition in regard to the *juiz do povo* but also supported two contrasting conceptualizations of Kriston de Geba identity. In the past, Geba's *juiz do povo*—as a representative of the *grumetes*—had to be, as a rule, a nominal Christian born in Geba. The Kriston de Geba identity itself, however, has undergone significant changes in the meantime—for instance, it has become increasingly ethnicized. Through this process, the Kriston de Geba identity has by now acquired a high degree of group cohesion or "groupness" (as against that of other creoles who identify themselves as *Kriston di Bolama, di Cacheu, di Farim*, etc.). The issue of identity, in this way, has become detached from the territory of Geba. As a matter of fact, most of those individuals who regard themselves as Kriston de Geba nowadays have neither been to Geba nor were they born there; for them, Geba is a place of imagination and identitarian reference. The increasing ethnicization of the Kriston de Geba identity is also borne out by Negado Fernandes's conversion to Islam. In other words, the Kriston de Geba identity appears to have begun dissociating from religious bonds as well. As a consequence, these transformations have led to an intergenerational and

interregional contestation between two factions. On the one hand, the elder generations of Kriston de Geba in Geba itself continue to adhere to the
earlier identitarian concept. Therefore, they consider the office of the *juiz
do povo* as a charge that is associated with both Geba (in regard to a candidate who seeks to represent all the Kriston de Geba) and Christianity. On
the other hand, the Kriston de Geba of Bafatá and Bissau, most of them
belonging to younger generations, tend to conceive of the Kriston de Geba
as a fully fledged ethnic group. In this way, the Kriston de Geba identity
has become strongly ethnicized, while its shared ethnonym and collective
memory continue to allude to Geba as the ancestral place of origin. At the
same time, the indigenization has proceeded to such an extent that the
Kriston de Geba feel at home not only in Geba but also in the whole of
Guinea-Bissau.

The installation of a *juiz do povo* in Bafatá can be interpreted as part of
the community's desire to be recognized as a full-fledged ethnic group.
From this perspective, any such ethnic group would ideally be headed by
a traditional leader. The (re)installment of the *juiz do povo* as the emblematic Kriston de Geba leader may thus have been modeled on the lines of
numerous other ethnic groups. The desire to be like other ethnic groups
consequently displays a collective self-assurance in the Kriston de Geba
identity. Negado Fernandes's emphasis of the former *juízes' do povo* alleged independence of chiefs and their presumed accountability for *all*
the Kriston de Geba do not necessarily represent any claims to power. Instead, his comments can also be interpreted to correspond to an increasing
ethnicization of Kriston de Geba identity and the community's collective
self-esteem. Meanwhile, the Kriston de Geba have reasserted their sociocultural boundaries against other ethnic groups by claiming to follow a
leader who is known by the traditional title of *juiz do povo,* as opposed to
the *régulo*—a word that is associated with Islam and with non-Atlantic
orientations in the context of Geba and Bafatá. In contrast, the title of *juiz
do povo* alludes to the former privileged social position and sociocultural
distinction of Kriston de Geba.

Caught in the Middle: The "Invisible" Creoles

Different from Cape Verdeans and Kriston de Geba another creole variety remains invisible, so to say. A profound ethnographic description and
analysis of creole categories of identification that are found in contemporary Guinea-Bissau is therefore adequate. The number of individuals
who belong to this creole variety supposedly does not exceed five thousand, and the majority of these reside in Bissau. Individuals who belong

to this variety refer to specific genealogies and their families' residence in the *praças*, while group cohesion is hardly developed among them. This means that even though references to family history, genealogy, and urban residence serve to construct common grounds between groups, their ethnicization remains rather weak.

In the case of creole individuals who are opposed to ethnic categorizations, self-perception and ethnic ascription fall apart. While individuals variously identify themselves as, for example, *guineense* ([Bissau-]Guinean); *sin raça* (without race, i.e., without ethnic affiliation); *raça ka ten* (there is no ethnic group); *misto* (mixed); *djagassi/djagassidu* (mixed); *di Bolama, di Cacheu*, etc. (from Bolama, from Cacheu—or from other former *praças*); *cristão*, or Kriston (Christian), these self-identifications are not reflected in their identitarian ascriptions. Often, external observers ascribe these creoles identities that allude to indigenous ethnic identities, such as Pepel, Manjaco, Fula, etc., or a Cape Verdean or Lebanese identity (*libanês, siriano*). Usually, and only upon inquiry, third parties stated to me that the individuals concerned were actually *misto*. Well-informed external observers occasionally pointed out that the family of a certain person is Christian and has been long established in one or the other former *praça* or that the individual's family has played a significant historical role in the *praças*. Ethnic or national ascriptions were normally rejected by the individuals concerned, at times even vehemently, with the argument that their ancestry was much more diverse or that they had nothing at all in common with the ascribed ethnic groups, since they neither spoke that language nor knew much about that particular ethnic group's cultural traditions. This indicates a definite, albeit low degree, of ethnicization—reflected in the individual's attempt to set him- or herself apart from "ordinary" ancestral ethnic identities. Regarding ethnic ascriptions, many interviewees claimed that they had little or nothing in common with people from the countryside and/or that they were actually opposed to the divisive effects of tribalism. All things considered, both identitarian self-perceptions and ascriptions can contain a reference to *praça* settings, while the majoritarian rural population is distanced through the drawing of cultural boundaries. Many individuals whose families have integrated Europeans or Lebanese among themselves in recent generations figure prominently among those creole categories of identification that reject any ethnic categorization (interviews AHVC; AP and RP; AH; AME; AS; CNDR; CR; CRR; CV; DCDA; FE; FMWF; HOS; ICDA; JDSC; JFGE; JH; MuJ; NGD; PPB; REMBDC; SC; cf. EHN; JJSDS).

Ambivalence of identitarian self-perception and perception by others is a crucial characteristic. A well-educated, middle-class man in his fifties possessed a heterogeneous ancestry with European, Levantine, and

African roots. When questioned about his ethnic identity, he replied that his parents had "lost their ethnic roots" and "cultural values" in colonial times because of their belonging to the "civilized" stratum. Therefore, he argued, he did not possess any ethnic identity (interviews AS). Another informant, likewise a well-educated, middle-class man in his fifties, responded differently. After quitting his job in the state bureaucracy more than fifteen years earlier, this interviewee had been working within civil society. His father had been a trader in Bolama in colonial times. When asked about his ethnic identity, my informant drew a family tree, stating, "My forefathers originated from the Lebanon, from France, and from Cape Verde. Some were Pepel, while others were Fula and Manjaco." He added that he could not speak any indigenous language because his mother tongues were Kriol and Portuguese. Given this "mixed" ancestry, he considered himself a *guineense* (interviews JH). A number of my interviewees perceived themselves as *guineense* or were explicitly against classifying themselves under any one ethnic identity. Hence, the co-occurrence of both ethnic and national identity is implicitly inherent in these self-identifications. In some cases, the self-identification as *guineense*, along with the simultaneous rejection of any ethnic affiliation, may date from twentieth-century assimilationist policies that the colonial state had imposed on the creoles who were classified as Portuguese citizens.

In contrast to these "creolized ethnics," the identity of those creoles whose identity supersedes "ordinary" ethnic identities ("decreolized creoles"), in most cases, is consistent with the ethnic ascriptions of third parties. However, as in the former case, both the individuals concerned and external observers usually allude to the individuals' families' length of residence in the *praças,* specific familial genealogies, and their Christian (Kriston) faith. The creoles in question themselves stated repeatedly that they had little in common with people from the countryside. Unlike the people from the interior, the former were "urbanized" and "detribalized," as some of my informants put it (interviews DCDA; ICDA; JH; etc.). Like those creole individuals who are opposed to ethnic categorization, they asserted that they were little or even not at all connected with their respective ethnic group's "ancestral" cultural representations, such as language or religion. Nevertheless, some of them valorized certain customs of the particular ethnic groups with which they identified. The identification with an indigenous ethnic group prevalent among these creoles, thus, can be interpreted as the result of a process of cultural decreolization. Instead of an increasing ethnicization, and eventually a *complete* replacement of original identities by a new, creole identity, the creole continuity is expressed in several creole categories of ethnic identification. This process was apparently accompanied by a de-ethnicization of creole identity and a simultaneous reapproximation of ancestral ethnic identities—a process that was presumably fostered by sociopolitical developments in the late colonial period, as described above. In other words, identity construction involved reinterpreting the original "ordinary" ethnic identities of one's ancestors instead of creating a strongly ethnicized creole identity with a pronounced group cohesion. Hence, transethnic common grounds between creoles are constructed on the basis of references to history, religion, genealogy, and residence (interviews DCDA; ET; FLCDAT; JCN; JHCDA; MN; cf. ICDA).

One of my informants, a man in his fifties, was descended from one of the oldest established creole families in Guinea-Bissau. His family's genealogy formed a very important part of his self-image. Before his retirement in recent years, he had been employed at a very high position within a ministry. According to him, his father was Pepel-born and raised in the *praça* of Bissau. However, he added, he did not know his father's exact roots. Nevertheless, in a census, he would classify himself as a Pepel. Shortly afterward, however, he further limited his identification with that community, stating that Pepel culture was not important to him. This was because he had spent his childhood in the countryside with his father's female cousin, who was a Mandingo. He continued to strongly identify himself with that group. He added that neither he nor his father had any knowledge of the Pepel language. Instead, he understood some Balanta because his mother belonged to that ethnic group. What is most striking in this particular case is the ethnic heterogeneity of this informant's familial origins, which gives rise to a multitude of possibilities regarding my informant's ethnic self-identification (interview MN).

Particular cases indicate that different self-identifications among creole categories of identification can occur even between siblings. The following example attests to the variability of possible ethnic self-identifications among creoles, mainly due to the diversity of their ancestral origins. My informant, a middle-class businessman in his fifties, told me in our interview that since many of his ancestors were Pepel, he usually classified himself as a Pepel in the census. He confided to me, however, that he actually regarded himself as a *mistura* (mixture). He attributed this identification to the fact that he was born in the eastern part of Guinea-Bissau, a stronghold of the Fula ethnic group. Since my informant was well informed about his family's history, which ranks among the most esteemed and oldest established ones in Guinea-Bissau, he knew that he also had Cape Verdean ancestors in the remote past. Apart from this, he added, his roots could be traced back to Banhum, Manjaco, and Bijagó origins. Despite this variety of ethnic ancestries, he was unable to speak any of these languages, not even Pepel (interviews DCDA). His younger brother, however, expressed a different response to this question. As a well-educated member of the upper middle class and an employee of the Bissau branch of a multinational organization, he admitted that he was not sure about his exact *raça*. Unlike his elder brother, he believed that even though his mother, who was born a Pepel, practiced the Pepel religious ceremonies, he would not classify himself as a Pepel, even if external observers frequently did so (interview ICDA).

What individuals of all creole categories of identification have in common, thus, is the repeated emphasis on their—or their ancestors'—urban residence and Christian beliefs. In particular, the references to the former *praças* play a major role in delineating the creoles' sociocultural boundaries against the non-creole rural population and rural migrants in town.

Creoles who identify with an indigenous ethnic group crystallize their view of the rural population and juxtapose it against their own urban way of life. One of my informants, an upper-class businesswoman in her forties who had matrilineally descended from a Kriston Pepel family and patrilineally from Kriston de Geba ancestors, shared her memories of the time of independence. Shortly after the victorious independence movement had peacefully entered the capital and taken over the government, she had observed, as a teenager, how the apartments of one of Bissau's few multistory residential buildings were changing hands. She recalled how supporters of the independence movement, who obviously originated from the countryside, moved into their new quarters, replacing the former Portuguese tenants who had already left the country. Exhibiting a lack of deeper understanding, she narrated in an ironic, mocking manner how these newcomers started to keep pigs in the balconies. She opined that unlike the older city residents, these countrymen did not seem to know anything about city life (interviews FVS; cf. FS). This reference to a collective urban creole we-group expresses the desire for drawing a boundary to exclude the rural population. The latter are implicitly perceived as being less "modern" and "developed," thus displaying an inferior social habitus. People residing in the countryside in colonial times were aware of this disrespectful sociocultural distinction. In their turn, therefore, they accused the "civilized" individuals from creole backgrounds who inhabited the country's few urbanized centers of "eating potatoes" with the Portuguese (e.g. interviews DCDA). This vegetable is widely associated with a European lifestyle in Guinea-Bissau.

A significantly large number of individuals who identify themselves as belonging to one of the creole categories of identification reveal a pronounced genealogical interest in their ancestral lineage. My creole informants repeatedly disclosed their kinship ties with extended creole family networks. As discussed above, endogamy was prevalent in the twentieth-century colonial times. Apart from this, the older creoles of the long-established families, especially, traced their genealogies back to the nineteenth century, using this strategy to stress their difference and peculiarity and thus emphasizing their creoleness. Some of the interviewees were very proud of their descent from well-known and highly esteemed creole families—*famílias de referência* (families of reference)—of the penultimate century (interviews AJPB, CNDR, DCDA). Evidently, this interest seemed to have been fostered by the New State's aforesaid colonial ideology that emphasized the achievements of distinctive creole personalities who were depicted as the revered ancestors of Portugal's "civilizing mission" in Africa (see Gable 2002: 316). Trajano Filho suspects that the New State found in the creoles fertile ground to spread its ideology by redefining them as an elite group dating back from the late nineteenth century, believing in a mystical historical image of itself (see Trajano Filho 2006b: 9). As a result, one reason for this genealogical interest was also to ascertain oneself that one's ancestors did, in fact, originate from Europe or Cape Verde. It appears that these beliefs are still founded on the implicit racist assumption that the lighter-skinned Europeans or Cape Verdeans are culturally superior to the dark-skinned Africans, consistent with the former colonial ideology.

Hence, apart from references to urbanity and genealogy, phenotypical markers, in some cases, can also be decisive in the ascription of a certain identity, as the following examples illustrate. One of my informants was a well-educated upper-class woman in her fifties who held a good position in the Bissau branch of an international organization. She descended from a family whose patrilineal ancestors had migrated from Cape Verde to Guinea-Bissau about one hundred years ago. Her mother, however, was a Pepel from Bissau's hinterland. A couple of years earlier, a census-taker had asked her about her ethnic affiliation. Since her mother was a Pepel, and given the fact that the Pepel have a matrilineal descent system, my informant replied that she was a Pepel. However, the census-taker further inquired whether she was sure about this ethnic identity. He alluded to her light skin color and proposed to register her as a *misto* on that basis (interview IMMN). Apart from highlighting the significance of skin color, this vignette testifies to the arbitrariness of census classifications. Another singular episode clarifies how racial markers are still used, in conjunction with references to history and colonial practices of racial prejudice and discrimination, within concurrent creole family branches. An upper-middle-class informant in his fifties, who was descended from one of the oldest established creole families in Guinea-Bissau, explained that his family was of Cape Verdean origin. This would be the reason for the lighter skin color among his family members, he argued. However, there were some people who bore the same family name and counted themselves among his extended family. Since these individuals were rather dark, my informant opined, with an air of mystery, these people could not possibly belong to his family. He advanced the view that their ancestors had, in fact, been slaves kept by one of his ancestors who was a slave trader. Subsequently, the former slaves adopted his ancestor's surname. Thus, although they shared the "dignified" family name, these dark family members did not have any blood relation with him, asserted my interviewee. While the counterparty rejected these insinuations, my informant confirmed the existence of this intrafamilial dispute based on skin color (interviews CNDR; MN).

In summary, the Portuguese colonial state managed to influence the construction of identities, albeit in a more indirect way as it continued to be characterized by weakness. By trying to impose legal norms that sought to classify the colonial population (*civilizados* vs. *indígenas*) and by means of the underlying dive-and-rule agenda, the colonial state was able to contribute to transformations of creole identities in Guinea-Bissau since the early twentieth century. While Cape Verdeans were encouraged and manipulated in their belief of sociocultural superiority, colonialism did not exercise enough power to impose identities that were rejected by people, as, among others, the case of the Kriston de Geba illustrates. This also applies to the central characteristic of creole Kriston identity and its intersection with other identities, such as European/Portuguese, African, Cape Verdean, white, black, *djagassidu, grumete, fidju di tchon, civilizado,* and *indígena*. Since the eve of independence, suppressed debates about ethnicity emerged, and in the light of the independent state's favor of an emphasis on national unity, some individuals of Kriston descent now managed to (re-)embrace African identities while other ones, orientated toward "civilized" European role models in colonial times, continued to stress their "mixing," portraying themselves as "true" "[Bissau-]Guineans" (Kohl 2016).

Notes

1. Urbanity cannot be measured merely in terms of population strength. Former *praças* never had a population exceeding a few thousand or even some hundreds inhabitants. According to Amin and Graham (1997: 417–18) a city entails "the co-presence of multiple spaces, multiple times, and multiple webs of relations, tying local sites, subjects, and fragments into globalizing networks of economic, social, and cultural change."

Chapter 3

Building the Nation

A fter having elaborated on the formation and development of creole identity in Guinea-Bissau, this chapter deals with the "transethnicization" of originally creole cultural representations. Transethnicization describes processes that entail the spread of cultural manifestations beyond the boundaries of the original group, thus being adopted by other groups as well. This leads to new, transethnic identifications and, as a consequence, to increasing interethnic and national integration, or nation-building from below. Closely related to transethnicization processes are, therefore, the associated terms of "nationhood" and "nation-building." In fact, there is a need to look at nation-building efforts from a bottom-up perspective because "we know little of how it was carried out on the ground" (Geschiere 2009: 171). Hence, what does this process look like and what have been the results in the case of Guinea-Bissau?

On the eve of decolonization, cultural representations such as the Kriol language, *manjuandadi* associations, and carnival celebrations had begun to spread beyond the boundaries of creole communities to which they had been restricted. By now, what previously had been exclusively creole cultural traditions not only reached new geographical areas but also spread among vast sections of Guinea-Bissau's non-creole population. In this way, the originally creole traditions have contributed to interethnic integration in Guinea-Bissau and helped to build a well-developed national consciousness. These integrating effects, however, have left intact the ethnic identities of the people who were affected by this process. Transethnicization was fostered by both the independence movement and the early postcolonial, one-party state.

Notes for this chapter begin on page 187.

National Integration, or: What's in a Nation?

Creole identity has played an important role in the process of postcolonial nation-building: countries in the Americas that obtained their independence in the late eighteenth and early nineteenth centuries were, in fact, founded, formed, and led by creole pioneers (Anderson 1999: 47). Creoles in other regions, too, have made crucial contributions in shaping both colonial and postcolonial statehood.

Early European nationalists were convinced that political, national, and cultural entities are congruent (Gellner 1998: 1; Hobsbawm 1999: 22–23). They believed that a culturally and ethnically homogeneous "nation" constitutes its own state—a nation-state. This classic European (or French) model of the nation has been paramount to date. The "concept of national unity as an integral and integrating ideal at all levels" implicated that "diversity became imperfection, injustice, failure, something to be noted and to be remedied" (Weber 1976: 9).

Given the absence of ethnic and cultural homogeneity in most newly independent African countries, popular as well as academic discourses have contested that these heterogeneous societies constitute "real" nations," dismissing them as "artificial" (Knörr et al. 2008: 30–31; 2010a: 360; cf. Hill 2005: 147–48, 151; Young 2007: 241; Kersting 2009: 7). Indeed modernization theorists in the 1950s and 1960s were convinced that ethnicity (or "tribalism") was a relic of the backward past that, after the African colonies achieved independence, would soon give way to the formation of new national identities. Eventually, Africans' "natural" and distinctively "tribal" affiliations would dissolve. Some African political leaders attempted to erase this "traditional" concept of ethnicity and replace it with a "modern," integrative concept of nationalism (Lonsdale 1996: 100–1; Mamdani 1996: 135; Young 2007: 241; Kersting 2009: 9). Nation-building was thought to be an inevitable teleological endpoint (cf. Vail 1989b: x; 1989a: 2–3; Berman 1998: 307–8).

Reality, however, did not comply with the script, and against all prophecies, ethnic identities have continued to exist in postcolonial Africa. In many African countries, "the promotion of an inclusive idea of the nation and a deliberate attempt to overcome and deny ethnic and tribal loyalties" (Frahm 2012: 25) did not materialize. Particularly the 1990s and 2000s saw a return of politicized "tribalism" and more exclusive, "new" concepts of the nation (Kersting 2009; cf. Geschiere 2009).

Politically, a pivotal means to unify the population had been to create a distinctive, integrated national culture, which was often formed only ex post—that is, after the foundation of the respective nation-state (cf. Gellner 1998: 2; Hobsbawm 1999: 71, 93–94; Barrington 2006: 20)—similar to

European countries like Italy, Germany, and even France that had sought to unite culturally diverse people under a national umbrella a century earlier (Weber 1976: 67–94; Weichlein 2006: 43; cf. Langewiesche 2000: 100). For this purpose, African nationalists supported those cultural representations that seemed suitable and appropriate for fostering national integration in an ethnically heterogeneous society. Postcolonial governments often only pursued or accomplished the creation of a national culture already prepared by its colonial predecessor. In this way, the colonial state became the "midwife" for postcolonial states, which had to cope with the territorial principle imposed by the colonial powers. African leaders borrowed the exclusivity demand of "one state = one nation" that had been left by the Europeans (Osterhammel 2009: 76–77).

Creole identities and representations often proved suitable for that purpose because due to their transethnic character they are not exclusive to a specific ethnic group but rather shared by various creole subcategories. This also occurs because creole culture conversely integrates heterogeneous elements of different ethnic and cultural sources, thereby creating conditions for local populations to transethnically connect to creoles (Knörr 2008: 13–14).

For this reason, the newly independent Bissau-Guinean state promoted the ideology and agenda of the ruling party by also using creole cultural representations. Even though the PAIGC lost its previous monopoly after the introduction of the multiparty system in the early 1990s, the authoritarian top-down, one-party state had nonetheless succeeded in leaving a lasting mark on nation-building, heavily referring to its "historical mission" to liberate, unite, and (re)construct (cf. Geschiere 2009: 171). This integrative claim continues to be cultivated, at least verbally and in its self-perception, by the PAIGC to date.

Generally, it can be acknowledged that African nations are usually not constructed according to the classic European model of nation-building. Widely spread are "unity in diversity" or "tree-as-nation" models, which view "smaller," more exclusive ethnic identities as its precedents or roots. From this perspective, national identities do not have to replace ethnic identities or make them obsolete. Quite the contrary, ethnicity has thrived in many postcolonial societies as both a constituent and an antithesis of nationhood. Against this background we can acknowledge the possibility of multiple conceptualizations of the nation. The recognition of the fact that nations do not necessarily have to follow the European model not only addresses analytical considerations but also mirrors popular discourses throughout the African continent. In fact, some African nationalists have based their ideologies on this very conceptualization of the nation. Yet, despite cultural and ethnic diversity, African citizens appear to largely accept the concepts of both nation and state these days (Kersting 2009: 8).

Transethnizication—termed "cultural pidginization" by Jacqueline Knörr—has played an important role in African nation-building processes. In contrast to cultural creolization, cultural pidginization involves the evolution of new, shared cultural features and the transcendence of identities without leading to the emergence of a new and common ethnic identity. Instead, the original ethnic identities stay intact. However, this process can lead to the creation of new transethnic identities. In the long run, therefore, the process of pidginization may—or may not—be resulting in creolization. It is cultural pidginization—rather than creolization—that commonly takes place in contemporary postcolonial societies with an ethnically diverse population (Knörr 2010b: 739). In this context, pidginization may—or may not—involve nation-building. Pidginization may result in new transethnic identifications. It may, for example, contribute to the development of a national identity, which transcends ethnic identities without replacing them. In this case a newly founded nation can unite heterogeneous ethnic groups and cultural representations under its umbrella. Pidginization should not be confused with homogenization, though: rather than creating cultural homogeneity, pidginization contributes to cultural integration by "replacing one diversity with another" (Hannerz 1987: 555; cf. 2002: 41–43)—depending on the varying degrees and modes of appropriation of new cultural forms by diverse local groups. Such models are translated in ways that fit the respective sociocultural contexts into which they are integrated. It is therefore appropriate to talk about "glocalization" (Robertson 1994) instead of "homogenization" (Appadurai 1996; Hannerz 2002; Latour 2005; Knörr 2009; 2010b; 2014; Kaufmann and Rottenburg 2012). Because flows of ideas and models do not occur unidirectionally but rather in a see-saw fashion (Czarniawska and Joerges 1996), the travel itinerary is often not traceable.

Some newly independent African states that sought to build their respective nations pushed forward transethnicization processes into a particular, well-defined direction. Yet, despite the fact that many newly independent authoritarian one-party states in Africa pursued a dictatorial top-down method of nation-building, "many people were eager to participate whenever they could" (Geschiere 2009: 171; cf. 172–74). In doing so, the postcolonial state could, starting from a top-down policy, trigger a popular-driven, grassroots process of interethnic integration that contributed to national integration. Notwithstanding these early efforts, nation-building seems "to have become a slogan of the past" (Geschiere 2009: 38, cf. 217) since the 1990s. To build a nation(-state), from the eve of independence, nationalists did not solely rely on purportedly "artificial" political ritu-

als like rallies, staged by youth and women's organizations of the ruling
single party (Geschiere 2009: 172–74). Rather, they top-down supported
cultural representations that seemed to be suitable and appropriate for
fostering national integration based on the principle of unity in diversity, as
in Guinea, Ghana, and Tanzania, for example (Bender 2000: 9–18; Askew
2002: 158–60, 203; Schramm 2003: 31–32; Coe 2005: 55–56, 65; Højbjerg
2007: 52).

However, what was originally planned as a unilineal top-down project
of nation-building actually depended on the consent and approval of the
population that created the nation by staging and celebrating national culture by means of a nationalism from below (Askew 2002:12–13, 290–93):
"Rather than an abstract ideology produced by some to be consumed by
others, nationalism ought to be conceptualized as a series of continually
negotiated relationships between people who share occupancy in a defined geographic, political, or ideological space" (Askew 2002: 12).

In Guinea-Bissau, creole representations played an outstanding role in
this regard. Here, they served the conceptualization of postcolonial nationhood in an ethnically heterogeneous society. This means, however,
that non-creole cultural manifestations could also contribute to interethnic integration, as long as they are not explicitly based on mono-ethnic
principles (as, for instance, sports associations). However, due to the transethnic character of creole continuities, creole representations appear to be
particularly suitable to contribute to this goal as they are often characterized by the fact that they are not exclusive to a specific ethnic group but
are rather shared by various creole subcategories. This also occurs because
creole culture conversely integrates elements of different ethnic and cultural sources:

> Because elements of the given local, ethnic cultures constitute integrated parts
> of many local creole cultures in ethnically heterogeneous societies today, local
> populations can find parts of their own (ethnic) culture reflected in them and
> thus may feel both ethnically (with regard to their ethnic "share") as well as
> transethnically connected with the creole culture while maintaining their own
> respective ethnic identities. (Knörr 2008: 13–14; cf. 2010b: 747)

For this reason, it became possible for the newly independent Bissau-
Guinean state to promote the ideology and agenda of the ruling party
by employing creole cultural representations. This integrative feature of
creole culture was supported by the indigenization of creole groups in
the Bissau-Guinean case, which prevented creoles and creole culture from
being regarded as alien elements.

Postcolonial processes of cultural pidginization that may contribute to
interethnic, national integration and the collective imagination of a com-

munity of solidarity, cutting across ethnic boundaries, do not necessarily proceed smoothly and undisputed. Rather, they can provoke counterreactions from those creole groups who regard themselves as the founders and therefore the original "owners" of the cultural representations in question. In such a situation, the "donor groups" often use the essentialist argument to support their claim over the representations, thereby seeking to separate their "genuine" representations from the "false," "unauthentic," or "copied" counterparts that have resulted from cultural pidginization processes (Eriksen 2007: 174; Knörr 2008: 4–5, 13–14). This implies that the donor ethnic groups might continue to regard specific cultural representations as "their own" ethnic markers, even as they come to be recognized as expressions of an integrated national culture and are no longer associated with a specific ethnic group.

Summing up, pidginization, in contrast to creolization, denotes a process of transethnicization that leads to the evolution of a new, common transethnic identity without entirely substituting the original diverse ethnic identities. How this process has unfolded on the ground in Guinea-Bissau will be analyzed in the subsequent sections, dealing with the creole language Kriol, *manjuandadi* associations, and carnival.

On Everyone's Lips: Kriol as Lingua Franca

> Criol i lingua ke tudu
> ginti ta papia na Guiné.[1]

In this section I will discuss the cultural pidginization, that is the transethnicization, of Guinea-Bissau's lusocreole language Kriol and its contribution to an interethnic integration from below. I will shed light on the emergence and geographic expansion of the creole vernacular that is nowadays known as Guineense (Guinean), or, more commonly, Kriol. In this context, I will also attempt to demonstrate the way in which Kriol became increasingly prevalent, finally assuming the status of independent Guinea-Bissau's lingua franca (cf. Chirikba 2008: 31)—thus uniting the nation linguistically across ethnic and cultural boundaries. Hence, Kriol contributes essentially to national integration. The fact that people share the same language does not mean, however, that they also have a national identity in common (Weber 1978: 1:395; Djaló 1987: 254). A nation "is not identical with a community speaking the same language" (Weber 1978: 2:922). Vice versa, multilingualism does not necessarily constitute an obstacle to national unity (Djaló 1987: 254). Yet, the shared mastery of a language facilitates the communication between different linguistic groups and thus contributes to interethnic conviviality and exchange, building solidarity and founding "a feeling of belonging and belonging together" (Weiß and Schwietring quoted in Figueira 2013: 88, cf. 89).

The current status of Kriol as Guinea-Bissau's lingua franca is best represented by the growing number of its speakers. In 1979, only about 44 percent of the Bissau-Guineans spoke Kriol, following the first census conducted after independence (Ministério da Coordenação Económica e Plano 1981: 156; figures are contradictory, cf. Lopes 1987a: 280). According to the census conducted in 1991, Kriol was spoken by more than 51 percent of the population (Instituto Nacional de Estatística e Censo 1996: vol. 1, tables 6.5A, B, C, D). Kriol continued rapidly gaining ground: by 2009 the number of creole speakers increased to 90.4 percent (compared to 27.1 percent Portuguese speakers), according to official census data (Instituto Nacional de Estatística 2009: 19). For the time being, Kriol predominantly remains the most prevalent language for interpersonal verbal communication, and it dominates not only the local audio-visual media but even parliamentary debates (cf. Augel 1998: 18–19). However, comparatively few print publications are released in Kriol (mainly ecclesiastical literature, belles lettres, comics, educational advertisements, and propaganda) (cf. Pinto Rema 1982: 913; Pinto Bull 1989: 119–28; Couto 1994: 54; Parente Augel 1998).

The origins of the creole language that is currently spoken in Guinea-Bissau and the Senegalese Casamance can be traced back to the sixteenth century. Its development was intimately connected with the foundation and development of urban *praças* (Rougé 1986: 36). It can be assumed that a pidgin or creole language had already emerged by 1580. Linguists suppose that it resulted from a simplified version of Portuguese that was even further simplified and spoken by local pidgin speakers (Couto 1994: 18–20, 34).

Both the origin and development of Kriol have been matters of contention among linguists. Some believe that Kriol first emerged in Cape Verde and was subsequently transferred to the littoral African mainland (Carreira 1984: 120, 123; 2000: 318–19; Lopes da Silva 1984: 31–32, 39; Green 2010). Another scholarly faction expresses the opinion that Kriol first emerged in the continental Upper Guinea coast, originating from *praças* like Cacheu and Geba (Pinto Bull 1989: 24). A third hypothesis assumes that Kriol evolved simultaneously in Cape Verde and in riverine West Africa. Another theory argues that the precursor to Kriol first emerged in Europe (cf. Rougé 1986: 30–31, 37). According to a fifth hypothesis, a luso-creole language used to serve as the first global lingua franca, connecting lusocreole-speaking communities in the Indian Ocean basin with Africa (São Tomé and Príncipe, Cape Verde, Guinea-Bissau, etc., see Seibert 2012)

(Thompson 1960; Valkhoff 1966; 1972; cf. Pereira 2006; Mello 2007: 66–67): ships' crews on the journey from Africa to Asia may have acted as transmitters of Luso-Pidgin elements (Cardoso 2010).

Historical evidence suggests that, by and large, Kriol continued to be limited to the few trading posts that were nominally controlled by the Portuguese in the mid- to late nineteenth century. A traveler reported in 1884 that Kriol was exclusively spoken by "Christian Negroes" in Bissau, Cacheu, Geba, and Bolama (Doelter 1884: 191, my own translation). The Kriston maintained plurilingual traditions and were thus able to act as economic and cultural brokers. In the 1890s Kriol did not constitute a monolithic language; instead, a number of creole variants could be distinguished in the handful of settlements. Contrary to the theory of its emergence as one language, three or four varieties of Kriol could be identified at the time. While those of Geba (cf. interviews FVS; JRS) and Cacheu were considered to be the oldest forms of Kriol, those spoken in Bissau and Cacheu were regarded as the most correct versions, for these *praças* had been seats of government. Meanwhile, the Kriol spoken in the then capital of Bolama was described as the most "Portugalized" version of the language (Marques de Barros 1897/99: 288, 296–98; cf. Couto 1994: 51).

After the turn of the penultimate century, Kriol was propagated further inland by Cape Verdeans who relocated to the country's interior. This caused the creole vernacular, which was still primarily restricted to urban settlements, to spread to Guinea-Bissau's hinterland (Havik 2007a: 58–59). After the Portuguese had seized control over the territory, they began to devaluate and legally suppress Kriol, which they regarded as a badly and incorrectly spoken Portuguese (Couto 1994: 54; Gomes 2001: 35)—though they never became powerful enough to enforce this policy.

The Basic Law of the colony enacted in 1914 granted franchise and eligibility to citizens provided they were able to read and write Portuguese (Lei Orgânica de Administração Civil das Províncias Ultramarinas: §§24, 44). One of the first bills that sought to distinguish between "civilized" citizens and indigenous subjects was passed in 1917. The law stipulated that applicants for citizenship should be able to read and write Portuguese, not merely Kriol (Carta Orgânica da Província da Guiné: §307). Later legislations retained this condition. Another law passed in 1917 heavily criticized the "constant use of crioulo" in public administration and schools, "as if it were the national language." Under this mandate, only the Portuguese language could be used in public administration and the education system (Portaria 38). It seems, however, that these endeavors to stamp out Kriol from Guinea-Bissau did not meet with success. Only a couple of years later the Portuguese governor complained in his annual report, "Rare are the Cape Verdeans who speak Portuguese. . . . Portuguese is heard spoken in Bolama and Bissau by some Portuguese public officials and merchants. The foreigners themselves, forced by their commercial life, are compelled to learn the language of the colony in which they are situated and speak Creoulo, ceasing to speak Portuguese! That is even an embarrassment!" (Velez Caroço 1923: 25; my own translation).

The conference of administrators that was held in Bolama in 1943 also discussed this issue, in which the administrators again advocated the removal of the "creole dialect" from the public service and the commercial sphere. The participants labeled the use of Kriol as unpatriotic, signifying the colonizers' "manifestation of inferiority," which they equated with "assimilating with the natives" (Colónia da Guiné 1944: 73–75, my own translation).

After the Catholic Church was entrusted with the responsibility of imparting rudimentary instruction to "indigenous" learners in 1926, it was stipulated that lessons had to be conducted in the Portuguese language, although the "indigenous languages" could also be used intermittently (Acôrdo Missionário entre a Santa Sé e a República Portuguesa: §16; Estatuto Missionário: §69; Estatuto Orgânico das Missões Católicas Portuguesas da África e Timor: §21a). The basic education that was provided to the citizens' children was based on the laws and provisions of metropolitan Portugal and was therefore conducted in Portuguese (Teixeira da Mota 1954: 2:109–10; see Errante 1998: 285–86). However, only 7.7 percent of the citizens (or 641 individuals) were able to read and write Portuguese in 1950 (Mendy 1994: 311). The remaining citizens—comprising more than 90 percent of the Bissau-Guinean citizens—who were not able to read and write Portuguese included a great number of Cape Verdeans, metropolitan Portuguese, and their legitimate children, who were not required to apply for citizenship and who therefore did not need to prove their ability to read and write Portuguese. These figures reveal the absurdity and hypocrisy of colonial legislation and ideology that pretended to spread Portuguese language skills as part of Portugal's civilizing mission.

These measures undertaken by the colonial state suggest that Kriol remained the urban lingua franca, and while Kriol speakers were obviously concentrated in the few urbanized settlements, it continued to spread in the countryside. The colonial authorities knew about this reality, and the 1940s saw the emergence of many debates and contentions that sought to distinguish between Kriol and the Cape Verdean creole language, presumably on the basis of racist considerations as part of the colonial ideology that favored Cape Verdeans over Africans. Apparently, the colonial administration feared that its overrestrictive measures might have completely alienated vast sections of the population from colonial rule (Havik 2007a: 61–62). Only in the mid-1950s, however, did the representatives of the colonial state and media begin to recognize the crucial role played by Kriol as an interethnic means of communication, contributing to overcoming "tribal isolation" (Teixeira da Mota 1954: 1:227–33; cf. Havik 2007a: 62).

Nonetheless, a Portuguese fact-finding mission that had been tasked in the late 1950s with studying local association movements in Guinea-Bissau—a project that has to be seen in the context of rising nationalism all over Africa at the time—continued to be critical:

> It is for sure that there is a lingua franca that all do understand—Crioulo, formed under the influence of Cape Verdeans; it is for sure that this fact reveals the influence of our culture but, it appears to me, merely an indirect influence, underlining the predominance that Cape Verde had over the colonization of Guinea, emphasizing the present insufficiency of our cultural influence. (Silva Cunha 1959: 62; my own translation)

In the early 1920s Kriol was predominantly restricted to the *praças* and was hardly understood in the countryside. Its influence expanded very slowly in the 1920s and 1930s. Only thereafter did it spread more rapidly, coincident with the expansion of colonial rule and infrastructure, which caused many people to migrate to the towns (Carreira 1984: 122–23). Indeed, until the 1930s Kriol appears to have been essentially limited to creoles, "Mestizoes," Pepel, and Manjaco in the western, littoral part of Guinea-Bissau that has been subject to transatlantic exchange for centuries (Sociedade de Geográfia de Lisboa 1939: 31).

The emergence of nationalist movements in the 1950s was strongly connected with urbanized speakers of Kriol. When the war of independence broke out in the early 1960s, Kriol served as a crucial means of popular mobilization. During the war, Kriol was employed as the training language for recruits as well as the communication medium in the fast-spreading basic primary schools run by the independence movement PAIGC in the "liberated zones" of Guinea-Bissau. Moreover, the PAIGC also started to broadcast messages, propaganda, and its ideology in Kriol on *Rádio Libertação* at that time (Carreira 1984: 122–23; Pinto Bull 1989: 78, 116–19; Couto 1994: 59); Nassum 1994; Embaló 2008: 105). Thus, reinforced by the war of independence, Kriol became even more widespread countrywide as a kind of interethnic lingua franca. In its program of 1963, the PAIGC demanded the "stimulation of the use of native languages and of the creole dialect; creation of a script of these languages" (quoted in Chilcote 1972: 360–66, here: 365). In this manner, the liberation movement did not only advocate a "unity in diversity" model but also highlighted the particular relevance of Kriol.

However, it was only after 1974 that Kriol manifested its full importance. Through its use, the different ethnic groups could identify themselves as one nation (cf. Askew 2002: 182), united by the same victorious struggle for independence that had promoted Kriol. In this way, Kriol was transformed from a language of colonization to a "language of liberation" (Bicari in Scantamburlo 1981: 5) and can be therefore interpreted as representing a sociolinguistic concept of independence (Lopes 1988: 230–31). Besides, Kriol was officially thought of as a unifier for Guinea-Bissau and Cape Verde (Couto 1990: 52). Although independent Guinea-Bissau made Portuguese its official language, Kriol was declared the "national language" (Scantamburlo 1999: 16, without indicating any evidence for his statement) and served as a national symbol that was spoken all over the country's territory. Interestingly, the creole speaker and nationalist Amílcar Cabral rejected teaching in Kriol and other local languages like Fula, Balanta, Mandingo, etc., instead favoring Portuguese as written language in Guinea-Bissau (Cabral 1990: 59). Understanding Portuguese as a unifying language, he declared, "Portuguese is one of the best things the tugas [i.e. the Portuguese] left us because the language is not proof of anything but a tool for men to relate with each other, it is a tool, a means for speaking, to express the realities of life and the world" (Cabral 1990: 59). Thus, the language issue was an ambivalent matter: by choosing the language of the former colonial power as the official language, Bissau-Guinean nationalists followed the path of many other former colonies, including those analyzed in America by Benedict Anderson (1999). However, to date the postcolonial state has not been able to enforce Portuguese, thus resembling the colonial state in its weakness (cf. Forrest 1993). In other words, because the postcolonial state appropriated rather than challenged the modalities of the Portuguese colonial administration (Kohl 2016: 198), it has been both unable to make Portuguese the de facto lingua franca and to develop alternatives, i.e. introducing Kriol. Thus, linguistic postcolonial nation-building was far less successful top-down than it was bottom-up and has not yet been able to match the "success" of the former colonial languages in Latin America, for instance.

Unsurprisingly, the new political leaders had a very low opinion of their own lingua franca. A linguist reported that a frontline politician had told him that Kriol was not a language as it neither possessed a grammar nor a dictionary (Couto 1989: 107)—a view shared by other politicians as well (cf. Godinho Gomes 2010: 93). What may have been the reasons for the decision against Kriol? Clearly, the emerging new elite in Guinea-Bissau, among them many creoles and former citizens, had been the social, political, and economic product of Portuguese colonialism and its socialization and education. The low esteem of Kriol can be consequently interpreted in terms of a colonially induced "self-hatred" (Fanon 2008). Further, producing educational material in Kriol might have been too costly whereas

Portuguese could be considered an international language, facilitating the access to Portuguese (and Brazilian) media, education systems, and labor markets (cf. Figueira 2013: 65–66).

When the well-known Brazilian educator and philosopher Paulo Freire started implementing an adult mass literacy program in 1975, it was decided by the political leaders—supposedly against Freire's own suggestions—to use Portuguese as the language of instruction. For this reason, the program failed because at the time only a small minority of the population was able to speak and write Portuguese: 5 percent Portuguese speakers were facing 45 percent creole speakers (Harasim 1983: 255, 268; Couto 1990: 53; Kirkendall 2010: 105–13; cf. Benson 1994). Despite this setback, there were attempts in the 1980s to standardize Kriol as a written language. However, these did not show any conclusive results (cf. Rougé 1988: 153–61; Ministério de Educação, Cultura e Desportos 1987), and to date PAIGC's original plans to scriptualize Kriol (and other local languages) remain unfulfilled.

Thus, whereas Portuguese continues to be a foreign language for most Bissau-Guineans, instruction is, at least officially, in this language, beginning from the first class. This also owed to the fact that Kriol textbooks and grammar guides are so far not available (Macedo 1989: 35–56).

As my own observations indicate, Kriol is at present understood by people throughout the country, independent of their ethnic affiliations. Exceptions include a few people from the elder generations, especially those living in remote rural areas. The radio stations that are active throughout Guinea-Bissau employ Kriol as the preferred communication medium, thus contributing to the spread of Kriol. In 2007, Guinea-Bissau's parliament passed a law demanding radio stations to broadcast 50 percent in Kriol, 50 percent in Portuguese (Embaló 2008: 103, 105), attempting to balance aspiration (Portuguese as official language) and reality (Kriol as countrywide spoken lingua franca). Similarly, Portuguese is reserved to specific social spheres: official publications like the law gazette are generally in Portuguese, although political debates in parliament, just like discussions and interviews broadcasted by Televisão da Guiné-Bissau, are mostly in Kriol. The same applies to many commercials, public advertisements, awareness campaigns (for example by the United Nations Development Programme), and almost all political debates and conventions. Although the low number of locally produced and marketed books and newspapers are almost exclusively in Portuguese (Parente Augel 1998; 2006: 79–87; Couto and Embaló 2010), the recent two decades has even seen the emergence of comics in Kriol (Couto 1990: 49; Parente Augel 2006: 77–79), even though the number of copies distributed is extremely low. Since Bissau attracts a significant number of people from the countryside who commute between their new and old homes, the capital can be perceived as a primary platform for the spread of Kriol.

Although Portuguese is supposed to be the official language of instruction, teachers—some of them poorly trained and barely able to write Portuguese flawlessly—from all over Guinea-Bissau frequently use Kriol during school lessons. Shortly after independence, the idea came up to introduce teaching in local languages, but results have been very meager (Couto 1989: 112; 1990: 55–56). In the last few years, there have been attempts to officially designate Kriol, by means of bilingual education, as a linguistic mediator between the various local African languages and Portuguese (Scantamburlo 2005).

Today, Kriol is not only a "language of unity" and interethnic communication but also a means of "business, practical communication at work, and personal contact in almost any local community" (Santo Vaz de Almeida 1991: 3). Kriol is the mother tongue of many Bissau-Guineans, especially in urban settings, and there is a strong trend toward Kriol-Portuguese monolingualism in Bissau. Nonetheless, most children and adolescents continue to grow up in bi- or multilingual settings, particularly in the countryside. Yet, some areas are marked by competing linguas francas, including geographic border areas (Fula in the east; Wolof in the northern part of Guinea-Bissau) and market zones where Wolof, Mandingo, and Fula dominate, also due to the foreign origins of many traders.

The spread of Kriol was apparently fostered by the fact that creoles (Cape Verdeans and Kriston), who originally spoke Kriol, are still not regarded as a "normal" ethnic group (such as Fula, Pepel, or Manjaco), according to various informants (interviews AJPB; AVHS). From that perspective, they are regarded as "mixtures" given their diverse ethnic, cultural, and geographic origins. From the analytical point of view, Kriol was, in fact, spoken by various ethnic groups in the *praças* who were united under the transethnic Kriston umbrella. Thus, Kriol bears only a weak ethnic reference.

However, Portuguese cultural workers criticized the spread of Kriol. For example, in the 1990s, the then director of the Portuguese Cultural Center in Bissau saw an "attack" on the Portuguese language originating from "foreign," i.e. non-Portuguese, organizations that promoted the spread of Kriol. He accused the French of supporting the use of French and Kriol "as much as they can" (Matos e Lemos 1999: 35–36; my own translation). Indeed, while no Portuguese artist had performed in Guinea-Bissau by the late 1980s, the country welcomed many French artists, and the French cultural institutions vehemently supported Bissau-Guinean culture and cultural research (Höhn 1987: 4). Contemporary witnesses remembered that in the 1990s, when then state president João Bernardo

"Nino" Vieira had won France as a new partner and Guinea-Bissau joined the Franc CFA zone in 1997, France sponsored road signs in French, to the displeasure of parts of the population (interview GP). By the 1990s, Portugal and France had indeed entered into a geostrategic competition, also affecting cultural and linguistic policies, although France had promoted its language in Guinea-Bissau as early as 1976 (Macedo 1978: 193; 1989: 37–38; Rodrigues Zeverino 2003: 71–77; cf. Couto 1990: 53–54). French was increasingly identified as a threat to Portuguese and even "as a competitor for the status of official language" (Figueira 2013: 253; cf. 254). The Swedish International Development Cooperation Agency (SIDA) and the Portuguese nongovernmental organization CIDAC were also criticized for weakening the position of Portuguese by trying to enhance the status of Kriol (Matos e Lemos 1999: 35–36; cf. Figueira 2013: 254). Hence, apart from French, Kriol was—building on Portugal's colonial anxieties—perceived as a threat to Portuguese cultural-linguistic hegemony.

The spread of Kriol and its increasing number of speakers have also influenced the language itself, to some extent. For instance, Kriol has been significantly influenced by two major developments in recent years. On the one hand, present representations tend to distinguish between *Kriol lebi* (light Kriol) and *Kriol fundu* (profound Kriol). The former is a "Portugalized" Kriol that has resulted from the ongoing process of linguistic decreolization. For the last couple of decades, Kriol has tended to become increasingly similar to Portuguese, due to which *Kriol fundu* is increasingly being replaced by *Kriol lebi*—which is primarily spoken by people with access to education. On the other hand, the substantial numbers of people who grew up speaking their local African mother tongues and who use Kriol only as a vernacular contribute to the simplification of the creole language (Rougé 1988: 8; Couto 1989: 121–26; 1994: 54–55).

Popular culture, notably music, is a major driving force that facilitates the spread of Kriol. Starting with famous bands like Cobiana Jazz in the 1970s, Guinea-Bissau has been home to the development of a lively musical scene over the past decades (Parente Augel 1997; 2006: 76–77). The scene has benefitted from a continuous, fruitful international exchange: many famous Kriol-singing artists have been shuttling between Lisbon and Bissau. Creole rap music has become very popular among young people. The rap groups communicate their messages critical of the government and bad governance almost exclusively in Kriol, thus not only expressing popular political discontent but also fostering the spread and popularization of Kriol in all parts of the country. Hence, this way, the role of Kriol as prime indicator of Bissau-Guinean identity is further strengthened (Barros and Wilson Lima 2012).

Apart from Kriol there are other popular cultural features that contribute to interethnic, national integration. Among these are so-called *manjuandadi* associations that transcend ethnic boundaries and contribute to a nationwide, transethnic integration; however, this process does not remain entirely uncontested.

Integrating the Nation from Below: *Manjuandadi* Associations

In Guinea-Bissau, *manjuandadi* associations are on the tip of many people's tongues, and their appearances are diverse. What then are the core characteristics of *manjuandadis?* Wilson Trajano Filho (1998: 399–405; cf. 2001a, 2001b, 2010), in a pioneering research on the *manjuandadis,* has characterized this institution as one that is based on the principles of mutual assistance and sociability. In general, the *manjuandadis* express solidarity among their predominantly female members by providing mutual aid and support. If any member of these associations is faced with personal or financial problems, the *manjuandadi* will collectively assist their fellow. Members foster friendly relations with each other by having fun together, drinking, eating, and chatting among themselves (also called *brinca* or *jumbai*). The origins of *manjuandadis* are heterogeneous—their roots can be traced back to both African and European cultural forms (Trajano Filho 1998: 335; cf. interviews CRL). Conversely, the origin of the term *manjuandadi* remains obscure.[2] In academia, the term was—to my knowledge—first mentioned in a study published in 1947 (Carreira 1947: images between 28–29, 101–2, 129, 147–49, 165–66; cf. Crowley 1990: 683, 687; Gable 1990: 165–66). It was subsequently used to generically designate "age classes" (Carreira 1961b: 665; 1963: 221; 1964: 408; cf. also 1967: 60; Rogado Quintino 1969: 906; Carreira and Rogado Quintino 1964: 79) and appears to be a creole neologism (Trajano Filho 1998: 316). This hypothesis is supported by linguistic research (Chan-Vianna and Mello 2007: 76–78). Correspondingly, Kriol native speakers associate the term with equality, referring it to people of the same age, the same social status, or generation (Djaló 2012, 30). In a wider sense of the term, *manjuandadi* is not only used to refer to age sets but can also refer more generally to friendship (*amizade*), comradeship (*camaraderia*), conviviality, solidarity, sociability (*konviviu*), and collegiality (*kolegasson*) (interviews FN and CRS; MASF and ERGM; cf. Cabral 1976: 173; Biasutti 1987: 150; Rougé 1988: 100; Pinto Bull 1989: 171; Massa 1996: 74; Montenegro 2002: 47).

Until the mid-twentieth century, *manjuandadi* associations were exclusive to Kriston communities that lived chiefly in the *praças* (interviews

CRL). Just like Kriol and carnival, they started to spread throughout the country at the time of independence—a process that was encouraged by both the PAIGC and the independent state.

The Diversity of the Manjuandadis

Although contemporary *manjuandadis* are characterized by a high degree of diversity, they are based on the principles of sociability and mutuality (Trajano Filho 1998: 314–23). At present, Bissau-Guineans use the word *manjuandadi* to refer to both systematically organized, permanent associations (see sequences one to four below) and loosely organized, mostly ad hoc networks of extended family members, neighbors, coworkers, and friends (see the last sequence; cf. interview JH and ZH). In both cases, the participants are known as *manjuas*, a term that is usually used to refer to individuals of similar ages.

The most striking of these associations is a special kind of *manjuandadi* that belongs to the first type. This type, in the form of music groups, enjoys an excellent reputation. As such, they can be easily distinguished by external observers because of their participants' attention-grabbing, colorful, identical printed dresses, which the members wear on festive occasions. Therefore, third parties often associate musical shows, singing, dancing, and the wearing of identical costumes with the institution of *manjuandadis*.

The following ethnographic sketches provide exemplary glimpses into the manifoldness of contemporary *manjuandadis* from different vantage points.

First Sequence:
Saturday, 31 March 2007, after 9 P.M., Bissau, Alto Bandim quarter, the Nightclub "O Rio": The Movimento Cultural Ubuntu (Ubuntu Cultural Movement), led by an upper-class, high-ranking staff member of the local United Nations headquarters and son-in-law of the businessman and former prime minister Carlos Gomes Júnior, had organized a cultural night. Ubuntu is a cultural society dominated by middle- and upper-class members. Tickets in advance sale were priced at 2,500 francs CFA (currently about $4.50) each. Several illustrious guests arrived before the commencement of the event, including leading politicians, businessmen, intellectuals, representatives of the civil society, and personnel from diplomatic missions, international organizations, and the development cooperation sector. The organizers of the event had already booked a variety of local musicians, both "traditional" and "modern," to perform that night.

The third group to perform was the *manjuandadi* called Nivaquina from Bissau's quarter of Belém. The performance included songs sung by seven female singers who also beat the *palmas de madeira* (literally, "wooden palms" that vaguely resemble castanets). The women were accompanied by seven male musicians: one singer-dancer, two *siko* drummers (a *siko* is a small, quadrangular hand drum played with bare hands), one *singa* drummer (a *singa* is a hand drum made by covering a mortar with skin), one *tina* drummer (the *tina* is also known as the *tambor água* or "water drum," which is actually an idiophone that usually consists of a bowl made of plastic or metal that is filled with water and covered with a halved calabash as a membrane), and two *palmas* beaters. All the artists were dressed in identical, wide, brownish-ochre print dresses. The audience watched the performance in hushed silence. After their performance, which went on for about forty minutes, the group was rewarded with thundering applause.

Second Sequence:

Friday, 17 November 2006, 4:30 P.M., Bissau, Bra quarter, in front of the Palace Hotel: The event was a conference convened by the União das Cidades Capitais Luso-Afro-Américo-Asiáticas (UCCLA, Union of Luso-Afro-Americo-Asiatic Capital Cities), and many participants, including the mayors of several cities, were expected to arrive at the above hotel. In the morning, a cheerful group of people had moved around in vans on the outskirts of Bissau, chanting "Jomav, Jomav"—the nickname given to Bissau's then mayor (and today's state president). At 4 P.M., I was waiting in front of the city hall in downtown Bissau for members of the Jamanodiata *manjuandadi* from the Cupilon de Cima quarter. As their leaders had informed me, Bissau's mayor had invited the association to welcome the conference delegates at the airport. However, only four women turned up, festively dressed in identical orange print dresses. I learned that the municipality had provided them neither transport facilities nor traveling expenditure. Consequently, we hired a taxi and drove to the conference hotel. Crowds of people were assembled in front of the complex along the arterial road that links the airport with the city center, while women belonging to different attendant *manjuandadis* were grouping together separately. Dressed in their identical costumes, some of them sang joyfully and beat their *palmas*. Members of a *manjuandadi* named Boa Esperança di Bande (Good Hope of Bandim), one of the country's most popular groups, had gathered next to us. Only fourteen members of the association had turned up. The women, who were identically dressed in dark-green skirts and white blouses (*ropon*), sang and beat their *palmas*, while a man in a t-shirt and trousers played the *tina*. Just a few meters away,

there was another *manjuandadi* named Quinhentos Padida (Five Hundred Caring Parents). Their members were dressed in green print dresses
that had been sponsored by a cleaning company, adorned with matching
turban-like headpieces. This association originated from the Reino quarter. Its members informed me that their group was a Muslim *manjuandadi* that was founded in 1971. They said that even now, some of the aged
founding members continued to actively participate in the *manjuandadi*
performances. Next to this group were situated members of the Nivaquina
manjuandadi. This group was dressed less festively. In contrast to the other
attendant associations, there were only male *manjuas* representing the
Nivaquina *manjuandadi*. They sang as they beat their skin drums, but they
did not play the *tina*. Since I had already met and interviewed some of the
attendees a few months ago, they were pleased to meet me and invited me
to join them in the traditional *badju di tina* (*tina* drum dance). Meanwhile,
I discovered another *manjuandadi* called Dona (Madam, Landlady), which
had assembled across the street. Theirs was a recently founded association
that hailed from the nearby Bairro Militar quarter. The exclusively female
members were likewise dressed in identical colorful print dresses.

Third Sequence:

Sunday, 18 March 2007, afternoon, Bissau, Sintra quarter: On my way to
a friend's house, I was walking through a labyrinth of residential houses
and narrow paths when I accidentally observed a *manjuandadi* reunion
in one of the backyards. While the female participants, who were identically dressed in pink prints, danced and played their *palmas,* the few male
members beat the *siko, tina,* and *singa* drums. This *manjuandadi* was called
Amizade (Friendship) and comprised members of diverse ethnic groups,
such as Mancanha, Balanta, and Pepel. These ethnic groups, however, are
considered to be predominantly Christian.

Fourth Sequence:

Thursday, 5 April 2007, after 5:30 P.M., Bissau, Belém quarter: An aged
member of the Boa Esperança di Bande *manjuandadi* had passed away in
the previous week. In memory of their deceased *manjua,* about twenty
members of the association met in the backyard of another member's
house on that afternoon. There, they handed around an empty halved calabash and asked each of the attendees to contribute 500 francs CFA (currently about $1.00). This amount served to reimburse several members
who had provided for *kaolange* (a homemade mixture of rum, milk, sugar,
and other ingredients, whose name is supposedly derived from the Irish
cream liqueur Carolans) and *feijoada* (a dish made of beans and different
kinds of meat, served with rice). As a guest, I had brought along a crate of

beer. After a certain amount of time, we started dancing the *badju di tina*, cheered by the *kinti* (literally, "hot" — but used here in the sense of "fast") drumming of the *tina* until late in the night.

Fifth Sequence:

Thursday, 1 May 2006, early afternoon, Bissau, Bissalanca quarter, close to the international airport: I had arranged to meet an employee of a restaurant that was located next door to my residence; we were to meet at the abovementioned location at noon. Some weeks prior, I had asked her whether she would introduce me to her *manjuandadi*. In reply, she had suggested that May Day would be a good day to become acquainted with her *manjuandadi*, since we could celebrate together. Our taxi took us to a shady area close to the airport, where a friend of her family's ran a small takeaway sales stall. There, I met my informant's *manjuas* — all of them were members of her extended family (her sister, the sister's husband, her uncle, and her cousin). As the day progressed, more and more family members and friends joined us, Christians as well as Muslims. After a while, the women started to prepare food, while the men and the takeaway owner were busy arranging for ice to cool the beer and commissioning a ghetto blaster. Spirits ran high and we had a nice evening with lots of merry-making, eating, drinking, and chatting with each other. Night had already fallen by the time we decided to leave. By then it was already 9 P.M. — we were all in a good mood and took a *toca-toca* (public transport van) home.

By describing these selected sketches from among my ethnographic field observations, I wished to demonstrate the highly diverse nature of contemporary *manjuandadis*. In the subsequent section, I will examine the possible origins of these groups.

Origins and Development in Colonial Times

Historical evidence suggests that the present-day *manjuandadis* have their roots in African age-set organizations on the one hand and Christian confraternities on the other.

Age-set-based organizations are very common among many ethnic groups inhabiting Guinea-Bissau. Age sets — that is, groups of persons united by age — are common among the Manjaco, Cassanga, Mancanha, Pepel, and Mandingo (own findings and Person 1968: 64–72; Jao 1989: 57–60; cf. Carreira 1961b: 663–71).

By contrast, confraternities have existed in Italy and the Iberian Peninsula at least since the late Middle Ages (Chauchadis 1986; Black 1989; Lahon 2001). A confraternity can be roughly defined as "a voluntary association of people who come together under the guidance of certain rules to promote their religious life in common. Normally this is a group or brotherhood of laymen, and is administered by the laity" (Black 1989: 1). More precisely, they were "secular associations organized around the veneration of a patron saint that provided welfare among their members, supported the service in chapels or churches, and promoted forms of worship among the population, not only directly by celebrating masses but also indirectly by conducting their own processions on the day of the patron saint or by participating in other processions" (Bethencourt 1998: 385; my own translation).

In the fifteenth century, Portuguese confraternities (*confrarias*) were exclusively reserved for Europeans. Subsequently, Africans—encompassing both slaves and free men—who constituted up to 15 percent of Lisbon's population were allowed to join "mixed" confraternities. The first black confraternity can be traced back to 1460 (Rosa Pereira 1972: 10–11). In the late sixteenth century, the idea of purity of blood became increasingly important, leading to the exclusion of blacks, among others (Lahon 2000: 277–82; 2005: 261; 2004: 55). In the wake of these exclusions, some of the confraternities split into separate black and white institutions, while others were dissolved. Later, separate black confraternities emerged, associated with their members' (supposed) ethnic or geographic origins (for instance, Angolans were known as Congos, West Africans as Minas, those who originated from Mozambique as Indios, etc.) (Lahon 2000: 294; 2004: 68–71).

Portuguese confraternities were usually either organized on a professional basis or formed in the parishes, and these bore a corresponding emblematic name, such as Irmandade da Nossa Senhora do Rosário (Confraternity of Our Lady of the Rosary). Mixed and black confraternities often elected their managing bodies, called *mesas* (managing boards), which comprised a treasurer, a secretary (*escrivão*), a judge (*juiz*) and a number of sextons (*mordomos*) (Rosa Pereira 1972: 15; Lahon 2000: 276, 300; 2003: 124). In addition, a member could become an elected *príncipe* (prince), *rei* (king), *duque* (duke), *conde* (earl), *marquês* (margrave), *cardeal* (cardinal), or any other dignitary within the confraternity (Rosa Pereira 1972: 23). Several confraternities possessed a female queen (*rainha*), who was generally accompanied by a prince and a princess (Lahon 2000: 301; 2003: 124). The *reis* and *rainhas*, often as a couple, were usually designated using an ethnic or geographical reference, for example, the "*rei/rainha de Angola*" (King/Queen of Angola) (Lahon 1999b: 70–71, 73; 2003: 142–44; 2004: 68–69; cf. Mac Cord 2005). Although women did not always seem to have access to posts of responsibility, in at least one confraternity in the eighteenth and nineteenth centuries, women formed the majority (Lahon 2000: 311; 2003:

124). The Lisbon-based confraternities usually had an influential member who acted as their patron and protector—sometimes the king himself (Lahon 2003: 124). In addition, some confraternities enjoyed financial privileges. Some of them even obtained from the Crown the right of "demanding and requiring the freeing and manumission of any black man or woman who is a member of the confraternity" (Lahon 2005: 265).

Moreover, these confraternities provided for their members' religious tuition, prayers and masses, mutual assistance, charity and solidarity—granting financial aid inter alia to members or their families in case of death or disease. Within this context, the confraternities requested obligatory alms from their members, along with an annual payment that served to cover the burial expenses of deceased members. In general, however, the confraternities did not have huge resources at their disposal (Rosa Pereira 1972: 17, 26; Lahon 2003: 123–44).

The global spread was due to the fact that Christian confraternities were founded wherever the Portuguese established colonial presence throughout the world. Thus, the "movement of organizing confraternities developed rapidly throughout the entire empire, constituting one of the principal processes of transferring European structures to other regions of the world" (Bethencourt 1998: 385–86, my own translation). However, this "transmission" was no one-way street. Rather, European models encountered diverse, locally specific thought-worlds that led to the unplanned translation of ideas, turning them into different substances (Czarniawska and Joerges 1996; Kaufmann and Rottenburg 2012). Sociocultural values, norms, and features were often selectively appropriated by emerging lusocreole groups—both intentionally and unintentionally—and subsequently integrated and adjusted to their own needs and cultural structures (cf. Walker 2005: 195). In Portugal, Christian confraternities existed until their abolition in 1869 (Lahon 2003: 123; cf., however, Rosa Pereira 1972: 23); however, they survived elsewhere in modified forms to date. Whereas the confraternities in former Portuguese India, São Tomé and Príncipe, and Malacca have subsisted to this day, those in Japan were short lived (Teixeira 1963: 27–31; Rocha 1973; d'Costa 1977; Thomaz 1981–82: 38–39; Eyzaguirre 1986: 257–58, 382–84; Marbeck 1995: 7–9; Kawamura 1999; Baxter 2005: 12, 17).

By contrast, a few black confraternities continue to exist in Brazil, where they are known as *irmandades*. There, the practice of electing kings and queens within confraternities of black slaves was also practiced until the nineteenth century. At that time, black confraternities in Salvador de Bahia, among others, were organized along ethnic lines; within these *irmandades*, competitions between Afro-Brazilians of different origins occurred (Lahon 2001: ch. 9; 2004: 68; Reis 2003: 332–33; Mac Cord 2005; Reginaldo 2011). Ultimately, the few surviving black confraternities in Greater Recife were dominated by a few influential families that sold burial places on their own account. After this scandal became public, the archdiocese decided to put them like other, non-Afro-Brazilian confraternities, under supervision (interviews FR).

In Cape Verde, the existence of *confrarias* has been recorded since the late sixteenth century at the earliest (cf. Brásio 1964: 80–81). *Tabancas* that share some characteristics with confraternities continue to exist until today in the islands of Santiago and Maio (cf. Meintel 1984: 142–45; Trajano Filho 2001b; 2006a; 2009a; 2009b; 2012; Jesus Tavares 2005: 46–48; Gonçalves 2006: 29–34; Semedo and Turano n.d.). While the word *tabanca* is still used to designate "villages" in the Upper Guinea, in Cape Verde, however, it exclusively refers to this kind of association (Monteiro 1948: 14; Scantamburlo 2002: 598; Hawthorne 2003: 121–22; Trajano Filho 2016). Like their Bissau-Guinean counterparts, the *tabancas* are based on a system of mutual assistance, and their members are given special titles, such as *rei* and *rainha* who are assisted by a *conselheiro* (councilor). The queen commands the *mandoras* (lutanists), *cativos* (captives), and *filhas-de-santo* (abigails). Apart from a juridical and military section, the *tabancas* also manage a "nursery" and a "prison" (Gonçalves 2006: 30).

Historical sources suggest that the Kriston communities in the *praças* like Bissau, Cacheu, Geba, Farim, and Ziguinchor were also organized into Christian confraternities, facilitated by the close contact with Portugal since the fifteenth century. As in metropolitan Portugal, these brotherhoods were dedicated to specific female saints (Lopes de Lima 1844: pt. 1, table inserted between 72–73; Havik 2004: 133).

The earliest account of Christian communities—and tacitly, of confraternities—is supposed to have been written by the priest Manuel Álvares around 1615 (Álvares 1990). Christian confraternities and their activities in Cacheu were sponsored by wealthy local traders in the late seventeenth century. Apart from organizing annual festivities in honor of their respective saint, the confraternities also celebrated Catholic holidays (such as All Saints' Day, All Souls' Day, and so on). They also fulfilled the basic functions of providing for mutual solidarity and support, for example in the case of funerals (Havik 2004: 134).

Generally speaking, we know little about the character and activities of confraternities. In the early 1820s confraternities in Cacheu, Ziguinchor, Farim, Geba, and other settlements served as miniature governments, consisting of deputies elected by Kriston communities in the *praças*. They assumed the right to pass judgment and legislation in the area under their control. Therefore, they challenged the colonial administration's authority. Their political activities resulted in conflicts between the *praças* and the neighboring "indigenous" dwellers. As a consequence, the confraternities were outlawed (Senna Barcellos 1905: 326–27, 348; Barreto 1938: 185–86). Hence, it is not surprising that official reports of the time condemned confraternities, which were mostly headed by influential creole traders, because they were feared as parallel governments (Barreto 1938: 186; Havik 2004: 134–35). Yet it remains unclear how former Catholic confraternities are related to present-day *manjuandadis* that bear some similarities to colonial brotherhoods.

Anyway, since the mid-eighteenth century, reports surfaced that portrayed popular festivities that might be attributed to *manjuandadis*, resembling their contemporary manner to fete. A Portuguese officer who visited Bissau in 1858 has presented an irritated account of nocturnal festivities that he had to endure. The details contained in his description might allude to the style of music and dance that are nowadays cultivated by the *manjuandadis*. The officer narrated that *grumetes* used to wander in Bissau's alleys and assemble in nearby houses at night. He was disturbed by "litanies sung between shrill laughter and furious screams, yet with *mornas* [Cape Verdean dance and music genre], *batuques* [drumming sessions ascribed to Africans], and other dances capable of routing the most hardbitten European" (Correia de Almeida 1859: 50; my own translation, original emphasis). Based on the author's account, these probably occurred on the occasion of Ascension, a Catholic holiday, on 13 May.

It appears that some female Kriston singers among the *manjuandadis* enjoyed a good reputation in the mid- to late nineteenth century. A number of their songs, called *cantigas de pretos* (Negroes' songs) became very popular at that time (Marques de Barros 1882: 728–29; 1900: 44–65; Semedo 2007: 76–77; 2010: 79).

Another Portuguese officer described a noisy and colorful crowd of "indigenous Christians" who were feting in Bolama on Dia de Todos-os-Santos (All Saints' Day) and Dia dos Finados (All Souls' Day) on 1 and 2 November 1898:

> They come out of their dwellings and gather at the door of the local church, whence they proceed with little lights, walking in procession through all the streets, singing the Ave-Maria intermixed with African songs.
>
> Men and women with fantastic costumes, as if it were a carnival, and swigging aguardente [spirit] and palm wine, wander about for three entire nights in this manner until after daybreak; then they disperse, everyone returning to their dwellings, to come out again at night, and spend all day on the 2nd in singing and dancing. The groups combine this with alcoholic drinks and engage in lewd behavior, which debauchery attains its peak during the night of the 2nd until dawn, when after several hours of rest, the finale of the commemoration takes place, which consists of feasting and more drinking, inside or in the open air at a place some distance from the settlement, afterwards singing once again

Ave-Marias for the souls of all the departed. (Brooks 1984: 1 translating Dias de Carvalho 1944: 73–75, 238–39; cf. also Marques Geraldes 1887: 503–4)

As the officer remarked, such "absurd" processions were banned by the authorities in 1904 (Dias de Carvalho 1944: 75). Although the term is not explicitly mentioned, the observation *may* be a description of the *manjuandadis*.

On Thursday, 28 May 1936, a British journalist made an observation in Bissau that may be attributed to a *manjuandadi* festivity. On that day, which was the Portuguese national holiday at that time, he followed "some sort of a *festa*" inside Bissau's Amura fortress:

> Then the old fort is gay with bunting and in the evening a *batuque* is held in the great barrack square which a century or more ago was the warehouse of the slaves. The Bissau blacks are Christians, blasé and unexcitable, and they stroll about the town in sun-helmets and European clothes, but as I watched the *batuque* . . . one spectator after another would suddenly shed his sophistication with a whoop and plunge madly into the shouting crowd which shuffled and swayed in the dust—utterly unconscious of anything but the drugging, maddening rhythm of the drums, the wild chanting of the drummers, and the fire which burned in his blood. (Lyall 1938: 291; original emphasis)

The indication that the festivities are held by "Christians" points to the Kriston community. The general frolicking, dancing, and playing of drums refer to the *manjuandadi* music and dance—notably the frantic *badju di tina*. Another point to note is the reference to a national holiday. As aged female former activists stated (interviews LC; MaCF; SG), until the 1960s the Portuguese administration used to invite *manjuandadis* to perform on the occasion of official visits, national celebrations, governors' birthdays, and other state-related events. Apart from these occasions, it is also possible that the festivity was linked to Catholic Whitsunday, which was celebrated on 31 May that year.

We can only speculate about the way in which the male-dominated confraternities were transformed into *manjuandadis*—in which women typically outnumber men. Ahistorical depictions of *manjuandadis* act on the assumption that they have been always dominated by females (Domingues, Freitas, and Gomes Ferreira 2006). Indeed, some of my aged Kriston informants whose experiences with *manjuandadis* went back to the 1920s confirmed that women outnumbered men even at that time (interviews VFR, MaCF; cf. Parés 2013: 135–36). They argued that men, in fact, often remained absent from the *manjuandadi* meetings, despite paying their membership dues, because of work obligations. Currently, my own observations indicate that women constitute as much as 70–80 percent of the *manjuandadi* members. According to Trajano Filho, the average number of male members in 2007 was slightly higher than it was at the time of his fieldwork in the mid-1980s and early 1990s (personal communication, Wilson Trajano Filho, Universidade de Brasília, April 2007).

As the historical sources quoted earlier may suggest, *manjuandadis* developed their own dynamics over a certain period of time in the nineteenth century. In this way, they eventually became self-contained creole cultural manifestations, independent of the state and Church authorities. One can only speculate if the impetus for this process might have been the colonial administration's attempts to restrain confraternities since the 1820s—perhaps suggesting that the colonial administration identified male members as troublemakers and subsequently managed to oust them. In contrast, women may have been regarded as apolitical, thus following the spirit of the time. If this was the case, it might have been possible that women were allowed to continue running *manjuandadi* associations. Ultimately, *manjuandadis* might have chosen to camouflage themselves as carnivalesque groups when confronted with the growing colonial presence. Such a solution was chosen, for example, by Afro-Brazilian cultural representations: coronations of the Rei do Congo that were closely connected to black confraternities in Recife transformed in the course of the nineteenth century into *maracatus*, nowadays known as popular carnival groups. They can either be interpreted as caricatures of the former coronations or as expressions of Afro-Brazilian cultural agency and claims (Mac Cord 2005: 258–59). In an analog way, Cape Verdean *tabancas* benefited from room left by the colonial state, in a complex space between resistance and domination (Trajano Filho 2006a). On the other hand, the Catholic Church may have taken action against *manjuandadis* because they had lost their original, religious purpose. Thus, they may have faced a similar fate as feasts organized by religious confraternities in nineteenth-century France:

> The clergy had always shown a certain hostility to popular rejoicing as essentially pagan; feasting was gross, libertine, leading to violence and keeping peasants away from church services. Unable to eliminate such feasts, the Church incorporated them but did not cease to treat them with suspicion. Around mid[-nineteenth] century the hierarchy set about purification.... Religious congregations and fraternities, especially penitents, had lost sight of their original purpose.... They had become social and drinking societies ... or political clubs.... They were replaced with associations specifically dedicated to prayer and to pious works. (Weber 1976: 366)

The last known founding of a "revived" Catholic confraternity that occurred in Bolama in 1884 (Dias Vicente 1992: 434, 470) supports this hypothesis.

Old and New: Differences between Past and Present Manjuandadis

Based on interviews with members (and their relatives) of old-established creole manjuandadis, representatives of current associations, and cultural activists (interviews AJVDB; ADZ; BC, ADS, JS, and IC; CRL; DGF; DN; EDP; GSD; HA; IDC; IsDC; IMMN; JC; LC; MASF and ERGM; MC; MDL; MV; NN; NR; SG; TL; VDC; VFR), a number of similarities and differences between "old" Kriston and "new," present-day *manjuandadis* can be identified.

Membership:

Until the 1960s, only Kriston could become members of *manjuandadis,* thus their members shared the Christian faith. Kriol obviously served as the main medium of communication. As some aged former activists informed me, Cape Verdeans and Europeans usually declined to participate in *manjuandadis.* Moreover, the *manjuandadi* members typically belonged to the lower or middle class. As my findings suggest, upper-class individuals were apparently alienated from this culture of carousal, raunchy behavior, tomboyish appearance, and feasting and frolicking that was cultivated by the *manjuandadis.* Instead, upper-class Bissau-Guineans often rejected *manjuandadis* in favor of Portuguese-style proms and violin music in colonial times.

Age-Set Organization:

Former creole *manjuandadis* were organized according to age sets until the 1950s or 1960s. However, most contemporary groups do not follow this principle, a fundamental shift that has induced aged Kriston former *manjuandadi* activists to claim that true *manjuandadis* no longer exist. As mentioned above, Kriston *manjuandadis* corresponded to a type of social organization that was recognized in both Guinea-Bissau and Europe. Age-set and age-grade systems are widespread among various ethnic groups in Guinea-Bissau's interior, and the Catholic Church initiates its adherents into adulthood by means of Communion and Confirmation. Informants affirmed, however, that their *gusto* (liking) sometimes motivated individuals to join *manjuandadis* that did not correspond to their age. Witnesses agreed that the members of younger *manjuandadis* were considered subordinate to those who belonged to older groups. Further, older *manjuandadis* were responsible for raising individuals of later-founded, younger *manjuandadis*. In case the juniors showed a lack of respect, they were disciplined by means of a spanking.

Since the early 1960s only a few *manjuandadis* in nonrural areas have continued to be organized on the basis of age sets. My informants opined that this was because of the war of independence. At that time, *manjuan-dadis* often discontinued their activities because so many associations had lost members and their relatives in combat operations. However, Trajano Filho (1998: 330) has conjectured that, in fact, political repression by the Portuguese security apparatus may have intimidated *manjuandadi* activists into discontinuing their activities.

Further, contemporary witnesses I spoke with suggested that the institution of *manjuandadis* (and thus their pronounced age-set-based organization) was increasingly seen as reserved for backward people. A woman of creole and highly diverse ancestry in her early seventies (interview DN) clearly stated that in the 1950s and 1960s, when she was still young, *manjuandadis* were something for "*tongóma*" (*tungumá*) and "*gurmetu*" (*grumete*) but nothing for "*senhoras*" like her. Originally neutral notions, both *tungumá* and *grumete* over the past decades have transformed into derogatory terms to denote individuals who did not frequent school. My interviewee's mother, who had been born in 1918, had, however, been a member of a *manjuandadi*. She and her husband (cf. interviews MaCF), though, as "educated people," had been members of *grupos* (groups) like Trovadores (Troubadours), then Embaixada (Embassy), and finally Famílias Unidas (United Families) that were not to be confused with *manjuandadis*. Obviously, these groups attracted socially advanced people and offered more sophisticated pastime, accelerating the disappearance of old-style age-set-based *manjuandadis*. The strict age-set organization became more flexible around the same time. This suggests that the newly founded associations were constituted in a less uniform fashion.

Moreover, a few groups might have clandestinely served as platforms for the independence movement, which could have resulted in the abandonment of the age-set principle. Although some of my informants disclaimed this idea, this role of the *manjuandadis* might have caused the colonial state to restrict their activities after the outbreak of the war—similar to the actions undertaken by the Portuguese authorities against the Cape Verdean *tabancas* (Trajano Filho 2006a). A possible starting point for this restriction could have included requiring the groups to obtain official permission for *batuques* by paying fees (cf. the municipal scale of fees in Duarte 1946: 628; 1948: 975). Elderly activists indeed remembered that if the *manjuandadis* did not obtain formal permission from the city council, the police would appear to put a stop to their activities (interviews LLDC; MaCF).

Like the contemporary *manjuandadis,* the former age-set-based Kriston *manjuandadis* bore emblematic names (cf. also interview MB). In the past, *manjuandadis* existed autonomously in each of the *praças*, that is, without central leadership. The names of the *manjuandadi* branches were identical, at least in earlier times. Nevertheless, the names of these associations could vary from *praça* to *praça*. The news of the establishment of a new age-set-based *manjuandadi* would spread by word of mouth within the creole community and to other settlements. When members moved to another *praça* or returned after spending a long time abroad, they would be welcomed by counterparts from other *manjuandadis* representing the corresponding age set. This aspect is affirmed by a report drafted in the 1950s: although it does not mention "*manjuandadis*" but instead refers to "clubs" for "entertaining purposes," the characteristics may allude to this kind of association:

> All clubs organize periodic feasts, generally during festive days of the Europeans. They usually consist of collective meals, followed by dance (batuque). Apart from these feasts others are organized when the local clubs are visited by delegations of other clubs. (Silva Cunha 1959: 40; my own translation, underlining in the original)

Offices:

Organized *manjuandadis* are also characterized by the existence of various offices resembling those of the Cape Verdean *tabancas* and (former) Portuguese and Brazilian black confraternities. A similar practice was reported on so-called "clubs" in the 1950s:

> The organization of the clubs is rudimentary. None of them has written statutes and the hierarchy of the leaders (that are chosen by the members) is in all respects similar to and imitating, in their designation, the Portuguese political and administrative hierarchies and social categories. Frequently, there are designations like that of governor, military commander, district administrator, judge, medical doctor, juridical doctor, police captain, customs director, finance director, etc. (Silva Cunha 1959: 41; my own translation)

The contemporary *manjuandadis* that I was able to observe possess an executive committee, which appeared to be more differentiated than it was in the past. Between different *manjuandadis*, there may be slight variations with regard to office designations and the assignment of tasks. The most important charges (*cores*) are that of a *rei* (king) and a *rainha* (queen). In addition, nowadays there are further subordinate offices, such as that of the *meirinha* (bailiff, magistrate), *cordeiro* (synonym for a lamb, Jesus Christ, or a gentle person), and *tesoureiro* (treasurer) (e.g. interview FN and CRS). At the time of independence, reports indicate that *manjuandadis* elected only a queen, a vice-queen, and a man who was responsible for handling the association's affairs with the public administration (Urdang 1979: 275). Many *manjuandadi* offices were supposedly created recently, such as *polí-*

Name of the *manjuandadi*	Formation
Kakre (Cancer, Crayfish)	ca. 1895?
Lamparas (Lamp; refers to any light producing object)	?
Melga (Crane Fly)	?
Mosquito (Mosquito)	?
Kombéfina (kombé = shell/cockle; fina = thin?)	ca. 1900–05?
Flor d'Ouro (Golden Flower)	ca. 1905-10?
Estrelas (Stars)	ca. 1915–20?
Raiz, Riz (Root)	?
Melga Nova (New Crane Fly)	ca. 1920–25?
Coral (Coral)	ca. 1920?
Coralfina (coral = coral; fina = thin?)	ca. 1925
Ferredja (Forge)	ca. 1930?
Pé di Mesa (Table-leg)	before ca. 1935
Pé di Kombe (Part (?) of a shell/cockle)	before ca. 1935 (ca. 1930?)
Pé di Banco (Bench-leg)	ca. 1940
Strelinhas di Cacheu (Small Stars of Cacheu) (origin: Cacheu); former name: Bom Conta (Good Story, Tradition)	ca. 1940
Pé di Mocho (Bench-leg)	ca. 1945?
Bolamense (From Bolama); former name: Argentina (Argentina)	1952
Ramo (Bough)	ca. 1970
Kodé di Ramo (Youngest Brother of the Bough)	early 1970s

Figure 3.1. Age-Set-Based *Manjuandadis* of the Past. This table provides only a fragmentary and approximate overview of the chronology of Kriston *manjuandadis* organized according to the age-set principle.

cias (policemen), *financeiros* (financiers), *vice-reis* (viceroys) (cf. Domingues 2000: 479, 482; Domingues, Miranda Freitas, and Gomes Ferreira 2006: 95), *presidentes* (presidents), *conselheiros* (councilors), *condes* (earls), *mamés* (mothers), *papés* (fathers), *orientadores* (guides), *coordenadores* (coordinators), *secretários* (secretaries), and *padrinhos* (godfathers). The innovative addition of new offices attempts to advocate gender equality by creating male and female counterparts for each office, as the representatives of one *manjuandadi* informed me (interviews DC and PS; cf. Domingues 2000: 479). Ordinary members are called *soldados* (soldiers). All members are obliged to pay *abotas* (membership fees) (interviews IMMN; MASF and ERGM; cf. Trajano Filho 1998: 368, 371–79) and make special contributions on the occasion of members' weddings, funerals, etc. (cf. Silva Cunha 1959: 40–41). Fees are collected and administered by the *tesoureiro*. As in the past, administrative fines (*multas*) can be imposed on members who arrive too late for sessions or who disobey the *rei*'s orders.

Festivities Celebrated:

Contemporary *manjuandadis* tend to celebrate secular events, such as the anniversary of the group's founding, which is regarded as an important day of celebration. Further, weddings, funerals, birthdays, *tocachors,* and other rituals of various types have been an excuse for indulging in *jumbai* and *brinca*. On such occasions, members gather together in order to drink, joke, laugh, dance, and make music. These shared activities give rise to friendship and sociability within the group. Before any event, members pool money in order to pay for the food and beverages consumed.

Although many present-day *manjuandadis* continue to celebrate holidays such as Christmas, carnival, or Easter together, the religious (Christian) context is far less emphasized today. This is especially true in the case of the for more recently founded *manjuandadis,* some or all of whose members are Muslims, and who therefore do ignore the Christian holidays that were previously celebrated by the Kriston *manjuandadis*. Some elderly Kriston *manjuandadi* activists mentioned, in fact, that the celebration of religious holidays was very pronounced in the past. This suggests that, in the past, *manjuandadis* had rather strong ties with the Catholic Church In the 1930s and 1940s, for instance, elderly Kriston activists from Bolama remembered that *manjuandadis* used to celebrate religious days such as a local church holiday that was commemorated annually on 15 August (interviews MaCF). On that occasion, various *manjuandadis* representing different age sets would gather together in order to celebrate the day. These celebrations were also marked by aspects of secular sociability and entertainment. The *manjuandadi* groups used to sing in front of people's homes, whose owners, in turn, had to pay a contribution to the *manjuandadi*. Similarly, the creole *manjuandadis* used to celebrate carnival—also a holiday associated with Catholicism—at that time.

Appearance:

Most of the *manjuandadis* that nowadays perform as musical groups present a striking sight due to their members' eye-catching "full dress." These identical costumes are often made from the same printed cloth (*légos*) that has become available only in recent decades, but they can also be made from other fabrics. The generic terms used to designate festive dresses are *uniforme* or *farda* (uniform). Creole *manjuandadis* in the past would wear different festive clothes to their assemblies and performances, and they still do today every once in a while. These garments normally comprised white chemises (*ropons*), combined with traditional handmade *panos di pinti*—made of black and white yarn—which were worn over the *ropons*. The *ropons* could be blue, yellowish cream, or pink in color. However, when in mourning, members traditionally wore white in order to show their respect. During festive occasions, however, my elderly informants remembered that their costumes consisted of white *camisas de soca* (long robes) adorned with a crocheted pattern around the neckline and very short sleeves. These dresses stretched from neck to feet and are very rarely seen today.

Originally, each *manjuandadi* possessed a *bandeira* (flag), or *vara* (stick), which served as their corporate symbol and was exhibited at public events. However, my observations suggest that the majority of today's *manjuandadis* have abandoned the tradition of possessing a *bandeira*. A contemporary *bandeira* consisted of pieces of fabric of different colors that were fixed to a wooden pole about six feet (two meters) long. Several informants explicitly explained to me that the flag was apparently a reference to military traditions. Flags were apparently also used by Afro-Brazilians, among others, on the occasion of the coronation of *reis* and *rainhas* connected to rosary festivities celebrated by black confraternities, as a drawing from the early nineteenth century suggests (Reis 2003: photograph 2). Similarly, Cape Verdean *tabancas* continue to creatively combine flags of their respective patron saint with various kinds of other flags (national flags, flags of football teams, depicting icons of international music culture, etc.) during their processions (Trajano Filho 2012). It remains unclear, however, if the tradition of *manjuandadi bandeiras* can be traced back to confraternities or even flags formerly used by Portuguese military orders. The use of musical instruments has also undergone changes. Formerly, the *tina* was the main instrument played by Kriston *manjuandadis*. Although the Christian groups continue to play the *tina*, the Muslim *manjuandadis*—usually founded after independence—generally do not use this musical instrument (interview, e.g., FN and CRS). Former Kriston *manjuandadi* activists mentioned that in the past, the *tina* was made of halved wine barrels. Moreover, the *siko* drum, which is played all over West Africa, was obviously introduced during the war of independence (personal communication, Trajano Filho, Universidade de Brasília, May 2009). Evidently, the wooden *palmas* that are common at present were quite rarely used in the past, if they were used at all. Instead, the musicians used to clap their hands. The *cocos de mango*—a type of rattle that is filled with mango kernels and worn around the ankles—were also used in former times. Informants and former members recalled that their *manjuandadis* used *gaitas* (harmonicas) in the 1950s and 1960s, which were fitting accompaniments to their three traditional rhythms (*niná, morna,* and *komboi*). However, my informants declared that this instrument seems to have disappeared around independence. Within this context, they mentioned that the *tina* became less popular in the 1950s and 1960s, given the increasing use of portable phonographs, thus introducing new genres of European and American music to the *manjuandadi* repertoire.

In summary, the historical overview indicates that *manjuandadi* associations have undergone diversification and differentiation accompanied by a simultaneous process of secularization. As a result, the ties between *manjuandadis* and the Church weakened and then finally dissolved, even if members label themselves as "Kriston." The following section will explain how these changes were apparently prompted by the independence movement PAIGC and the postcolonial state apparatus established by the movement.

Manjuandadis *as a Means of Mobilization after Independence*

Independence and the subsequent installation of a leftist one-party state under the leadership of the PAIGC signified not only a fresh start for *manjuandadis* but also their gradual transformation into organizations that were deemed "traditional" (Askew 2002: 171) and supposed to support the politics of the new state (cf. Trajano Filho 1998: 402; cf. Gacitua-Mario et al. 2006: 28). The PAIGC tried to turn the *manjuandadis* into monopolistic mass organizations: these "were designed to mobilize support for government and party and to channel the energies and enthusiasms of the people exclusively in directions by the leadership. They were not intended to be the means by which the people could control the leadership or even influence their decisions" (Galli and Jones 1987: 86).

Whereas other mass organizations were suppressed (Koudawo 1996: 78–79), all women—particularly those in the party's stronghold Bissau—

were required to take membership of the party's women's wing, for most of the time known as UDEMU (over time, the PAIGC's women's organization was known by different names; UDEMU—União Democrática das Mulheres da Guiné n.d.; Chilcote 1972: 341–46, 1991: 73, 134; Andreini and Lambert 1978: 45; Urdang 1979: 267–68; Godinho Gomes 2013). According to a leading party member, UDEMU's aim was to "mobilize the mass of women in the struggle for their emancipation—that is, for the elimination of the unjust position of inequality in relation to men in which women are still placed in our society" (Aristides Pereira quoted in Galli and Jones 1987: 84).

Despite this commitment, UDEMU was, in reality, severely constrained by the party leadership, and it actually remained an underfunded and understaffed organization, concentrated in the capital. This situation merely mirrored the low priority given to women's rights issues by the government, assigning UDEMU a merely symbolical role (Galli and Jones 1987: 84–86, 93–94; Forrest 1992: 127; cf. Ly 2015).

The first president of UDEMU was Carmen Pereira (1936–2016). Although she was born in Bissau, her family stemmed from Bolama, Geba, and Cacheu—former centers of Kriston culture. During my conversation with her (interview CP), she described herself as a *guineense*, underlining that she had Cape Verdean, Portuguese, and French ancestors. Carmen Pereira was later succeeded by Francisca Pereira (born in 1942, no relation), who headed UDEMU from 1981 to 1998. Her family likewise originated from Bolama and Cacheu. Francisca Pereira opined that although her mother was a Pepel, she regarded herself as a *Kriston di Bolama* and believed that she was a *guineense* without any *raça* (interview FP).

These descriptions make it clear that the first two leading figures of UDEMU were familiar with Kriston culture. What is even more significant, however, is that they were both familiar with *manjuandadis*. Francisca Pereira's mother had been a member of the Pé di Kombe *manjuandadi*. As a result, it seemed only logical for her to use *manjuandadis* for mass-mobilization on behalf of PAIGC and UDEMU (cf. Trajano Filho 1998: 319, 402). It was in this very spirit that Carmen Pereira declared the following in 1976: "They [the *manjuandadis*] will form the basis for organizing women in the towns. We have begun working with them in order to organize them politically and mobilize them for the continuing work of national reconstruction. They are giving strong support to the Organization of Women [i.e. UDEMU] and are beginning to participate in our work" (Carmen Pereira quoted in Urdang 1979: 276).

Part of UDEMU's strategy was to mobilize female folklore groups from Guinea-Bissau's Muslim communities. New Muslim *manjuandadis* were neither organized according to age sets nor concerned with the Christian heritage cultivated by the Kriston *manjuandadis*. We cannot preclude the possibility that Muslim organizations had been supported by the PAIGC long before independence. In fact, it is quite likely that the seemingly un-suspicious *manjuandadis* served as clandestine support bases for the in-dependence movement during its struggle against the colonial state (cf. interviews CRL). This is indirectly suggested by the history of one of the oldest Muslim *manjuandadis* in Bissau, Jamanodiata (Mandingo for "Time Pleases"), which was an ally of the PAIGC and the late state president Vieira for decades. One of the group's leading members mentioned that some precursor associations had been founded in 1956, and these had only merged with Jamanodiata after independence in the mid-1970s. In fact, Muslim migrants from the hinterland had founded mutual solidar-ity organizations in Bissau by the mid-1950 (Proença Garcia 2000: 162). The *rainha*'s husband had organized a football team in colonial times that was secretly linked to the PAIGC. Francisca Pereira refuted the idea that *manjuandadis* were founded at the behest of UDEMU through financial grants. Instead, she asserted that UDEMU respected people's feelings and assisted the associations by managing their transport and logistics and organizing beverages and food for the associations. However, some of my informants (interviews cf. DC and PS) recalled that when UDEMU would invite *manjuandadis* for gatherings, the associations were, in their turn, re-quested to communicate political messages and slogans of the PAIGC and UDEMU via their songs (cf. Geschiere 2009: 174–75). Although UDEMU did not organize competitions between *manjuandadis,* they did arrange for mutual visits among groups. According to Francisca Pereira, the attempt to enlist entire *manjuandadis* as national flagships to international con-gresses failed due to the lack of funds. Nevertheless, individual *manjuan-dadi* activists, usually high-ranking *manjuandadi* members like the *rainha,* were occasionally invited to international events as representatives of a certain social class.

The reorganization of *manjuandadis* after 1974 resulted in the emergence a new politicized name genre among *manjuandadis*: the names of some new groups reflected the legacy of the victorious war of independence. For example, the Grupo Cultural Vitorino Costa (Vitorino Costa Cultural Group) *manjuandadi* was named after a combatant, whereas the Grupo Cultural di Antigos Combatentis (Cultural Group of Veterans) consisted of war veterans and their family members.

The Boa Esperança di Bande is another new type of *manjuandadi* (in-terviews DC and PS). Its members were of varying ages—most of them between thirty and fifty years old, although the founding members were older (fifty to sixty-five years). Many of its members were related to the public service. While the majority of members were Christian, there was a

Muslim minority. The group was originally founded in 1977 and adopted the present name in 1983. The *rainha* of the *manjuandadi* acted as UDEMU's chairwoman in the neighborhood.

In the 1980s the *manjuandadi* introduced new musical instruments to the genre. Its leading representatives asserted that during their interactions with other musicians they learned that it was necessary to incorporate elements of "modern" studio music in their "traditional" performances. The renowned, late guitarist Aliu Barri (Parente Augel 1997; Kohl 2007) performed with Boa Esperança di Bande from 1987 and was designated as the group's *padrinho.* Throughout the 1980s and 1990s, the group earned popularity as one of the most esteemed *manjuandadis* of Guinea-Bissau. Between 1987 and 1989, the group won the first prize in a public musical competition organized by the Bissau-Guinean state.

Even after the dissolution of the one-party state in the early 1990s, Boa Esperança di Bande's success story continued. On the one hand, the group continued to have political ties: even though its members performed for an opposition candidate during the 1999 election campaign, they supported Vieira's presidential election campaign for an appropriate fee and wore festive print dresses bearing the victorious candidate's countenance in 2005. On the other hand, they remain active within the cultural sphere, both nationally and internationally. In 1998, the group was awarded a quasi-official status as the "national band" of Guinea-Bissau and was subsequently sent to represent the country in various West African festivals.

In the 1980s and 1990s, the *manjuandadis* began to be confronted by profound challenges that threatened their survival. On the one hand, that era was characterized by a change in generations. Many former leaders of Kriston *manjuandadis* were passing away. Simultaneously, the number of *manjuandadis* decreased due to the diminishing popular support for these associations. In this regard, individual musicians started to appropriate rhythms and musical instruments that had previously been exclusive to *manjuandadis.* On the other hand, the eventual introduction of multiparty democracy and the accompanying withdrawal of the state since the late 1980s stripped UDEMU and PAIGC of their monopolistic character. Indirectly, this development also affected the *manjuandadis,* which had thrived on the support of the one-party state.

Guinea-Bissau's first multiparty elections in 1994 signaled a final flare-up of the *manjuandadis* — at least for that time. For the last time, the *manjuandadis* aligned unanimously with UDEMU in order to campaign for the PAIGC and state president Vieira in Guinea-Bissau's first-ever free elections (Koudawo 1994: 36; 1996: 85). Before the elections, those *manjuandadis* supporting the PAIGC had founded a strategic platform in September 1993 that was named the Associação de Mandjuwandades do Sector

Autónomo de Bissau (AMSAB) (Association of Mandjuwandades of the Autonomous Sector of Bissau). AMSAB was supposedly a union, or "free association," of all *manjuandadis* in Bissau. However, the umbrella association was patronized by the wife of the state president and chairman of the PAIGC. The president of AMSAB was Adriano "Atchutchi" Gomes Ferreira, a personage who has been involved in the art, culture, and media sectors since independence and known to be an ally of president Vieira. Hence, the *manjuandadis*—which appeared to be unsuspicious traditional associations for sociability and mutual assistance in times of sociopolitical and economic upheaval at first glance—had turned into single-party- and government-controlled election campaign machines. The AMSAB served its purpose, as the election results showed. Before it disappeared over allegations of corruption and mismanagement during the civil war of 1998–99, the AMSAB had purportedly been transformed into a nongovernmental organization (Koudawo 1994: 18–19; 1996: 79–81, 87).

On the whole, it appears that the postcolonial one-party state laid the foundation for the countrywide proliferation of a formerly creole cultural representation, which rapidly spread across ethnic and religious boundaries. The fact that *manjuandadis* had originally not been identified with a specific ethnic group was certainly conducive to this process. This was because, although the earlier *manjuandadis* had been associated with the Kriston, the transethnic Kriston identity encompassed various "ordinary" ethnic identities.

Commodification and Politicization

Both Boa Esperança di Bande and AMSAB had set the tone for the future development of *manjuandadis*. In view of the aforesaid challenges that confronted the *manjuandadis* in the mid-1990s, these associations had to conceive of new strategies for the future if they intended to survive. In other words, they had to find new sources of funding due to the collapse of the one-party state and worsening economic conditions that had led to widespread unemployment and growing social disparities since the late 1980s. In these circumstances, the strategies that were finally employed by some of the *manjuandadis* led to their commodification and politicization. Looking for new partners and sources of funding, *manjuandadis* established ties with other political parties apart from the PAIGC, lent themselves to prosperous nongovernmental organizations in order to communicate their agendas, and, supported by radio stations and cultural activists, began to market their music effectively. By the end of the 1990s, there was a revival of *manjuandadi* music—a boom that persists to date.

After the introduction of multiparty democracy, *manjuandadis* have successfully managed to disengage from the PAIGC and UDEMU. Since that time, along with their music and dance performances, many of them have become popular mouthpieces of various solvent political parties during electoral campaigns—in contrast to the situation in the single-party era. Despite the end of the single-party rule, however, the PAIGC and UDEMU have remained important political patrons and beneficiaries of *manjuandadi* performances. For members of such *manjuandadis* who mostly belong to the lower and middle social classes, participation in electoral campaigns signifies a potential source of income (interviews BC, ADS, JS, and IC).

In contrast to earlier times, *manjuandadis* in recent times seem to be increasingly characterized by a growing sense of commodification. For example, in earlier times, they would perform only on the occasion of state receptions held by or for colonial governors (e.g. interviews ADZ; EDP; LC; MaCF; SG) and, postindependence, for political parties and their rallies. However, nowadays even ordinary citizens, by paying a suitable fee, can book some *manjuandadis* to perform at a private wedding, birthday, or any other festivity. Since electoral campaigns are held once every few years, *manjuandadi* members cannot exclusively depend on this source of income, even if some politicians continue to patronize "their" *manjuandadis* after election times.

Apart from the presence of *manjuandadis* in electoral campaigns, these associations have successfully made inroads into civil society, leading to a kind of "NGO-ization" of *manjuandadis* (e.g. interview MASF and ERGM). Since the 1990s, many of them have, in fact, partnered with nongovernmental organizations. *Manjuandadis*—just like other groups—are hired by nongovernmental organizations that wish to spread their messages through *manjuandadi* performances. Members perform at competitive cultural festivals organized and patronized by nongovernmental organizations. In some cases, *manjuandadis* enter into a close and enduring cooperative arrangement with certain nongovernmental organizations. For an appropriate fee, the members participate in various campaigns organized by the nongovernmental organizations at their respective events. These campaigns often address socially sensitive issues, such as women's and children's rights and HIV/AIDS sensitization. As I realized during my fieldwork, nongovernmental organizations pursue at least two objectives: On the one hand, they seek to promote their own organization's and its leader's reputation. On the other hand, their objective is to effectively communicate and promote their messages, agendas, and slogans to the public. In this manner, *manjuandadis* hope to attract both money and work (Domingues, Miranda Freitas, and Gomes Ferreira 2006). It remains doubtful, however, to what extent they are able to meet their own commercial expectations, in terms of increasing the members' incomes. One difficulty in this regard is the excess supply of *manjuandadis* as compared to the limited demand.

The revival of *manjuandadis* and their musical genre was ultimately fostered by public and private radio stations. For more than a decade, the media have been responsible for the increasing popularity of this style of music. This popularization of the *manjuandadi* musical genre apparently started during the Military Conflict of 1998–99, as the editor in charge of the *manjuandadi* format at the public Rádio Difusão Nacional (RDN, National Radio Diffusion) informed me (interviews CRL). According to her, RDN aired the Domingo de Tina (Tina Drum Sunday) broadcast for the first time in December 1998. Since then, the format has been broadcasted every Sunday afternoon, when the recorded musical performances of different *manjuandadi* groups are presented to the public. Most private radio stations have subsequently added similar formats to their programs. These broadcasts also serve to promote the respective groups. RDN also organized a festival every year, at locations that change from year to year, but which are usually limited to the former *praças*. From 8 to 10 December 2006, this festival was held in Bolama. Numerous *manjuandadis* from Bolama, Cacheu, Bissau, and other towns took part in the festival. However, it is important to note that Muslim *manjuandadis* were not invited. Many of these associations had been founded in the recent past, in the 1990s or even in the new century by younger generations. One *manjuandadi* that originated from Bolama had been founded only a few months before the festival. Thus, such festivals—regardless of whether they are sponsored by the state, nongovernmental organizations, or the media—appear to have the general effect of creating new groups.

The Bolama festival started in the late afternoon. A number of *manjuandadis* performed on stage after being introduced by a radio presenter. Due to the lack of appropriate technical equipment, it was not possible broadcast the performances live—instead, the musical presentations were recorded by RDN and aired on the following Sunday in the *Domingo de Tina* broadcast. During this festival, the eldest inhabitant of Bolama was publicly interviewed and recounted aspects of Bolama's past. Apart from the official performances, there were parties and revelries held every evening, which ended only early in the morning of the following day. On the last day, a committee of judges announced the name of the winning *manjuandadi*.

This transformation in the basic character of the *manjuandadis*—which nowadays more resemble semiprofessional musical groups whose main objective is breadwinning than groups that promote sociability and mutual assistance—is also mirrored in a gradual semantic shifting. A Kriol dictionary published in 1999 continued to define the term *manjuandadi*, consistent with previous reference books, as "a group comprising members of the same age." However, it offered a second meaning, equating a *manjuandadi* with a "folk music group" (Dieterle 1999: 98). This means that although the term *manjuandadi* continues to have various connotations (Trajano Filho 2001a: x) associated with solidarity, conviviality, and mutuality, there appears to be, in recent times, a prominent tendency to associate the word with a group that performs "folk music." This new, more restrictive meaning has emerged from the commercialized music and dance performances that some *manjuandadis* present in public. This does not imply, however, that the previous, broader meaning is lost. As we shall see below, age-set associations in the countryside are increasingly known by the Kriol term *manjuandadi*—an indication of the ongoing drastic semantic shifting that accompanies cultural pidginization.

Functional Incorporation of Manjuandadis

Due to the rapid spread of Kriol in the past decades, the term *manjuandadi* has been adopted by the population in the country's interior. These people have attached the notion—previously reserved for the creole, age-set-based *manjuandadis*—to their own age-set groups. Similarly, representations that have no relation to age sets but are based on the principles of sociability and mutuality are likewise increasingly referred to as *manjuandadis*. This applies, among others, to traditional age-set groups from the interior—associations that also provide for sociability and mutual assistance—and rotating credit associations that are incorporated under the Kriol umbrella notion of *manjuandadi*. The term also continued to denote loose networks of friends and family members.

Traditional age-set associations continue to be valued in the countryside because they provide for mutual assistance and sociability among the group members—these seem to be increasingly termed as *manjuandadis*. An informant of mine (interview CGC)—a waiter who was about thirty years old—was born in Biombo peninsula, which is regarded as the *tchon* of the Pepel ethnic group. He had been brought up partly in his village and partly in Bissau. Many of his coevals originating from his village or the neighboring villages also resided in the capital. Sometimes, over the weekend, he returned to his village in order to visit his family and his male *colegas* (individuals of the same age or profession). Ever since he participated in the *fanadu* with other boys of the same age set, when they were adolescents, they have been members of a *manjuandadi* named after the American rock musician Jon Bon Jovi. When we talked in Kriol about his group, he used the Kriol term for *manjuandadi* instead of the corresponding Pepel word. This example shows how people translate their rural versions of age-set associations into *manjuandadis*. Like in other *manjuandadis*, the *colegas* pay membership fees. According to my informant, their group members gave mutual assistance to each other and also partied together.

Another informant, an employee of a Bissau-based international organization, was born in the early 1960s into a Cassanga family in a small village in northern Guinea-Bissau (interview JB). He explained that his exclusively male *manjuandadi* still existed in his home village. Like the previous case, he used the Kriol word for *manjuandadi* instead of the corresponding Cassanga term. He stated that he, along with the other boys of his age set, used to work together in the *bolanhas* (rice fields) and peanut fields; they had also performed the *fanadu* together. The main objective of his *manjuandadi* was for members to provide mutual assistance to each other, my informant opined. This included helping one another in times of illness, at weddings, and at funerals, among others. However, due to his demanding profession, he was not able to invest much time in his *manjuandadi*, which nevertheless carried on without him. He pointed out that many of his *manjuas* have left their village in search of better living conditions. My informant continued to maintain contact with some of his *manjuas* via telephone, and he assured that these relationships are very important to him. Occasionally they met, for instance, if a *manjua* passed away.

Apart from the traditional age-set associations, there are other, entirely new types of groups in the countryside that are incorporated under the umbrella term of *manjuandadi*. This is exemplified by the recent spread of associations that are founded and controlled by women, independent of party or state influence.

In early 2007 I visited a village in the southeastern region of Tombali. The village was situated in a very remote area, and the majority of its inhabitants were Fula and Balanta. A middle-aged woman explained that she, along with other women from the same village, had founded a *manjuandadi* after the civil war of 1998–99. My informant (interview UW) likewise employed the Kriol term to describe her association. She remarked that neither their village nor the region had seen a similar institution in the past. This group seemed to prioritize the aspect of sociability, for the group members usually assembled in the event of funerals, weddings, and other festivities, in order to *brinca*.

The *abotas* constitute another kind of association frequently labeled as *manjuandadis*. These are rotating credit associations, also known as rotating savings and credit associations, which are widespread in West Africa and other parts of the world, particularly in developing countries (Ardener 1964: 204–6; Besley et al. 1994: 701). These associations "are formed by a core of participants who agree to make regular contributions to a fund which is given, in whole or in part, to each contributor in rotation"

(Ardener 1964: 201; emphasis omitted). The distribution of lump-sum funds usually occurs at fixed intervals (Geertz 1962: 243).

To my knowledge, scholars first mentioned *abotas* in the mid-1990s as one of the key actors of informal economic cooperation (Duarte and Gomes 1996: 110). However, they appear to have a long tradition that dates back a number of decades, at least (Lourenço-Lindell 2002: 130–32). They are widespread in Bissau and other towns of Guinea-Bissau and are often related to day workers and commercial spheres. Friendship and mutual confidence are essential prerequisites of *abotas* (Domingues 2000: 445–48; 2005; Gacitua-Mario et al. 2006: 28; 2007: 31–33). Like *manjuandadis,* they ensure solidarity and mutual assistance among their members (Lourenço-Lindell 2002: 130). In contrast to *manjuandadis,* however, individual financial interests are paramount in *abotas.* This goal is achieved by the rotating disbursement of a lump-sum fund to one of the members who can use it for his or her own individual purposes (Domingues 2000: 445, 447; Lourenço-Lindell 2002: 130).

I became acquainted with the system of *abotas* while traveling in Senegal in January 2007, when I chanced to meet a Bissau-Guinean woman who was almost fifty years of age (interview MJ). During our conversation, she informed me that she was Fula and that for a couple of years she had been a member of a *manjuandadi* that was based in her hometown Gabú in eastern Guinea-Bissau (cf. Borszik 2008: 67). Her *manjuandadi* was founded in 2000 and bore the name Grandeza di Moda (Splendor of Fashion). My informant stated that almost all of her association's seventy members were Muslims, most of them women. They belonged to different ethnic groups, such as Fula, Mandingo, and Sarákole. These members included mobile traders, soft-drink sellers, and shop owners. The association possessed a *rei,* a *rainha,* a *vice-rainha,* a *conselheiro,* a *tesoureiro,* and a public relations officer. In addition, they possessed identical print *uniformes* that they wore on festive occasions such as weddings. Prior to the wedding of a group member or similar such festive event, an extra sum of money would be collected from among the other members, which would finally be handed over as a gift.

Given all these details, I was convinced that her group was a *manjuandadi* in the wider sense of the term. Later, however, she added to my surprise that her association neither sang nor danced in public. Instead, they *brinca* to the music on the radio, she said. According to my informant, each member of her group had to pay a weekly membership fee of 1,000 francs CFA (currently about $1.75). The lump sum collected from all the members would eventually be handed over to two chosen members. These members were responsible for investing the lump sum in purchasing attractively priced commodities from neighboring countries. Upon returning to Gabú, the members would sell these commodities. My informant finally confirmed that her *manjuandadi* was also called an *abota*, employing both notions interchangeably.

These findings suggest that the term *manjuandadi* increasingly incorporates other types of associations or even simple ad hoc networks that differ from conventional *manjuandadis*. Transitions can be seamless: in reality, it may not be possible to clearly and analytically distinguish between *manjuandadis* and other similar associations, for example, *abotas*. What all these associations and networks have in common, however, is that they provide for sociability and solidarity within the group, thus indicating a *"manjuandadi*zation" of functions. Since this process has been accompanied by the spread of Kriol all over Guinea-Bissau, the term *manjuandadi* has also become popular, along with its connotations.

The Relevance of Ethnicity and Religion

The growing popularity and spread of *manjuandadis* throughout Guinea-Bissau in the last decades brings to mind the relevance of both ethnicity and religion in a culturally and ethnically heterogeneous country like Guinea-Bissau. In this context, it is crucial to pay particular attention to the newly founded Muslim *manjuandadis*, which are often given differential treatment from Christian ones.

Most present-day *manjuandadis* are organized according to their members' residential background. In other words, locality subordinates ethnicity. As regards ethnicity, quantitative research data collected in the mid-1990s in Bissau showed that the vast majority of *manjuandadis* (86 percent) were multiethnic in their membership (Domingues 2000: 466–67). This implies that *manjuandadis* are different than other types of cultural associations that expressively serve to unite one specific ethnic group only, such as the Senegal-influenced *sociétés* (or *pkumel*) of the Mancanha, for instance (interview ADSM; Jao 1992: 65–66; cf. Domingues 2000: 432). Thus, according to the survey, only a minority of *manjuandadis* comprised members that belonged to only one and the same ethnic group. However, as far as I was able to observe, many *manjuandadis* are dominated by a specific ethnic group. Consequently, they are identified as associations of a certain ethnic group by external observers. Another reason for the existence of monoethnic *manjuandadis* is that the members are usually recruited from among extended families, neighbors, coworkers, and friends. The fact that people of the same ethnic origin often dwell close to each other precipitates the numerical dominance of a certain ethnic group.

Contemporary *manjuandadis* rather tend to be divided along religious lines into Muslim and Christian associations, a differentiation that seems to have become increasingly important in recent years. Based on the afore-mentioned survey, in the mid-1990s, 54 percent of the *manjuandadis* were Christian, 13 percent were Muslim, and the remaining 33 percent were mixed (Domingues 2000: 467; cf. Trajano Filho 2010). Muslim *manjuanda-dis* bear a number of characteristics that differ from their Christian coun-terparts. Unlike Christian-Muslim or solely Christian *manjuandadis,* they have partly integrated structures previously cultivated by different Mus-lim ethnic groups. In addition, they have incorporated some changes in regard to the functions and names of their respective *manjuandadis.*

One of the largest and oldest Muslim *manjuandadis* in Bissau went by the name of Jamanodiata (interview BC, ADS, JS, and IC). The headquar-ters of this association was situated close to the presidency in the Cupelon de Cima quarter. Nevertheless, many of its members resided in other quarters as well. In November 2006 the association comprised around 150 members of different ages. Internal estimates indicate that 90 percent of the members were female; moreover, some of the leading activists as-sessed that about 99 percent of the members were unemployed. Member-ship was ethnically diverse, consisting of Mandingo, Beafada, and Fula, who accounted for 80 percent of the total number of members, according to internal estimates. Furthermore, some Balanta and Pepel women who had converted to Islam and some Christian members who resided in the neighborhood had also joined Jamanodiata. The most prominent member was state president and former chairman of the PAIGC, "Nino" Vieira. Activists proudly recounted that he occasionally would join in the associ-ation's activities and had even invited members to his private home.

With regard to Jamanodiata's internal structure, like other *manjuan-dadis* it was characterized by a range of charges, including the offices of *presidente, rainha, tesoureiro, orientador, conselheiro, merinha,* and an official responsible for deployment and propaganda. The group's internal orga-nization was quite complex, since Jamanodiata was made up of differ-ent age grades and their subgroups. As members explained, individuals ideally pass through a number of stages. Jamanodiata was thus mainly composed of the middle-aged grade. This meant that there were several aligned subgroups for the elder and younger members, which coexisted with the middle-aged grade. Moreover, the *manjuandadi* had a male divi-sion called Amizade. The members of this division, however, did not play music—at the time of my field research, the division was about to become a nongovernmental organization instead.

In response to my questions regarding their performances and festivi-ties, my informants explained that they did not consume alcoholic bever-ages because the majority of the members were Muslims. Like other Mus-lim *manjuandadis,* moreover, they did not play the *tina.* Although members asserted that their *manjuandadi* was not politically oriented, since its establishment in the mid-1970s the association has been connected to the PAIGC. In 2005 Vieira invited the *manjuandadi* to support his electoral campaign for the presidency. They accepted and performed in return for a stipulated fee. Apart from this, they took part in competitions organized by the civil society all over the country, in which they have frequently won prizes. In addition, they have been invited to perform at discotheques, nightclubs, and restaurants, while CDs and tapes of their recorded performances are also sold.

A few months later, in February 2007, when I was staying in Bafatá, I became acquainted with another Muslim *manjuandadi*. This association, which had been founded in 1987, was named Vizinhos Unidos (United Neighbors). According to the association's *rainha* (interview AlS), theirs was the first group to play a drum other than the *tina*. External observers classified the association as a Mandingo *manjuandadi*. As a matter of fact, however, other Muslim ethnic groups, as well as a few Christians, were likewise represented in this group. I was informed that since all the members were affiliated to UDEMU, the Vizinhos Unidos always supported the election campaigns of president Vieira and the PAIGC. By 2014 this had changed: the *mamé* explained that the group had recently campaigned for a non-PAIGC presidential candidate (interview FSD). What is noteworthy is the fact that the *rainha,* in our conversation, employed the terms *manjuandadi* and *musso-kafó* interchangeably (cf. interview SeM). The Mandingo term *musso-kafó* actually refers to female age sets that are common among this ethnic group.

I also became acquainted with another Muslim *manjuandadi* in Bafatá that, just like the abovementioned group, did not play the *tina*. This association was known by the Fula name of Lislámica, which was translated as "Muslim Friendship" by one of its leaders (interview BM and FB). According to an activist, they called their *manjuandadi* "*huondiral*" in Fula, which means "sitting together" or "exchanging words together." Most of the members of this *manjuandadi* were female. According to the activists, they were all members of UDEMU. The members were of varying ages. Their representatives informed me that although the group had been formally established after independence, it had its roots in the late colonial era. Third parties regarded this association as a Fula *manjuandadi* despite the fact that there were Mandingo members in the group as well—this may be because the group's founders were Fula, while its subsequent members are of different ethnic origins.

As these descriptions suggest, Muslim *manjuandadis* did not differ fundamentally from Christian and mixed *manjuandadis*. The main difference, in fact, concerned their non-usage of the *tina* drum. Leading cultural activists who work closely together with Christian associations opined that because they do not play the *tina*, Muslim *manjuandadis* could not, in fact, be regarded as "genuine" *manjuandadis*—instead, in their eyes, they were simple *grupos* or *agrupamentos* (groups, groupings) (CRL; NN; cf. JH and ZH). In other words, these activists regarded the *tina* as a necessary prerequisite for the group to qualify as a *manjuandadi*. This assertion was rejected by Muslim activists, who considered their associations to be Muslim *manjuandadis*. Although the latter agreed that they did not play the *tina* because they believed that this musical instrument was reserved for Christian *manjuandadis*, they did not consider this difference to be so significant that they should not be considered *manjuandadis*. Like the cultural activists, some members of Christian *manjuandadis* also strongly associated the *tina* with the Kriston communities inhabiting the *praças* in the past. They used this reference to highlight the antiquity and uniqueness of the musical instrument. According to them, the *tina* originated in the *praças*, where it was first crafted from wooden wine barrels centuries ago. Moreover, the activists proudly pointed out that the *tina* was not known anywhere else in West Africa (interviews CRL; DC and PS).

This refusal to accept Muslim associations as *manjuandadis* can be traced back at least to the early 1990s, and there is a reference to this in the statutes of AMSAB, which mention that the umbrella organization was also denominated "ALAHWARTA" (Associação de Mandjuwandades do SAB 1993: § 1, 1). Although activists who had been involved in AMSAB at the time did not know the meaning of this word, it is supposedly of Arab origin and may mean "Allah does not arrive," "Allah does not rescue," or "Allah does not manifest himself" (personal communication, Youssouf Diallo, Max Planck Institute for Social Anthropology, 22 April 2008). If this translation is correct, the expression may be directed against Muslim *manjuandadis*. AMSAB's successor organization openly conveyed its rejection of Muslim *manjuandadis* through its very name, the Associação das Manjuandadis-Tina da Guiné-Bissau (AMT-GB, Association of *Tina-Manjuandadis* of Guinea-Bissau). This new umbrella organization was founded in January 2007 by nine Bissau-based Christian *manjuandadis*. As per its statutes, all *manjuandadis* that did not make music or play the *tina* were excluded from membership (Associação das Mandjuandadis-Tina da Guiné-Bissau 2007).

How can we interpret this rejection of Muslim *manjuandadis* by a number of Christian *manjuandadi* members and other cultural activists? My findings suggest that this rejection can be perceived as a countermovement against further changes in the *manjuandadi* institution brought about by strangers, that is, non-creoles. It should be noted that most of the individuals who oppose Muslim *manjuandadis* are closely linked to specific Christian *manjuandadis* and are often descended from Kriston families.

They are aware of their creole cultural heritage and the fact that these associations were, in the past, exclusive to the Kriston communities in the *praças*. Hence, they consider this type of association to be their own cultural representation, which therefore has to be an expression of Christianity. Against this background of ethnocentric essentialism, the *tina* drum seems to have become the symbol of Christian *manjuandadis*, per se. According to their point of view, the Muslim associations that were founded after independence cannot be called *manjuandadis*. It is possible that the said activists feel challenged by the Muslim *manjuandadis*, which seem to question their cultural and interpretative privilege. This attitude can be traced to the colonial era, when Christianity was openly regarded as superior to other religions. After independence, the official preference of Christianity was omitted, and Catholicism became merely one among many other religions. The recent transformations in the *manjuandadi* institution, however, seem to prompt Christian *manjuandadi* activists to insist on the genuineness and originality of contemporary *manjuandadis* that play the *tina* on the one hand and have Kriston precursors on the other. Meanwhile, Muslim *manjuandadis* are disparaged as merely imitators. The activists' firm conviction that the *tina* has always been associated with Kriston *manjuandadis* and their tacit implication that this musical instrument was invented by creole communities, however, seems to be contradicted by musicological evidence. In Mali and Guinea a musical instrument is played that bears a striking resemblance to the *tina*—they call it the *filendunun* (Nketia 1979: 98; Blanc 1993: 17; Brandily 2001: 67–68). Ironically, if this resemblance does not prove to be a mere coincidence, it might imply that the *tina* actually originated from the Islamized societies of Africa's interior and not from the Atlantic Euro-African, creole encounter.

At the same time, however, a musical instrument that closely resembles the *tina* is also reported from the Caribbean. This instrument, known as *bastel* in the island of Curaçao, is closely connected to the slave trade and used to be played by slaves who originated from the African continent (personal communication, Suzette Maduro and Andrehina Paulina, CPost International, 15 and 16 September 2015). Using a halved calabash that was placed facedown in a tub of water and played with drumsticks (Campbell 2014), the *bastel* could confirm the oral narratives that associate the *tina* with the Atlantic slave trade and colonial times.

Celebrating Unity in Diversity: Carnival

Carnival has been celebrated in present-day Guinea-Bissau for over a century. What began as a creole cultural representation in a few trading posts (e.g. interviews AJPB; AMV; DDC; ECDC; JC) has more recently been transformed into a mass event that has rapidly spread beyond the boundaries of the few former *praças*. Formerly a loosely organized festivity, carnival turned into a state-run competition shortly after independence. Later, carnival became a nationwide celebration. Today, carnival enjoys such mass popularity that it is even staged in remote areas.

Crucial is the connection between the state and carnival and how they have influenced each other. The significance of the state has changed throughout history—from that of a powerless spectator confronted with nationalistic manifestations of a carnival celebrated by creole government agents in the late nineteenth century to that of an actor that appropriated and politicized the festival after mid-independence. The postindependence state succeeded in transforming the creole carnival into a mass event attracting people of various ethnic origins. The one-party state initially reinvented carnival in order to mass-mobilize the population on behalf of the ruling party, the new state, and the state ideology. As my findings suggest, the state thereby significantly contributed to the cultural pidginization of the originally creole representation. Following the state's active promotion of the carnival in the 1980s, the festival has become increasingly commercialized after the introduction of multiparty democracy in the early 1990s. Political parties and nongovernmental organizations have played an important role in this process by using the carnival for promoting their own purposes, thus fueling the spread of carnival.

How did carnival manage to appeal to people across ethnic boundaries? Apparently, this process was catalyzed by the multilayered character of carnival, because carnival can be regarded as a secular ritual that cannot be "entirely separated from everyday life" (Mitchell 2006: 384). Since the performance of rituals

> is a reality apart from its participants, the participants may not all experience the same significance or efficacy. . . . the performance is bound to mean different things to different people. In the absence of any exegetical canon one might even argue that there was no single "correct" or "right" meaning for a ritual at all. The performance is objectively (and socially) validated by the participants when they share its action and intensity, no matter what each person may individually think about it. (Schieffelin 1985: 722)

From this, it follows that a shared identity is constructed "through the interaction of the performers and participants" (Schieffelin 1985: 722) despite the different meanings that the ritual in performance might have to different individuals. In this manner, shared performances help to overcome ethnic boundaries at the community level and thus contribute to the construction of postcolonial nationhood and the appropriation and adaption of carnival by Bissau-Guineans. Because of their own cultural repertoire, they could identify with carnival or traits of it, discovering parallels to their own culture. In other words, "pieces of reality, however much borrowed from or imposed by others, are woven together through the logic of a group's own locally and historically evolved bricolage" (Ortner 1995: 176). Hence, performances can pursue different agendas, even though they appear to be similar on the surface.

This integrative feature of carnival is reflected by the fact that it is, at present, celebrated countrywide and proudly regarded as a unique national festival by Bissau-Guineans. This process has benefited not only from the binding effects of shared performances but also from the fact that carnival—to an even lesser extent than *manjuandadis*—had not been associated with a specific ethnic group, because its celebration is not restricted to creoles but is also widespread in many parts of the world. Following the prior elaborations on *manjuandadis*, therefore, I will mainly examine the ways in which, through the medium of joint performances, carnival not only contributes to interethnic sociability, integration, and cohesion but also to nation-building—despite the fact that this popular festivity takes place only for a short period once per year (cf. Fischer-Lichte and Warstat 2009: 9).

Nowadays widely regarded a popular festivity that attracts all generations of people, including, very prominently, children and adolescents, carnival and related carnivalesque performances are in many parts of the world expressions of popular jollity, cultural diversity, skillful dance shows, shrillness, etc. Carnival has been celebrated for centuries in several countries in Europe and Latin America, including Portugal and Brazil, where it was also but not exclusively associated with black confraternities (cf. Leite de Vasconcellos 1982: 145–70; Veiga de Oliveira 1984: 17–58; Braga 1985–86: 2:191–92; Coelho 1993: 299–300; Lahon 1999b: 170–71; Mac Cord 2005). According to historical references, not only was the internal organization of these confraternities carnivalesque, in the sense that they caricatured the royal courts by introducing charges such as *reis* or *rainhas*, but their festivities were also performed in a rambunctious, carnival-like manner (Braga 1985–86: 1:293, 300; Lahon 1999a; 1999b: 70–76; 2001; Mac Cord 2005). What is even more interesting is the fact that black Christian confraternities used to organize carnivalesque fancy-dress parties. The *carnaval* or *entrudo*—as the carnival was known, at that time—was an inherent part of the festive life of these confraternities in the mid- to late nineteenth century Lisbon (Lahon 1999a: 170–71). Carnival also became tremendously popular throughout Portugal's former colonies and possessions, where the festival has been adopted by the local population (Crowley 1989a: 143–44, 146–47). One such place where carnival continues to be celebrated is Guinea-Bissau.

Historical Transitions: Weak Colonial State, Unpredictable Carnival

Pictures taken at the turn of the twentieth century indicate that carnival was at the time celebrated by both Europeans and Africans (Governo da Guiné 1952; cf. Matos e Lemos and Ramires 2008: 142). Carnival served as a platform to criticize the colonial policies and politics and to perform resistance. Indeed, scholars like Mikhail Bakhtin have pointed early to carnival's potential to bring forward criticism of rulers and to perform resistance (Bakhtin 1993; cf. Trajano Filho 2006a). At the time, carnival was closely associated with urban, creole settings where it was first celebrated.

An early written account of carnival in Guinea-Bissau dates from 1888 and was originated from a confidential telegram sent by the colony's governor, Francisco Teixeira da Silva, to the Portuguese Overseas Ministry.[3] In this telegram, the author complained that a big masquerade had taken place in Bolama on Friday, 17 February. The small town had been declared capital of the colony in 1879, after the administrative separation of Portuguese Guinea from Cape Verde. The masquerade was composed of local soldiers under the leadership of Coronel Eusébio Catella do Valle, commander of the Bolama-based riflemen battalion no. 1, the colony's short-term interim governor in April 1887, and former secretary general. The writer accused the locals, notably Catella do Valle,[4] of wanting "to govern this province." Catella do Valle was accused of populism, treason, and of possibly being the author of the masquerade that had turned into "an element of disorder" from the moment he had started to govern the province of Portuguese Guinea. Catella do Valle had reportedly "lost his head" and even recommended to replace the governor. The text also alludes to the Franco-Portuguese commission that had been installed to accurately delimit the Portuguese's colony's borders with French Senegal.

At the 1884–85 Berlin Conference both France and Portugal had decided to resolve several territorial conflicts in Africa. Both countries had signed a treaty in May 1886 that stipulated an exchange of territories, thus delimiting their colonies' boundaries. The new boundaries in West Africa were to the disadvantage of the Portuguese: whereas the Casamance with its capital Ziguinchor, by then one of Portuguese Guinea's most valuable areas, was ceded to French Senegal, the Portuguese merely received some mangrove swamplands in the most southern Rio Cacine area—truly a bad bargain. However, the delimitation was only implemented from February 1888 (Esteves 1988; Pélissier 1989: 172–74), which is around the time of the portrayed carnival episode. According to the descriptions in the telegram, the crowd parodied French officials and caused general disorder. The Franco-Portuguese Border Delimitation Commission included two French officials, Captain Henri Brosellard Faidherbe as head of the French mission and Lieutenant Clerc (depicted as "Clerk" in the document), both of whom were mentioned in the telegram. On 28 January the French mission, altogether nineteen individuals, including soldiers, had reportedly arrived in Bolama; they left on 4 February, heading to the Rio Nunes area in the southern part of present-day Guinea-Bissau (Esteves 1988: 183–87).

As early as Pancake Day on 14 February, the report continued, a masquerade had emerged from the casern and passed in front of the government house without permission. The crowd had carried along a banner bearing Portugal's national colors and the word "commission." This was accompanied by a safe that bore the inscription "Money, a lot of Money" and a big box labeled "Cape Roxo" — a reference to the cape that marks the Senegalese–Bissau-Guinean border. A buoy labeled "Mind the Buoy" was followed by five masked figures representing members of the commission. According to the report, the falsework had reportedly been constructed by local soldiers, possibly of Cape Verdean origin as many soldiers in Portuguese service at the time originated from the archipelago off the West African coast. Finally, the telegram accused the indigenous population, i.e. supposedly Kriston and Cape Verdeans alike, in general, and the local soldiers, in particular, of being traitorous. This did not come as a big surprise given the fact that creole government agents were already showing a nationalist stance in their protest against the Franco-Portuguese agreement and Europeans were being repeatedly targeted by their sarcasm and insults. Eventually, Bolama's municipal administrator was interviewed by the author of the telegram and asked why he had given permission to organize the masquerade. The administrator replied that he had been convinced that the masquerade was something "innocent." The author, however, did not accept this justification and exonerated the administrator who had breached his responsibilities as, de jure, only the general secretary, apparently of the provincial administration, was allowed to grant permissions. In a subsequent letter to the ministry, the governor explained that Catella do Valle had justified his involvement in the parody in that he wanted to "defend himself" and "abreact from his responsibilities." Catella do Valle declared that he lived together in the barracks with his officers, possibly Bissau-Guinean and Cape Verdean and/or Angolan creoles, who knew how to produce masquerade pieces. As stipulated in his military personal record card, Catella do Valle was exonerated by decree of 28 February 1888 from his position as commander of the riflemen regiment and was retired in 1890.

Carnivalesque behavior and performances, however, were not limited to the actual carnival period. This is indicated by the aforementioned account relating to the celebration of All Saints' Day and All Souls' Day in 1898 in Bolama. Apart from suggesting that the event was celebrated by *manjuandadis*, which were then only to be found within the Kriston community, the account indicates the freedom granted by the state to the performance of carnivalesque events at the time (Dias de Carvalho 1944: 74–75, 238–39). This was affirmed by an aged Kriston former *manjuandadi* activist who recalled that her *manjuandadi* used to perform publicly on the occasion of the carnival in the 1920s, 1930s, and 1940s (interviews MaCF). The group members, wearing festive dresses, would gather in front of residences in Bolama's city center and dance (interview MaCF). If the house owner liked the performance, he was obliged to give them some money.

The Estado Novo: Attempting to Restrain Carnival

However, times were changing. Little by little, the colonial state extended its influence and sought to control the social and cultural life in Guinea-Bissau. Especially after the effective colonial seizure of the territory was completed in the 1930s, the New State regime attempted to restrict the people's freedom. The following example reveals how the colonial state attempted to control public festivities like carnival. This example also demonstrates that the street carnival remained a unique creole cultural representation that was limited to the *praças*.

A Kriston informant who was born in the early 1920s remembered his young days in the *praça* of Cacheu (interviews AJPB; cf. also DCDA on Bissau). On the occasion of the carnival, the local *manjuandadis* would assemble together, while other people would dress up as "tribals" or representatives of specific occupational groups. One of his friends, for instance, decided to disguise himself as a seaman and had fabricated a corresponding paper headdress. In this respect, people often wore folded paper hats that reached down as far as the neck. My informant added that he and his peers would make masks from scraps of paper that were stuck together using natural glue (cf. Sigá 1995: 11). For this purpose, parts of baobab fruits were mixed with water and then heated. This pulp was sculpted into clay masks by the addition of mud from the swamplands adjoining the nearby Cacheu River. The masks usually represented the faces of animals, although smiling human face masks could be intermittently detected (cf. also interviews DCDA; VFR). The latter were feared by children, who used to take to their heels at their sight. The same applied to the "tribal people," my informant stated, because they did not know anything about a carnival. *Máscaras novas* (new masks) were made from paper that had been sewed together, covering the wearer's head like a hat. In addition to this, people painted their faces. Moreover, carnivalists frequently wore colorful paper dresses around the upper part of the body; these dresses consisted of a number of paper layers that were cut in a jagged manner. While strolling through the town, one would meet many *entrudos,* that is, people wearing masks. In the evenings, balls were organized that were primarily attended by Europeans. My interviewee's elder brothers used to play the violin and viola at such balls (interviews AJPB).

Parade floats were also constructed for carnival. Built of wood and possessing wheels, they could be from twenty-five to thirty-three feet (eight to ten meters) long. My informant said that he and his friends decided to construct a parade boat on their own initiative, after they had collected some money. Moreover, some *brancos* (literally, "whites") had contributed to its construction, while friendly local carpenters helped them with the woodwork. Hidden in the interior of the float, which resembled a ship, four or five men moved the construction. The ship's exterior was covered with a white paperboard, and a chimney was fixed in the middle. Smoke was generated for the latter by igniting grass or straw. Some individuals dressed as seamen stood on top of the parade float. During the course of this interview, as we sat on my informant's veranda, he even recalled two songs that he and his fellows used to sing (see figure 3.2.).

In accordance with the spirit of the time, the young carnival activists had evidently chosen a military topic because many Portuguese colonial officials were navy officers. Ostensibly, it would seem that it was intended to suit the representatives of the colonial regime, also reflected by the fact that the songs were sung in Portuguese instead of the officially despised Kriol. Although the state did allow Bissau-Guineans some freedom when it came to harmless, nonsuspicious festivities (such as wearing masks and disguises), the colonial state nevertheless appeared to have attempted to influence or control carnival. In addition, the state had already managed to drive a wedge between the colony's local populations. Following the introduction of the Native Statute, those who were classified as citizens were henceforth expected to conform to the Portuguese, Catholic lifestyle if they wanted advancement within the colonial social status reward power system. This especially concerned those citizens who belonged to the upper social classes. These circumstances are evident in the following two episodes.

An informant from an upper-middle-class family with Kriston Pepel ancestry, who was born in 1914, remembered a carnivalesque event that occurred in Bissau in the mid-1940s (interview LLDC). While the male adolescents of her age had decided to dress up as seamen and play violins and mandolins, she and other young women were dressed in Portuguese-

Somos marujos,	We are seamen,
do alto mar,	from the high sea,
somos navegantes,	we are the navigators,
dos nossos navios,	of our vessels,
somos marujos,	we are seamen,
do mar de guerra,	of a war zone,
português guerreiro,	Portuguese warrior,
contra os canhões!	against the canons!

O nosso tempo,	Our time,
que já chegou,	has already come,
tempo ta vai,	time goes by,
tempo ta vem,	new times arrive,
adeus carnaval,	goodbye, carnival,
carnaval já chegou!	carnival is here again!

Figure 3.2. Cacheu Carnival Song

style long, wide gowns. Most of her fellows were Portuguese. Together they promenaded along Bissau's main road to the government house. There, they attracted the interest of the colony's governor, who left the building in order to greet the group. Since he liked their performance, and especially their costumes, he gave them some money. My interviewee concluded that she was not at all concerned with carnival, which she associated with frivolous festivities in the streets. Hence, it remains an open question if the event was carnival or if it was a parade on a different occasion. Nevertheless, the costumes and the joyful atmosphere reminded my informant of carnival.

Another contemporary witness recounted how carnival was celebrated in Farim (interview ECDC). He was born in the early 1920s in this former *praça*, educated in Portugal, and was a clerk by profession. His Kriston parents used to live in the city center, away from the "uncivilized indigenous" population, as he expressed it. According to him, carnival was a popular festival that was exclusive to the "civilized" population. A number of Europeans who worked as commercial agents in the town also participated in the carnival (cf. interview LH). Attendees often masqueraded as chiefs or "tribal folk." Carnivalists from different parts sauntered around the city, converging at its center. Socially higher-ranking inhabitants met in the nearby Sports and Recreation Club to celebrate.

In the 1950s, carnival was increasingly exposed to European and American influences. The opening of cinemas popularized Zorro and characters from the American Old West, which inspired carnival fantasies. These figures were henceforth added to the traditional costumes. Simultaneously, carnival slowly started to spread. Missionary-led schools for the indigenous population allowed the celebration of carnival. Children used to wear horned devil headpieces and masks. Around the same time, each of Bissau's neighborhoods began to have its own carnival, and the most esteemed of these took place in the Chão de Pepel quarter (Rambout Barcelos et al. 2006: 181–14).

Suppression in Times of War of Independence

Since the 1950s, the clandestine nationalist movements were increasingly, vehemently advocating self-rule and independence of the autocratically ruled colony. These movements were usually led by creole urban dwellers. Protests against the colonial regime reached their peak in 1959, when a dock workers' strike was violently quelled by the colonial regime (Pijiguiti Massacre). The nationalist movements continued their agitation, and in January 1963 the war of independence began with an attack by the PAIGC. As early as the mid-1950s, however, the colonial state must have started to become increasingly nervous about these developments, which threatened the state's sovereign authority. From this it follows that the colonial state must have perceived carnival as a potential means to exert some control over nationalist activities and their indoctrination. Accounts by informants suggest that carnival seemed to have been banished from the capital's city center in about the 1950s, limiting the popular festivities to the suburbs (interviews DCDA; SG; MaCF; cf. FV). Later, the Avenida do Brasil that circled colonial Bissau turned into a spot of popular street carnival (interviews DCDA, JDC; LR; MaCF; cf. AJVDB).

Further legal measures were taken in 1961, with the governor issuing a decree aimed at curtailing the *entrudo*. The decree stipulated that "carnivalesque events" had to follow a number of restrictions: alongside uncontroversial clauses, such as the prohibition on blocking traffic or using dangerous or inflammable objects in public spaces, the regulation also issued a ban on "masks and other disguises which occult or garble the bearers in a form that does not permit to identify her/him rapidly." Moreover, the "usage of personal costumes of administrative authorities, the army, navy, police, customs, Mocidade Portuguesa, and the fire brigade by individuals who do not belong to these institutions" was henceforth forbidden. Finally, the performance of any dance or entertainment event, whether in public or private spaces, needed a special license from then on (Portaria 1,301; my own translation). Subsequent to these regulations, one of my informants' friends was arrested during a carnival in the 1960s because he had worn a military police uniform as a costume (interviews CR). It seems that the street carnival was eventually banished entirely from Bissau's *praça*, from where it moved to the Chão de Pepel neighborhood (cf. Rambout Barcelos et al. 2006: 183).

It seems that private parties and festivities of a nonsuspicious nature were excluded from this prohibition on carnival celebrations in the public streets. This included orderly carnival balls organized by sports clubs like the União Desportiva Internacional de Bissau (International Sports Union of Bissau), Benfica, and the colony's chamber of commerce. Carnival balls organized by the latter, in particular, were chiefly frequented by European and Lebanese merchants. It was primarily the elite who attended these balls, and tickets were comparatively expensive. Private carnival gatherings were often organized by local people (interviews ECDC; ER and JF; LH). A descendant of a long-established upper-middle-class Kriston family who was born in the early 1950s told me about his carnival experiences in the late 1950s and 1960s (interview DCDA; cf. FV; JJSDS). Many European and creole middle-class families lived in his quarter—the Chão de Pepel neighborhood—at that time. As in his father's time, informal associations continued to exist among circles of friends and coworkers, usually craftsmen. These workers' networks would party together after pooling money to pay for food, drinks, and costumes. The parties began around 9 or 10 P.M., with people having drinks in either bars, taverns, or the backyards of their residences. If these parties were held in the backyards, the people would also play disc records originating from either Europe or Africa. Another informant from an upper-middle-class trader family, born and brought up in Bissau in the 1950s, recalled that in the late 1960s and early 1970s, a famous carnival pub existed in the Santa Luzia quarter where the festivities commenced as many as three or four days before carnival was officially launched (interview LH).

Apparently, the street carnival found a refuge in the Chão de Pepel quarter. Many of my informants remembered the *entrudos* of that time (interviews CR, ECDC, ER and JF; VFR; etc.). These *entrudos* were actually individuals, usually elderly men, wearing big masks. At times, *entrudos* were referred to as a *homem morcego* (batman) when they were dressed in ugly, messy, black clothes (interviews DCDA; cf. interviews TL). These masked figures were feared by some, especially by children, for the *entrudos* used to scare minors by growling and beating them with *chicotes* (whips). In time, the *chicote* came to be rarely used by the *entrudos* because the instrument was popularly associated with the colonial police. A contemporary witness opined that this was also because some papier-mâché masks caricatured members of the Portuguese government and their local colonial representatives. According to this informant, the Portuguese colonial authorities had already lost control over carnival by 1970 (interviews LH; cf. CR). According to him, these carnivalists occasionally clashed with Portuguese soldiers in the late 1960s and early 1970s. Although some European residents used to come down to the quarter in order to take photographs of this street carnival, the majority of the Europeans remained in the city center and participated little in "popular" carnival festivities, informants recounted (interviews AJVDB; DCDA; ECDC; FV; TL). It seems that the colonial state might have finally attempted to enlist the support of the street carnival participants for its own cause. Reportedly, Bissau's carnival of 1972 was dominated by the youth, due to which its duration was extended by one day. It is possible that by pandering to the youth's likes, the Mocidade Portuguesa intended to use the carnival for its own purposes (Sigá 1995: 12).

In summary, carnival was apparently limited to Bissau and a few other urbanized settlements throughout the 1960s and the early 1970s and was largely celebrated by the country's creole population. There seemed to be increasing segregation: members of different social classes and ethnic groups (Europeans and Lebanese, Cape Verdeans and Kriston) celebrated the carnival in different ways. This conclusion is based on the fact that many of my Bissau-Guinean informants, for instance, did not know how the Portuguese residents celebrated carnival. This segregation may have been due to the fact that Africans were put under general suspicion during the war. Since the colonial state seemingly feared the appropriation of the street carnival by masked nationalist followers, the festival must have represented an incalculable risk. In this way, the carnival's role extended far beyond simple public masquerading and boisterous partying in the streets. Instead, it constituted a social performance that merged the private and political spheres.

The Postcolonial State: Carnival Goes Political

Following Guinea-Bissau's independence in 1974, carnival entered a new stage, characterized by its politicization by the state. The postindependence leftist one-party state reorganized carnival as a competitive event under its aegis in the late 1970s. Interestingly, carnival—which is actually characterized by antistructure, disorder, social and political critique, and resistance—was transformed into a ritual of structure and order. Hence, carnival was turned into an instrument to mass-mobilize the population and to communicate agendas and slogans on behalf of the state and its ruling party. Against this background, carnival eventually managed to spread all over the country, reaching new sections of the population, in both ethnic and geographical terms.

The party-run youth organization JAAC was mainly responsible for the postindependence revival and reshaping of the carnival. Founded in 1973, the "youth avant-garde" organized voluntary works, reunions, education campaigns, and music and drama performances; its members also participated in mass demonstrations. In this way, JAAC's objective was to enlist the youth's participation in the commemoration and construction of both the party and the state (Andreini and Lambert 1978: 43–44, 90–91; Harasim 1983: 217, 238; Galli and Jones 1987: 84; Forrest 1992: 53). JAAC also served to draw the youth into the PAIGC in order to familiarize them with the party's ideology and deployed adolescents for cleaning the streets. Despite this, JAAC's influence fell far short of UDEMU's reach, mainly due to the fact "that most of the organization's activities were centred in the capital" (Galli and Jones 1987: 84; cf. Barros and Lima 2012: 92).

According to different sources, carnival was revived in either 1978 or 1980–81 (Sigá 1995: 12; Rambout Barcelos et al. 2006: 184). The principal figures responsible for this revival included JAAC's adjunct secretary general at that time and present-day cultural activist Adriano "Atchutchi" Gomes Ferreira and the former JAAC activist and leader of a local nongovernmental organization, Carlos "Pepito" da Silva Schwarz, who—according to the former—had come up with the proposal to revive the carnival as early as 1978. Both of them came from an urban background and had been born into "civilized" families (interviews AGF).

JAAC's functioning relied on the organizational capacity of neighborhoods, schools, and other associations in Bissau. Ever since the revival of the carnival, an organization committee has arranged for a parade passing through Bissau's city center. A jury, situated along the route, is responsible for selecting the winners for three events: best group performance, best mask, and carnival queen; these winners are then awarded prizes (interviews LR; JDC; cf. Cassama 2011). Every year, there is a new official theme for the carnival. The public administration generated new sources of income by issuing licenses to those who wish to take pictures of the carnival or set up *barracas* (sales stalls for drinks and food) along streets that are highly frequented for weeks before and after the carnival. A carnival queen has been selected since 1991. Moreover, the authorities have introduced participation fees for those wishing to compete (in the best group performance, best mask, and carnival queen events) (Sigá 1995: 12–14). Contemporary witnesses observed that in the early and mid-1980s JAAC's revival of the carnival predominantly attracted children and teenagers. This was obvious during the Sunday parade, where masked children and adolescents marched through Bissau in an uncoordinated manner, segregated by gender and organized into groups. The vast majority, roughly 90 percent of the participants, were male. The observers counted about forty groups, and each group's strength ranged from six to fifty individuals (Crowley 1989a: 76–78; Ross 1993).

The takeover of the central carnival organization by the General Directorate of Culture in 1984 marked an important step toward the wider spread of the carnival. Carnival became increasingly professionalized, which culminated in the creation of a "National Commission for the Organization of the Carnival" within the Ministry of Culture in 1990. This government body sought to spread the tradition of carnival parades in the country's regional areas. Subsequently, the regional capitals were expected to compete with each other for national classification (Sigá 1995: 12–13). However, this attempt to popularize the carnival did not succeed in the beginning. Therefore, the carnival continued to be organized on an exclusively regional basis from 1981 to 2001. During these years, the JAAC arranged for carnival competitions at the sectoral level. The person who was formerly responsible for organizing the carnival under the secretariat of state for youth, culture and sports—José da Cunha—informed me in retrospect that by reviving the carnival across Guinea-Bissau, the government body had intended to attract tourists in order to show them the various "tribes" inhabiting Guinea-Bissau (interview JDC). The carnival was thought to present the country's "ethnic diversity in national unity," underlining the prevailing harmony in ethnic terms. Hence, the main focus was on displaying the country's "original culture." According to him, this improved procedure was also aimed at attracting an increasing amount of financial resources since the 1990s, thus initiating new dynamics and publicity.

During the 1980s, the production of giant masks was professionalized, with some artists gaining considerable fame and honor for their creations (e.g. Jon Capé in Bissau in the early 2000s in Bafatá, for instance; interview JMM). At the same time, loose groups without any formal membership began to join the carnival. The composition of these groups varied from year to year, since the membership was not constant. These groups began to take part in the carnival contests. One group, Alegria do Povo (People's Joy), produced two carnival queens in the early 1990s. Because of the significant number of *burmelhos* in this group, it was popularly known as the "Cape Verdean group." Most of its members, however, resided in Bissau's city center. The group became active exclusively in the carnival season and counted 150–200 contributors annually. It was linked to the Escola de Música (Music School), whose director made the public building's rooms available for the group's preparations. Each year before the season commenced, the group's organizer started to mobilize the contributors. These individuals comprised friends, neighbors, and principally the participants' classmates. Money that was required for costumes and other paraphernalia was collected from various government bodies via personal petitions. The group was organized into different sections—for example, some rehearsed the Brazilian style of dancing while another practiced "tribal" dances. For the actual performances, participants wore corresponding dresses and makeup (interviews ISTC). This demonstrates how urban dwellers disguised themselves as "tribal people" and therefore contradicts Crowley's observations of "large village groups" that reportedly appeared in the "local festival dress" of "finely braided short or long grass skirts," in stark contrast to the "urban Creoulos" (Crowley 1989a: 81–82; 1989b: 147; cf. Rambout Barcelos et al. 2006: 192). My informants repeatedly asserted that carnivalists who were disguised as tribals did not necessarily belong to that particular ethnic group in reality. Quite the contrary, ethnic cross-dressing was the standard norm. With the outbreak of the Military Conflict in 1998, however, the Alegria do Povo group ceased to exist.

The takeover of carnival, the subsequent formalization of its organization, and the introduction of contests and parades by the one-party state for political purposes signaled the beginning of the carnival's spread all over the country. The concentration of carnival festivities in Bissau after 1974 popularized the celebration among a large group of migrants from the hinterland, for the population of the capital had grown tremendously during and after the war of independence. These people, mostly young men and women, continued to stay in contact with their rural kin and thereby transported the idea of the carnival to the countryside. In this way, carnival became popular in the countryside independent of the official carnival contests that had been organized by the state since the 1980s. Given the involvement of the state in the organization of carnival, its consequent proliferation all over Guinea-Bissau—and through it, the spread of the state ideology advocating national unity—has been described as follows: "This Carnival is obviously being modified by the government to serve as a national festival which might provide some cohesion and identity in this ethnically-diverse country" (Crowley 1989b: 147).

This integrative transformation had already become visible in the mid- and late 1990s. Reports indicated that adolescents had begun participating in carnivalesque activities in Bula, a small town and sectoral seat in the region of Cacheu, in 1995 (Rambout Barcelos et al. 2006: 189). By 1997, carnival was already deeply rooted among the inhabitants of Canchungo, the administrative seat of the Cacheu region. Although originally propagated by the state, carnival had become popular on its own merits, independent of the Ministry of Culture's efforts. This may have been due to the crisis that the state underwent at the time. However, even during times of crisis, carnival was hailed as a countrywide festivity that was "celebrated in most of the smaller cities and towns as well as rural villages" (Pink 2001: 106). Canchungo town dwellers proudly regarded carnival as "the biggest festival" in Guinea-Bissau. Since the carnival celebrations in Canchungo were not supported by the state at the time, "the competitive and 'officially' structured aspects of carnival were abandoned" (Pink 2001: 106). Nonetheless, the population had fun without even realizing that the "official" carnival had been canceled.

Carnival at Present

The period following the introduction of multiparty democracy in the early 1990s was characterized by the state and the former single ruling party's loss of monopoly over the country. Although the state has subsequently continued to organize carnival contests, both PAIGC and its youth section JAAC are no longer involved in organizing the carnival. It is possible that this withdrawal of influence has contributed to reviving rites symbolizing subversion and antistructure. In the meanwhile, carnival was able to shake off the state's paternalistic intervention and partially renew its critical attitude toward the state and politics. As a result, the carnival has acquired a new kind of freedom, although the state continues to organize the festival. Carnival in Guinea-Bissau has turned into a popular festivity that continues to spread throughout the country. At the same time, it has become subject to new commercial and promotional interests and partnerships in the last few years. In this respect, carnival resembles *manjuandadis*, which have also turned into "spectacles" in recent times.

Regional carnival commissions, established in 2004, and sectoral commissions, founded about the same time, organized annual knockout competitions. The sectoral winners could take part in regional contests, while the victors of these regional parades, in turn, were delegated to Bissau. In 2007, Bissau's "official carnival" — or *carnaval oficial,* as it was termed by government representatives — started on Saturday, 17 February, and continued until Pancake Tuesday on 20 February. The official carnival theme of 2007 was *"Kê di bambaram di nô mames"* (What is from our mothers' baby sling). Even some weeks prior to the beginning of the festive season, those who arrived on the outskirts of the capital could see *barracas* constructed of dried, braided palm leaves along the main arterial road in the Bairro de Ajuda quarter. The municipality had permitted the construction and operation of these stalls for the sale of drinks and food.

The "official carnival" parade started Monday afternoon after 3 P.M. A crowd of cheerful children and adolescents — all shouting, singing, and dancing in great hilarity — moved toward Pijiguiti port. They were accompanied by a flatbed truck carrying huge loudspeakers that played music and intermittently blared loud, incomprehensible, carnival-related announcements and advertisements for a cell phone company. After the carnivalists had gathered at the port, the groups started to slowly move toward the destroyed former presidential palace. While some groups represented various regions of Guinea-Bissau, others represented each of the quarters of Bissau. Yet others were sponsored by the Portuguese Cultural Center or local nongovernmental organizations, displaying slogans corresponding to their sponsors' activities. Some of them wore fancy papier-mâché headpieces and big, colorful masks representing devils and dragon-like creatures, while other participants played drums and other musical instruments. The majority of the headpieces were related to current grievances in society and politics and thus represented people, sometimes even politicians, who were allegorically inserted into the thematic context. Others contained appeals for national unity, democracy, and solidarity. Some juvenescent and childlike male members wore traditional outfits, and many of the groups had female members who paraded in rows. One of the participating groups was the Grupo Harmonia de Missirá (Group Harmony of Missirá) from Bissau's Missirá quarter. Among other performances, the group presented children's dances. These were followed by adolescents who performed dances of the country's different ethnic groups. Each section wore distinct costumes displaying features popularly associated with the respective tribe. This particular carnival group comprised members of a *manjuandadi* called Kimbum de Estrada de Bór (Kimbum of the Bór Road). According to one of its leading representatives (interview ERGS), they had adopted the name of Grupo Harmonia de Missirá in order to represent the whole neighborhood and promote their *manjuandadi,* because they were looking for opportunities to perform at tourist events or cultural centers in order to raise some money. Only a few spectators wore masks, wigs, or costumes.

The carnival jury was seated in front of the former presidential palace and was composed of appointed representatives of the civil society as well as the carnival-organizing committee from the State Secretariat of Culture, which was responsible for nominating the jury. The jury awarded prizes for the categories of best group performance, best mask, and carnival queen; the prize money ranged from $600 to $3,500, according to the president of the organizing committee, Lúcio Rodrigues (interview LR). In 2007, 30 percent of the prize money had been contributed by private sponsors, mostly from the development cooperation sector (interview LR; cf. AS/JUM 2007). At dusk, Bissau's city center was filled with masses of spectators, many of whom, after returning to their neighborhoods, continued to celebrate the carnival with their friends, neighbors, and coworkers—at home, in bars, or at the food and drink stalls.

The parade on Tuesday was said to represent the carnival of the people. Huge crowds strolled through the city center, and the improvised masquerades and carnivalesque makeup were more pronounced. A number of male adolescents had dressed up as women, while hordes of male teenagers wore the traditional black-and-white or colorful *panos,* complemented by headscarves, Wellingtons, and ruffs made of bast fibers.

In comparison with the "official" carnival contest held in Bissau's city center, the carnival at the regional (interviews JL; JMM on the situation in Bafatá), quarter, and sectoral levels appeared to be even more multifaceted, underscoring the commercial and promotional character of the official festival. These differences likewise highlighted the integrative, interethnic character of carnival. The carnival, in this way, has often remained a season that promotes sociability and conviviality among people at the community level, irrespective of their ethnic affiliations and beyond the sphere of official contests.

In 2007 the international nongovernmental organization "Plan International" (cf. interview IsDC) organized a children's carnival in all the schools run by the organization in the sectors of Bafatá region. The organization's objective was to communicate and promote its messages and activities—that is, children's rights—through its carnival. The closing event was organized on the Saturday following Ash Wednesday. The children originated from different schools in the sectors of Bafatá. They paraded in traditional costumes and performed dances, songs, poetry recitations, and street plays that dealt with children's right to education, health, and nutrition, among others. Representatives of UNICEF and Bissau-Guinean politicians were also present at this event (cf. J. U. Mendes 2007).

Since 1998, a Carnival Organizing Commission has been planning the festival in Bissau's Bairro de Ajuda quarter. This body comprised twenty members in 2007 and has been reconstituted ad hoc every year. The commission's aim is to work with children in order to prevent youth vandalism and arrange for their fraternization and entertainment. Before this commission started its work, there had been no attempt to organize any kind of carnival in the quarter. At present, the children and adolescents who participate in this carnival come from different social, ethnic, and religious backgrounds from the nearby churches, kindergartens, and schools in Bairro de Ajuda and its neighboring quarters. While there have been no competitions held among the groups as yet, the groups do rehearse "ethnic dances" for two or three days before performing. The members of the commission work together on a voluntarily basis. However, they were supported both materially and financially by residents, the kindergartens in the vicinity, a local mobile phone provider, and an international nongovernmental organization (interviews JDSN, SF, and ANM).

By now, carnival has even spread to the southernmost region of Tombali. Apart from the official contests held in the regional capital of Catió, the carnival has been celebrated in the sector of Cubucaré since 2003, an area chiefly populated by Balanta farmers. People from the area who worked or attended school in Bissau formed the Associação de Estudantes e Filhos de Cubucaré (Association of Students and Sons of Cubucaré) at the turn of the century. After returning to their homeland, they began to organize festivities such as the carnival, among others, based on their experiences in Bissau. People of diverse ethnic origins unite on the occasion of carnival in order to sing, dance, and parade on the streets wearing masks and fantastic or tribal costumes. With a view to represent different cultures, various ethnic groups in Bedanda annually perform traditional songs and dances on Carnival Saturday. In this regard, it often so happens that the participants end up representing other ethnic groups apart from their own. The nongovernmental organizations who wish to sponsor carnival donate the resources that are subsequently distributed in the form of cash prizes (interview AC).

In the former *praça* of Geba, carnival was revived in 2007. In that year, carnival was celebrated for one whole week—from Monday to Sunday. It was organized by a young man who had grown up in the village. His initiative was supported by a considerable number of children and adolescents from different ethnic groups. Many participants attended school in

Bissau or Bafatá and used to return to Geba only during the weekends or on holidays. On the days of the carnival, a small but festive parade moved through the village, with children as well as adolescents wearing masks representing the faces of animals. The carnivalists were mostly dressed in workaday clothes, although many girls had dressed up in club wear. The highest point of the evening was a disco party organized in Geba's school (interviews AJVDB; CR; DCDA; FD).

Thus, since the early 1990s, carnival has managed to assume an autonomous existence independent of state influence. While nongovernmental organizations and private companies sponsor carnival to promote their own interests, many disadvantaged people regard its organization and their participation in carnival contests as an opportunity to get some money. Recent years have seen the increasing geographic spread and popularity of carnival, predominantly fostered by adolescents. Carnival brings people together by promoting sociability and conviviality among the participating friends, classmates, coworkers, and neighbors. Through this, it creates a sense of unity in diversity. Therefore, the fact that carnival is celebrated by all members of the community, irrespective of their ethnic background, indicates that the shared performance and celebration of this secular ritual contributes significantly and pragmatically to the construction of national consciousness. This integrative appeal is reinforced by the fact that for the last two decades at least, Bissau-Guineans have been frequently and with great pride referring to "their" tremendously popular carnival as a unique national festival in all of West Africa.

Shared Performances as a Means of Integration

The construction of a shared identity is supported by the multilayered character of carnival, which implies that different participants and spectators see different meanings in specific carnivalesque performances while collectively sharing in the experience. Conversely, people of different cultural backgrounds are able to identify with carnival because this complex festivity mirrors certain performative actions and expressions that are similar to those in their own original cultures. Hence, carnival—like creole culture, in general—has succeeded in appealing to the masses by flexibly and perpetually absorbing various cultural influences. Because of its multilayered nature, carnival is able to provide multiple answers to a multitude of questions, depending on the individual observer's cultural and social imprint. For this reason, the question of whether carnivalesque performances display an upside-down world or the real world largely depends upon individual perceptions. Carnival performances at the grassroots level have therefore facilitated and fostered the spread of carnival across ethnic boundaries, thus contributing successfully to the cultural pidginization of carnival, and consequently, to national integration.

As indicated by the previously mentioned description of carnivalesque performances on the occasion of All Souls' Day and All Saints' Day in 1898, such occurrences are not necessarily connected to the Church-related pre-Lenten period (cf. Braun 2002: 11). On the contrary, carnival acts as a special platform for performances involving any kind of masquerade and disguise—in other words, it allows performers to play with their identity. The general characteristics of carnivalesque performances can be listed as follows: First, carnivalesque performances are comical and embody some deviance from everyday behavioral norms. Second, since they are intended to parody daily routines, the performers often exhibit coarse, mannerless behavior. Third, carnivalesque performances are exotic—for instance, the performers wear alien, fantastic costumes. Fourth, such performances can be characterized by eroticism. Fifth, certain demonical aspects—as represented by masks, for example—are an intrinsic part of carnival and its associated performances. Sixth, carnivalesque performances are historical, as the participants as well as spectators proudly refer to the historicity of the festival. And, finally, carnivalesque performances bear military aspects, as represented by orderly parades and uniform costumes (Mezger 1980: 213–19). Although the Bissau-Guinean carnival shows all these characteristics, they are by no means restricted to this festivity. On the contrary, these characteristics are also to be found—entirely or in part—in other rituals performed in the country's interior on different occasions and at different times, as I will demonstrate.

This gives rise to the question of what incites people to participate in carnivalesque performances. Carnival is apparently popular because carnivalesque rituals address certain human and social needs. One vital aspect of this viewpoint is that carnivalesque events allow for a departure (such as cross-dressing, overtly caricaturing and criticizing politicians and businessmen, etc.) from daily routines. Carnivalesque rituals aim at a dialogue with everyday life, thus disclosing the discrepancy between real and carnivalesque life. By displaying abnormal behavior, aberrant costumes, and mummery, individuals can metamorphose into other characters and slip into new roles. This allows for new, unusual opportunities of communication, because the anonymity granted by costumes and masks can serve to disguise one's own origins, social status, and personality. Therefore, carnival has been described as an expression of an upside-down world. The escape from daily routines meets people's social and psychic demands, since it paves the way for expressing social grievances. Hence, it is not astonishing that throughout history, carnivalesque events have been repeatedly forbidden or restricted at different times and places (Mezger

1980: 205–11, 220–23; 2000: 116, 129–31; Braun 2002: 10). For centuries, carnival has oscillated between acceptance and constraints, being claimed by
different social classes. Studying medieval and early modern-era carnival in Europe, Mikhail Bakhtin (1993) has pointed to the antiauthoritar-
ian and antidogmatic, extremely rough, salacious, and grotesque-comical
character of the original "folk carnival" — in contrast to manifestations of
carnival established at later times. Similar to Europe where medieval carnival deteriorated after it had been appropriated by the ruling class, transforming the formerly wild ritual into courtly masquerades, parades, and
feasts, carnival was also domesticated in Guinea-Bissau, not only in colonial times but especially thereafter. Here, carnival was restrained or even
prohibited in this manner in 1888 and the 1960s and early 1970s, at a time
when social and political discontentment challenged the colonial state's
rule. In order to prevent such carnivalesque excess and thus any disagree-
able critique, the postcolonial state decided to appropriate carnival for its
own propagandistic goals. Thus, carnival was temporarily domesticated
by the independent state. However, following the introduction of the multiparty system, the Bissau-Guinean carnival regained in the 1990s, at least
to some degree, its critical stance toward politics and partially reverted to
its role of being a ritual of rebellion. For instance, in the late 1990s, carnival
in Canchungo contained several allusions to corruption. A neighborhood
teenager dressed up to perform "a local image of economic success" — he
was made up and behaved like a local businessman. In reality, however,
the adolescent did "odd tasks for people about their homes." In the same
carnival, there was a group of young men in costumes who parodied the
smartly dressed people in everyday life. One of them was dressed in a suit
and wore odd shoes and dreadlocks in his hair. While the group danced
around him, they also slipped crumpled banknotes into the fellow's
mouth. When questioned about the meaning of this action, they explained
that the receiver represented the president of Guinea-Bissau, who "ate
money" (*kume dinheiro*) — a local phrase to describe a person who accepts
bribes or is corrupt (Pink 2001: 111–12). By these means, irrespective of
their ethnic identity, the performers obviously intended to playfully vent
their anger regarding the unjust and unbearable political circumstances
and social distress that they daily experienced as socially disadvantaged
youth in Guinea-Bissau, which they subverted and symbolically reversed
during carnival.

Similar motives, though nonpolitical, may have influenced the choice
of clothing worn by certain male adolescents during the 2007 carnival in
Bissau. One of them appeared along with his girlfriend. Wearing a short
skirt, top, and baseball cap, he paraded through one of the capital's central
squares with her. The multilayered aspect of carnival allows for differ-

ent explanations for each performance, without there being a "correct" or "incorrect" meaning underlying the given performance. Hence, cross-dressing may be interpreted simply as a fancy masquerade or, in contrast, as a silent protest against the social disapproval of transsexuality and homosexuality or even as an expression of one's own hidden sexual desires, for instance. Analogical conclusions can be drawn from the dresses worn by female adolescents, who often dressed up in scanty club wear during carnival and on other occasions. Such a style of dressing can be interpreted as either a symbolic escape from a burdensome life in poverty or a rebellion against the parental generation or a reflection of a self-confident, hedonistic, or narcissistic cult of the body.

However, as the military coup of April 2012 has demonstrated, specific political events allow for the (re)taming of carnival by the state. Carnival of 2013 could have been a platform of rebellion, an opportunity to criticize the unpopular transitional regime that was backed by the military and lacked democratic legitimacy. That carnival had lost again its critical, subversive function was best expressed by the fact that, among others, both Bissau-Guinean army officials and military representatives of ECOWAS (Economic Community of West African States)—the regional organization that had approved the regime in power—took their seats in the gallery to watch the official carnival parade in Bissau's city center on Carnival Monday, 11 February, and Pancake Day, 12 February. Although some papier-mâché headpieces were topped by peace doves or bore inscriptions that called for peace, some dance performances were marked as "peace dances," and some adolescents wore military uniforms, parodying army marches, criticism was very mild—or restrained, so to speak. However, Bissau-Guinean spectators applauded enthusiastically when, as part of a kindergarten group's carnival dance performance on Friday, 8 February, a young girl called for peace and reconciliation in her speech to the carnival committee. Thus, carnival continued as a commodified festivity centrally organized by the state apparatus—carnival enthusiasts being careful of criticizing the rulers, including particularly the security forces that are known for their intimidating measures.

In a nutshell, carnivalesque performances are able to satisfy the people's need for criticism and parody of their circumstances as well as serve as an escape from social constraints. According to Victor Turner (1979: 83, 93; 1995: 128–29; 1996: 232), rituals—like carnival—temporarily suspend the forces of normal everyday role-playing. At the same time, the multi-layered character of carnivalesque rituals prevents unambiguous judgments regarding their meaning. The abovementioned needs are shared by people of different origins, irrespective of their ethnic affiliation. All these factors have facilitated the spread of the Bissau-Guinean carnival. After it was appropriated from the Portuguese during the earlier colonial period, carnival benefited from the fact that while it was not exclusively linked to a specific ethnic group, it was primarily associated with the Kriston as an ethnic category of identitarian classification. Moreover, carnival in Guinea-Bissau was dissociated from the Church very early in its history and instead became a distinct, popular, and secular festival (Mezger 2000: 110–11). In addition, carnival spread far and wide due to the aforementioned fact that its characteristics mirror qualities that are not at all alien to the societies in the hinterland but instead are inherent in some of their cultural manifestations as well. The attractive and multilayered nature of carnivalesque performances have contributed to the increasing popularity of the secular ritual in the countryside. Hence, the societies in the hinterland were able to integrate carnival mainly due to its manifoldness and malleability, which conversely also enabled the performers of the ritual to absorb, integrate, and reinterpret any alien influences. In retrospect, therefore, carnival's integrative potential renders it impossible to ascribe certain performative elements to specific ethnic or cultural groups.

The multilayered nature of meanings emanating from carnivalesque performances on the one hand and the symbolic association between specific carnivalesque aspects and different groups of people on the other are revealed, for example, in the previously mentioned episode about the construction of a ship float in colonial Cacheu. The building of such floats is entirely unknown in contemporary Bissau-Guinean carnival. The construction of the ship can be attributed to various cultural contexts, depending of the observer's point of view. Therefore, it is possible that the construction was a singular occurrence that was linked to the celebrations of the five hundredth anniversary of the colony's "discovery" by Portuguese navigators in 1446. Alternatively, the ship may have been intended as a more general tribute to the New State's army and navy, or the ship and warlike seaman's songs may have alluded to the ongoing World War II. Apart from such political deductions, the construction of ships can be also linked to Catholicism. Portuguese renaissance confraternities used to annually gift candles to people who set sail for the Upper Guinea coast (Rosa Pereira 1972: 15–17). In addition, for centuries, carnival has been known as a metaphor for the ship of fools: the idea of a ship of fools has ecclesial origins and stands in opposition to the nave (from Latin *navis*, "ship") of a church. The ship of fools served to show sinners and detractors the consequences of their misdeeds and misconduct. On Ash Wednesday, the believers had to leave the upside-down world embodied by the ship of fools in order to reenter the "normal" world (Moser 1986: 71–82; cf. Brant 1962). This implies that the carnivalesque ship scene, which can be understood as an encomium of Portuguese colonialism at first view, can also be interpreted as a hidden, mordant critique of Portuguese colonialism that was staged by Kriston contributors. Apart from these Eurocentric interpretations, carnival can also be understood in terms of a number of Afrocentric traditions. They allow us to understand how the local population could identify with carnival, mainly because of the similar performative expressions or similar interpretative meanings covered by both the carnival and the rural cultural expressions. For example, just to the north of Cacheu, in parts of Senegal and the Gambia, among others, there is a tradition of building and parading illuminated floats. These "man-made structures," which "are either carried or wheeled through the streets," are known as *fanaals* (Oram 2002: 77). They are constructed in the region around Banjul for the Christmas and New Year festivities and may have a Christian background. However, the tradition of building floats in the shape of ships has been discontinued in the Gambia. Processions in the Gambia are usually accompanied by singing, dancing, and drumming (Nunley 1982; 1985; Bettelheim 1985; Gamble 1989; Oram 1998, 2002). Historically, such float parades were also observed in the Casamance in the mid-nineteenth century (Reade 1864: 399; see Bettelheim 1985: 50; Gamble 1989: 2–3). This suggests the possibility that the ship float in Cacheu shared a symbolic repertoire with the *fanaal* parades conducted in other regions, including Ziguinchor, the main town of the then Portuguese Casamance. Another possibility is that the Cacheu episode can be interpreted as an expression of the maritime character of creole culture. As we have seen, some Kriston were even known as *grumetes* (meaning "cabin boys") at one time, with many of them serving as auxiliary seamen.

The multilayered meanings expressed by carnivalesque representations are also reflected in the use of cow horns. While cow horns are commonly used to adorn masks in carnival, they are also locally used during religious rituals and masquerades held in the country's interior (Rambout Barcelos et al. 2006: 181–82). On the Bijagó Islands, for instance, cow horns are used as ship decorations and are inherent parts of masks used in religious rituals (Bernatzik 1933: vol. 2, figures 23, 30, 151, 165, 167, 171–72, 181–83, 202–5, 216–18). While the horns mainly remind children of cows, the Catholic Church, in contrast, interprets cow horns as the devil's horns. Reportedly, however, the priests who directed the missionary schools in colonial times did not object to the use of horned pieces of cardboard (Rambout Barcelos et al. 2006: 181).

The multilayered aspect of meanings conveyed by carnival is also evident in the previously mentioned episode of the All Souls' and All Saints' Day celebrations in Bolama in 1898. This festivity was characterized by a congruency of different meanings. While the city's European and creole inhabitants may have regarded the festival as a Christian holiday, people with close links to the interior might have considered it a kind of harvest festival celebrated at the end of the rice harvest season. Tradesmen, in turn, might have regarded the festival as a celebration of their impending annual departure for their sales travels into the continent's interior (Brooks 1984).

This congruency of meanings that facilitated the successful spread of the carnival continues to exist even now. In Bafatá, for example, during the 2007 carnival, I observed the appearance of a *kankuran* mask, considered as an integral part of Mandingo culture and linked to age-set initiations. It consisted of a full-length costume made entirely of multiple brownish stripes of bark. The masked figure was equipped with a cutlass and sought to frighten children, who would scream in terror and take to their heels. The identity of the masked figure was kept secret, and he was assisted by some adolescent companions who served to detect hidden children. Even elders feared the *kankuran* and warned me against approaching the mask. Through this, I sensed that the mask was highly respected by the spectators. Nevertheless, I also realized that the protagonists of this scene—both children and the numerous spectators—were actually enjoying the performance. The audience was commenting and laughing about the way in which the frightened children ran away and hid themselves from the masked monstrosity.

The *kankuran* is regarded as a mechanism for male adolescents, young adult males, and their secret age-grade association to "establish its credibility, impartiality, and flexibility as a rule-applying structure" (Weil 1971: 286) in a society characterized by norm-setting and its application by male elders. Thus, a *kankuran* serves as a means to decrease the potential of intergeneration conflict. This is because the acts of the *kankuran* are attributed to the mask and not its wearer. On this account, the mask can often act with impunity (Weil 1971: 279; de Jong 2000: 154; 2007: 129–30).

A similar masquerade, called *kumpó,* is traditionally performed in the Lower Casamance and northwestern Guinea-Bissau. At present, the *kumpó* masquerade is performed mainly by the Jola ethnic group as a protection against witches as well as a means to enforce norms, regulate the migration of girls, and provide entertainment (Mark 1985: 124–25; de Jong 1999: 56–57, 62; 2007: 160; cf. interviews AJPB). The *kumpó* is dressed like the *kankuran,* namely in a full-length costume made of dried palm leaves. In this ritual, again, the *kumpó* seeks to frighten the children, with the masked figure developing an existence that is independent of its wearer. Like the *kankuran* masquerade, the *kumpó* is organized by secret age-set-associations (de Jong 1999: 52–53, 57; 2007: 157). A number of characteristics of both the *kankuran* and the *kumpó* are mirrored by the carnival. This includes the depiction of an upside-down world, which is inherent in the carnival as well as in the *kankuran* and *kumpó* performances, as is evident in the following statement regarding the *kumpó*: "During the hours that the masked dancer roams through the village, the rules by which men normally govern themselves are temporarily suspended" (Simmons 1971: 161).

This reversed social order was also reflected in the presence of *entrudos,* which were popular especially during the carnivals of Bissau in the 1960s and 1970s, apart from the *kankuran* and *kumpó.* In both these rituals, the personality of the mask-wearer remains secret while violence symbolically comes to the fore. Just like the *kankuran* and *kumpó* masked figures that hunt children in order to punish them, the *entrudo* whipped children and scared adults with impunity because the mask had adopted an identity beyond the mask-wearer's personality. As in the earlier case studies, the multilayered nature of the carnival implies that the *entrudos* can be interpreted according to a variety of meanings. Hence, the *entrudo* can be regarded as a parody of colonial police officers, who used to whip the actual or suspected delinquents with *chicotes.*

As these findings suggest, the cultural pidginization of carnival has been significantly facilitated by its multilayered character. The congruency of different meanings represented in carnival depends on the participants' or observers' individual cultural backgrounds. People of different origins, therefore, are able to retrieve their respective cultures through carnivalesque performances. Despite, or more correctly, because of these different meanings, carnival has managed to create a common identity among its participants as well as observers. People of diverse ethnic affiliations are attracted to carnival, a cultural representation that was promoted by the nation-state, following Guinea-Bissau's independence in 1974, in a move to implicitly advocate national unity. Ironically, the very same state's weakening control over the nation since the 1980s appears to have contributed to the nationwide expansion of carnival, a former creole representation.

Notes

1. "Kriol is the language that all people speak in Guinea[-Bissau]." Ordinary citizen in Bissau quoted by Couto (1990: 53).
2. We can only speculate about the origins of the term: lexicographer Luigi Scantamburlo assumed that the term *manjua* may be derived from French *mangier,* meaning "to eat (together)" (Scantamburlo 2002: 382). The rarely used Portuguese noun *manjar* can be translated as "food" or "dainties," the verb *manjar* as "to eat." The Portuguese ethnographer Ernesto Veiga de Oliveira, for instance, reported about "manjares ceremoniais"

during Portuguese carnival (Veiga de Oliveira 1984: 59–68). Such "ceremonial feasts" are, in fact, a usual event among *manjuandadis* as I will illustrate.

3. Telegram dated 20 February 1888, Arquivo Histórico Ultramarino (AHU), Fundo da Guiné, Livro 102. I am deeply indebted to Wilson Trajano Filho, who called my attention to this document and provided me with his transcript. See also Arquivo Histórico Ultramarino (AHU), Sala 12, 2.1 Secção-D1, No. 923.2, Pasta 10.A.

4. According to his military personal record card (Arquivo Histórico Ultramarino [AHU], Sala 12, 2.1 Secção-D1, No. 923.2, Pasta 10.A, Processo 97) Eusébio Catella do Valle was born in Luanda, Angola, in 1844, presumably into a creole family as no ethnic identity is indicated and his parents bore Portuguese names. As he is insulted as "sobba" (the Angolan-Portuguese term meaning "chief") in the telegram, he appears to be at least partly of African origin. Interestingly, carnival seems to have been well established in Luanda for centuries and was embraced by creole inhabitants (Birmingham 1987).

Conclusion

In this volume I have shown how creole identity manifests itself in contemporary Guinea-Bissau, how it has emerged and developed historically, and how it is related to other ethnic identities in terms of interethnic contact.

Following Jacqueline Knörr, I have understood creolization as a process that involves indigenization and, to varying degrees, ethnicization. Cultural creolization is a specific case of ethnicization and takes place primarily—but not exclusively—in colonial settings. Creolization implies the formation of a new collective identity that replaces a heterogeneous set of original ethnic identities over generations. Indigenization occurs as part of this process: over the course of time, creoles tend to increasingly identify with a certain settlement territory and come to be recognized as its founders and landlords.

Against this background I studied three varieties of creole groups whose identity has been ethnicized to varying degrees. I have discussed how individuals belonging to the different categories of creole identity identify themselves, which criteria they use to do so, and which identity is ascribed to them by others.

One variety of creole identity consists of the Bissau-Guinean Cape Verdeans, whose identity is strongly ethnicized. They or their ancestors originated from the Cape Verdean archipelago off the West African coast and migrated to colonial Guinea-Bissau in the past. The Bissau-Guinean Cape Verdeans maintain a distinct identity, distancing themselves particularly from the Kriston variety of creole identity. Kriston identity emerged in the *praças* during the sixteenth century. While the contemporary Kriston de Geba likewise possess a highly ethnicized identity, that of the third variety of creole identity is only weakly ethnicized. The Bissau-Guinean Cape Verdeans and Kriston de Geba can be regarded as *ethnic groups,* whereas the weakly ethnicized third variety can be understood as an *ethnic category.*

In this book I have tried to explain how the colonial state contributed to creating the different trajectories of creole identity. Colonial policy and ideology, enforced by the legal classification of Bissau-Guineans as either citizens or subjects, resulted in the transformation and diversification of creole identity, leading to the formation of creole groups on the one hand and creole categories of identification on the other. By imposing a classificatory grid on the population, the colonial state manipulated the Bissau-Guineans' identity in an attempt to make them governable, subjugating the inhabitants to colonial domination under the colonial social status reward power system.

Despite their tiny numbers—as compared to the country's total population—creoles in Guinea-Bissau have exerted a major influence on national identity. In fact, due to their manifold contributions to national identity, creoles can be regarded as precursors to Bissau-Guinean nationhood. Creoles of heterogeneous ancestry indigenized to a high degree, and it is because of this that they are still recognized as firstcomers and landlords in the former *praças*. Some of them openly reject any ethnic affiliation and portray themselves as *guineense* ([Bissau-]Guinean), thus ascribing to themselves a particular position that can be interpreted as superior to that of "ordinary" ethnic groups. They and their ancestors had been almost exclusively classified as "civilized" citizens under colonialism, and thus as "Portuguese." Hence, creole identity transcends the "unity in diversity" or "tree-as-nation" model that popularly conceives the nation as being composed of various ethnic groups.

Moreover, I have already shown how Christianity—which is strongly associated with creole culture—continues to retain exceptional significance in postcolonial Bissau-Guinean society, even encompassing Islam in its hierarchical opposition. Further, I have demonstrated how creoles contributed some of their own cultural traditions to national identity formation: cultural features that had been originally exclusive to creole communities, such as the creole language Kriol, *manjuandadi* associations, and the carnival, have spread all over Guinea-Bissau since independence. In this way, creole representations were transformed into expressions of Bissau-Guinean national identity, which was subsequently cultivated across ethnic and religious boundaries. Apart from this, creole nationalists actively engaged in the struggle for independent nation- and statehood. Leading nationalist politicians such as Amílcar Cabral—himself a creole—were influenced by European thinking and the European (or more precisely, French) model of nationalism, which was based on the assumption that the state, nation, and people were congruent.

This study seeks to contribute to a better, more comprehensive contextual understanding of the processes of cultural creolization. Contrary to some earlier approaches—this study has shown that one must employ analytical criteria to define identity as "creole." Thus, while the ethnonyms of the Krio in Sierra Leone or the Créoles of the Caribbean and Mascarene Islands contain the term "creole," for example, neither Cape Verdean nor Kriston de Geba ethnonyms bear a mention of the term (or its corresponding Portuguese version). It is only the name of the Bissau-Guinean lingua franca "Kriol" that alludes to its linguistic quality as a lusocreole language.

The Bissau-Guinean case demonstrates that cultural creolization does not necessarily constitute a one-way street, because the process can also be reversed. Thus, a creole identity can gradually de-creolize in later stages, reapproximating the various ancestral ethnic identities that had constituted the creole ethnic group when it came into existence. This seems to have occurred in the case of creole categories of identification that acquired a native ethnic identity. While their ancestors, in most cases, had developed an identity as Kriston, which encompassed diverse original identities, subsequent social and political developments—promoted and accelerated by the colonial state—led to the gradual de-creolization (or de-ethnicization) of their Kriston identity. This identity has subsequently reapproximated ancestral "ordinary" identities in some cases. These creoles identify themselves as "Pepel," "Manjaco," or "Mancanha," for example, while following only some cultural traditions of these ethnic groups. Usually, ethnic self-identification and ethnic ascription are congruent. At the same time, however, they distance themselves from other "ordinary" identities: many of them highlighted their and their families' length of urban residence and their inability to speak the language of the "ordinary" ethnic groups. Some also referred to the Christian faith as a distinguishing marker and admitted that they retained only a few customary practices of the "ordinary" ethnic groups. All in all, this weakly ethnicized variety of creole identity shares a rather vague reference to creoleness.

Furthermore, this study has demonstrated that processes of cultural creolization can involve different variations of indigenization. On the one hand, indigenization can occur through the construction of a specific, new identity. This is most strikingly exemplified by the Kriston de Geba, who identify with the former *praça* of Geba and even bear the place's name as part of their ethnonym. On the other hand, indigenization can occur through adopting a native ethnic identity. This is the case in those creole categories of identification that acquired a native ethnic identity as part of their creole self-representation. The latter variety of indigenization is apparently owed to the postcolonial self-redefinition of identity, attempting to shake off the formerly privileged "civilized" status of colonial times. The reconceptualization as "African" expresses the desire for taking sides with non-creole Bissau-Guineans.

These developments of creole identity formation are closely linked to colonialism, which provided a hierarchical sociocultural order that constricted social permeability (and therefore both social advancement and decline) along racial and ethnic lines. Creolization occurred in colonial societies that were marked by substantial migrations of people—some of which were forcibly imposed—causing cultural and ethnic heterogeneous societies. This does not imply that processes of cultural creolization occurred only under European colonialism. Although it is true that many societies in Africa, America, Asia, and Oceania that were colonized by European colonial powers—most notably Portugal, Spain, the United Kingdom, France, and the Netherlands—generated creole categories and groups, cultural creolization also occurred in settings not affected by European political and economic domination. This applies, for instance, to the east African Swahili Coast and the adjacent Comoro Islands, Zanzibar and Pemba, where Arabs and Persians had traded, settled, and ruled for centuries. Creole identities could emerge in these heterogeneous settings. In this way, cultural creolization processes are primarily founded on population movements and pronounced sociocultural hierarchies that result in varying degrees of ethnically and culturally diverse societies.

As pointed out, I differentiated the processes of cultural creolization from those of cultural pidginization. In contrast to creolization, which involves the emergence of a new collective identity based on a heterogeneous set of ancestral ethnic identities, pidginization constitutes merely the formation of shared cultural manifestations and transethnic identifications but not the formation of a new ethnic identity. For instance, cultural representations—such as Kriol, *manjuandadi* associations, and carnival— that had been unique dimensions of creole identity, primarily in the *praças,* have spread throughout postcolonial Guinea-Bissau across ethnic and religious boundaries.

In this book, I have shown how the countrywide proliferation of *manjuandadis* has been accompanied by a functional incorporation. This means that the term *manjuandadi* is now used to refer to cultural representations that are somewhat different than the original *manjuandadis,* in the strictest sense of the word. In other words, the term *manjuandadi* is being increasingly applied to describe formations that have little in common with the traditional Kriston *manjuandadis.* However, the core meaning of *manjuandadis*—the mutual provision of solidarity and sociability—has remained constant. The proliferation of *manjuandadis* was fostered by the fact that non-creole individuals associate solidarity and sociability with the Kriol term *manjuandadi,* which was consequently used to describe different types of organizations that were known by different names in the respective local languages. For instance, traditional age-set associations came to be increasingly called *manjuandadis*. Thus, both carnival and *manjuandadis* became popular due to the fact that individuals of different ethnic and cultural origins could identify with these features while keeping these institutions' core meanings intact.

Several different factors facilitated this process of pidginization (or transethnicization). One concerns the transethnic character of Kriston identity. Kriston identity has traditionally encompassed a diversity of ethnic identities, such as Pepel, Manjaco, Mancanha, Beafada, and Balanta, among others. Cultural representations such as the Kriol language, *manjuandadis*, or carnival were not exclusive to an ethnic subcategory of the Kriston. On the contrary, different ethnic Kriston subcategories claimed these representations as part of their creole identity. Any person could become a Kriston, regardless of his or her ethnic identity, by joining a creole community in any of the *praças*, converting to Christianity, and learning Kriol. Although cultural representations like *manjuandadis* or carnival were not ascribed to a specific ethnic subcategory of the Kriston, they were primarily identified with Christianity.

Another important factor is the leading role of the postcolonial state in promoting the nationwide spread of creole representations. By employing Kriol as a means of interethnic communication and *manjuandadis* and the carnival as a means of political mass-mobilization, the postcolonial state made what had been exclusively Christian features popular among Muslims as well. For the last decade or so, essentialist discourses by individuals of Kriston origin as well as cultural activists have argued against the cultural pidginization of *manjuandadis* and rejected the claims of Muslim associations to be recognized as *manjuandadis*. Nevertheless, both *manjuandadis* and carnival have managed to spread across ethnic and religious boundaries and have thereby produced a common identity. This is largely due to the fact that secular rituals like carnival do not convey any fixed meaning. On the contrary, different participants experience different significances and efficacies, depending on their respective socialization and enculturation, and regard these as representations of their respective ethnic identity. The construction of a shared identity is thus ensured by the participants' conjoint performance of rituals.

These developments were initiated by the postcolonial state in its attempt to construct a nation *after* the formation of an independent state. Therefore, the postcolonial Bissau-Guinean state had to create an integrated national culture by means of cultural pidginization. Through this, the state and its leaders attempted nation-building in line with the European ideology that propagated the congruency of the state, nation, and people.

Since a number of creole representations were shared by various ethnic subcategories of the Kriston, contemporary Bissau-Guineans do not appear to labor under the impression that a specific ethnic group exerts hegemony over others. Instead, cultural representations such as Kriol (interviews AJPB), *manjuandadis,* and the carnival seem to be ethnically "blind" and therefore unrelated to specific ethnic groups. This has enhanced conviviality and cooperation among Bissau-Guineans, thereby also stabilizing their national identity.

Bissau-Guineans distinguish clearly between state- and nationhood. While they are critical of their state's performance, they nevertheless identify as one nation. The state is most severely criticized by the masses of disadvantaged people who regard themselves as victims of their state. The Bissau-Guinean state can therefore be portrayed as an arena wherein different conceptualizations of the state—represented by different institutions, social layers, and interest groups, and including the poor people's image of the victimizing state—compete with each other. While the people's conceptualizations of the state may be fragmented, their identification with the nation is very pronounced. The nation's collective suffering under an anonymous state apparatus, which is seen as responsible for political instability and socioeconomic hardships, makes the population desperately long for a new redeemer. This feeling unites Bissau-Guineans across ethnic and religious boundaries.

When the Military Conflict broke out in June 1998 and foreign powers entered Guinea-Bissau, the nation stood united against a shared enemy, embodied by Senegalese, Guinean, and French army troops, thus forgetting any social, ethnic, and religious cleavages. National cohesion was intensified by narratives and historical facts relating to French colonial and postcolonial Senegalese and Guinean claims to Bissau-Guinean territories. In light of this history, Bissau-Guineans stood together as one nation to defend their country.

The Bissau-Guineans' strong commitment to nationhood has largely been fostered by the independence movement PAIGC. On the basis of a "unity in diversity" model, the PAIGC had actively encouraged national cohesion ever since the beginning of the struggle for liberation. The PAIGC ideology was developed by one of its cofounders and long-term charismatic leader, Amílcar Cabral, who was a Bissau-Guinean Cape Verdean born in Bafatá. Creoles—both Bissau-Guinean Cape Verdeans and individuals of Kriston origin—were strongly represented in the PAIGC leadership. Moreover, their commitment to national independence was largely based on their proximity to European culture, which provided them the European model of nation- and statehood. Given the determination of the Portuguese New State regime, which resisted any form of self-governance and independence, an armed struggle seemed the only possible way to achieve independence. Thus, despite their small number, Bissau-Guinean creoles have made a considerable contribution to Guinea-Bissau's achieve-ment of independent nation- and statehood.

Creole identity has transcended the rigid, popular dichotomy of a nation that encompasses a number of "tribes"—as delineated in Amíl-car Cabral's state ideology that sought to construct an integrated nation as an umbrella for various ethnic groups—in different ways. Some cre-oles explicitly portray themselves as "[Bissau-]Guineans" based on their self-representation as urban dwellers. While Kriston regard themselves as firstcomers and landlords of the *praças,* many other creoles of non-Kriston ancestry that had been classified as citizens in colonial times feel attached to urban life. In this way, these creolized ethnics assume a particular, and to some extent superior, position regarding the "ordinary" ethnic groups, thus refuting the popular unity in diversity model.

The exceptional role played by creole identity and creoles in the con-struction of postcolonial nation- and statehood is also reflected in a num-ber of other factors. For instance, creoles are aware of the fact that several of their cultural representations that had previously been largely restricted to urban creole communities, such as Kriol, *manjuandadis,* and carnival, have turned into representations of the new, integrated national culture. Moreover, references to Geba—a former cradle of creole culture—as Guinea-Bissau's first capital underline creoles' self-image as precursors to the contemporary nation-state. The portrayal of Geba and Cacheu as housing Guinea-Bissau's first church and chapel, respectively, and the la-beling of mosques as "(Muslim) churches" or "(Muslim) chapels" in Kriol demonstrates that Christianity—as one of the most important markers of creole identity—continues to encompass Islam, thus again highlighting the significance of creole identity and creole markers for the postcolonial nation-state. Last but not the least, Amílcar Cabral is even now regarded by most Bissau-Guineans as the national redeemer—a national hero and martyr whose life ended so tragically shortly before independence, pre-venting him from achieving his utopian ideal of constructing a powerful postcolonial nation-state.

With regard to the existence of influential creole groups, Guinea-Bissau is far from an isolated case, because creole identities and cultural repre-sentations can be found, to date, in various countries in Latin America, Africa, and Asia. Some of these creole identities are connected to the Por-tuguese colonial empire. Apart from Guinea-Bissau, such creole commu-nities can be found in Cape Verde, São Tomé and Príncipe, certain localities in India (Goa and others) and Sri Lanka, Macau (China), Malacca (Malay-sia), and Brazil, among others. Common features shared by many of these communities, for instance, include the role of Christianity and a specific language as important ethnic markers of creole identity construction. Cultural representations strongly associated with creole culture, such as Portuguese-based creole languages, carnival, and confraternities, for instance, can be found in many of the aforesaid localities. These representations, in fact, are "traveling models" that owe their global spread to Portuguese expansion since the fifteenth century. These cultural manifestations show that people in the colonies were integrated into global processes of cultural, economic, and social exchange and influence at a very early stage. Against this background, it could be very interesting and productive for theories of cultural creolization to perform a comparative research on the formation and development of creole identities and culture.

Further comparative investigation concerning the way in which such "traveling models" were locally appropriated, transformed, integrated, and embedded into larger sociocultural contexts on site may shed more light on different creolization processes. Such research could contribute to a better understanding of the role of creole identities and interethnic relations, Christianity's impact on locally significant religious practices, aspects of creole identities (whether they are strongly or weakly ethnicized, exclusive or inclusive, and how they transformed over time), and the effect of social status reward power systems, and thus the effect of power and domination, on the shaping of creole identities. In particular, a systematic comparison of confraternities (and their resultant cultural representations) and other types of creole associations in the various settings mentioned earlier would significantly contribute to the existing knowledge on the field. At present, there are only a few brief comparative studies in this regard—one deals with Cape Verdean *tabancas* and Bissau-Guinean *manjuandadis* (Trajano Filho 2001a,b) while the others study *manjuandadis* and Brazilian *irmandades* (Domingues 2005; Miranda Freitas and Domingues 2005; Domingues, Miranda Freitas and Gomes Ferreira 2006). The paucity of such analyses reveals that there has been very little comparative research referring to the Afro-American context thus far. Even less attention has been paid to the comparison of lusocreole cultures in Africa and Asia.

Further comparative research could also focus on processes of cultural pidginization, including the role played by creoles and creole cultural features in postcolonial nation- and state-building. Investigations from both the synchronic and diachronic perspectives could significantly contribute to a better understanding of the influence of creoles and creole identity on the formation of an independent nation-state. Studies should also examine which role-specific creole representations were used by political decision-makers and nationalist ideologues seeking to create an integrated national culture after independence. Such a research could focus on various creole settings in West Africa. To date, analyses of creole identity have largely neglected these issues: for example, studies regarding creole identity in the four communes of Senegal have concentrated mainly on creole identity in colonial times. The same applies to the Fernandino of Equatorial Guinea and the Gambian Aku. Although a number of new projects have focused on the Aguda (or Afro-Brazilians) of Togo and Benin, they too have largely disregarded the significance of creoles and creole identity for postcolonial nation-building. In contrast, several studies have explored the role of creoles in the processes of state- and nation-building in Sierra Leone and Liberia. Interesting parallels regarding contributions of creoles, creole identity, and culture to local conceptualizations and ideologies of nation- and statehood could emerge through a comparison between West African creole settings and those in the Swahili Coast in East Africa (Kenya, Tanzania, Comoros), South Asia (India, Sri Lanka), and Southeast Asia (Malaysia, Indonesia).

Interviews

AB, male, 55–60 years, Cupilun/Bissau, 19 March 2007.
AC, male, 35–40 years, Bissau, 30 March 2007.
ADSM, male, 45–50 years, Bissau, 27 September 2006.
ADZ, female, 75–80 years, Cacheu, 6 December 2006.
AF, male, 75–80 years, Geba, 30 November, 1 and 2 December 2006, 18 and 20 April 2007.
AFQ, male, 60–64 years, Farim, 16 November 2006.
AGF, male, 40–45 years, Bissau, 13 September 2006, 3 April 2007.
AlS, female, 45–55 years, Bafatá, 14 April 2007.
AH, male, 45–50 years, Bissau, 21 June 2006.
AHVC, male, 40–45 years, Bissau, 14 July 2006.
AJPB, male, 80–85 years, Bissau, 1 August 2006; 3, 4, and 29 April 2007.
AJVDB, female, 60–65 years, Bissau, 26 March 2007.
AME, female, 60–65 years, Bissau, 6 August 2006.
AMV, male, 65–70 years, Bafatá, 12 April 2007.
AP, female, and RP, male, 50–55 years, Bissau, 24 September 2006.
AS, male, 50–55 years, Bissau, 29 May 2006.
AuF, male, 55–60/60–65 years, Bafatá and Bissau, 7 February 2007, 9 March 2013.
AuF, JB, ACMV, MLF, and SMB, male, 55–60, Bafatá, 8 February 2007.
AVHS, male, 70–75 years, Geba, 2 December 2006; 16, 18, and 23 April 2007.
LVHS, male, 30–35 years, and NVHS, female, 50–55 years, Geba, 2 December 2006.
BC, female, and ADS, JS, IC, male, 40–50 years, Bissau, 10 November 2006.
BM, male, and FB, female, 45–50 years, Bafatá, 14 April 2007.
CF, JF, and LVHS, male, 30–35 years, Bissau, 19 November 2006.
CGC, male, 30–35 years, Cupedo and Bissau, 20 August 2006, 28 January 2007.
CNDR, male, 45–50 years, Bissau, 4 September 2006.
CP, female, 70–75 years, Bissau, 28 March 2007.
CR, male, 45–50 years, Bissau, 9 August 2006, 24 April and 3 May 2007.
CRL, female, 40–45 years, Bissau, 15, 23, and 24 November 2006.
CRR, male, 45–50 years, Bissau, 15 and 30 August 2006.
CV, male, 50–55 years, Bissau, 30–31 July 2006.
DC, female, 65–70 years, PS, male, 40–45 years, Caracol/Bissau, 31 March, 1, 4, and 5 April 2007.
DCDA, male, 50–55 years, Bissau, 6 and 19 July, 21 August 2006; 2 April 2007.

DDC, male, 60–65 years, Bafatá, 13 April 2007.
DGF, female, 60–65 years, Bolama, 12 December 2006.
DM, female, 20–25 years, Bissau, 27 July 2006.
DN, female, 70–75 years, Bissau, 28 September 2014.
DTN, female, 30–35 years, 16 April 2006.
DuN, female, 25–30 years, Bissau, 16 April 2006.
DuN, female, IM, male, and FN, female, 25–30 years, Bissau, 13 May 2006.
DuN, female, and IM, male, 25–30 years, Bissau and Chugué, 14 and 16 February 2007.
ECDC, male, 80–85 years, Bissau, 29 March 2007.
EDP, female, 95–100 years, Bissau, 22 March 2007.
EHN, female, 45–50 years, Bissau, 21 August 2006.
EHN and JJSDS, female/male, 45–50 years, Bissau, 9 September 2006.
ER and JF, female/male, 60–65 years, Bissau, 26 April 2007.
ERGS, male, 35–40 years, Missirá/Bissau, 9 April 2007.
ET, male, 35–40 years, Bissau, 3 October 2006.
FD, male, 35–40 years, Geba, 19 April 2007.
FE, male, 25–30 years, Bissau, 20 September 2006.
FGDL, male, 45–50 years, Bissau, 26 July 2006.
FLCDAT, female, 35–40 years, Bissau, 11 September 2006.
FM, male, 70–75 years, Geba, 20 April 2007.
FMWF, male, 45–50 years, Bissau, 16 August 2006.
FN, female, 25–30 years, Bissau, 5 May 2006.
FN and CRS, female, 30–35 years, Bissau, 17 July 2006.
FP, female, 60–65 years, Bissau, 27 March 2007.
FR, male, 40–45 years, Olinda, 6 July 2016.
FS, male, 45–50 years, Bissau, 6 and 24 September 2006.
FSD, female, 40–45 years, Bafatá, 21 September 2014.
FV, male, 50–55 years, Bissau, 5 and 7 April 2007.
FVS, female, 45–50 years, Bissau, 6 July and 21 September 2006.
GP, female, 50–55 years, Bissau, 8 November 2006.
GSD, female, 70–75 years, Bolama, 12 December 2006.
HA, female, 80–85 years, Bolama, 9 December 2006.
HOS, male, 40–45 years, Bissau, 29 August 2006.
ICDA, male, 45–50 years, Bissau, 1 August 2006.
IDC, DDSR, and MS, female, 40–50 years, Amedalai/Bissau, 10 August 2006.
IsDC, female, 20–25 years, Bafatá, 9 February and 12 April 2007.
IM, male, 25–30 years, Bissau, 15 May 2006.
IMMN, female, 50–55 years, Bissau, 2 May, 2 and 29 June 2006.
ISTC, female, 30–35 years, Bissau, 3 and 9 April 2007.
JB, male, 40–45 years, Bissau, 6 June 2006.
JC, female, ca. 80–85 years, Geba, 30 November 2006, 17 April 2007.
JCN, male, 45–50 years, Bissau, 21 June 2006.
JDC, male, 45–50 years, Bissau, 23 February 2007.
JDSC, male, 45–50 years, Bissau, 21 April and 10 July 2006.
JDSN, SF, and ANM, male, 25–30 years, Bairro de Ajuda/Bissau, 24 February 2007.

JFGE, male, 45–50 years, Bissau, 28 August 2006.

JH, male, 45–50 years, Bissau, 22 April, 3 and 15 May, and 13 June 2006.

JH, male, 45–50 years, and ZH, female, 25–30 years, Bissau, 16 June 2006.

JH and JFN, male, 45–50 years, Bissau, 18 June 2006.

JHCDA, male, 60–65 years, Bissau, 18 November 2006.

JJSDS, male, 45–50 years, Bissau, 6 August 2006, 24 March 2007.

JL, male, 40–45 years, Bafatá, 12 April 2007.

JMM, male, 30–35 years, Bafatá, 13 April 2007.

JN, male, 40–45 years, Bissau, 18 April 2006.

JRS, male, 45–50 years, Bissau, 26 August 2006.

JV, male, 20–25 years, Bissau, 30 September 2006.

LC, female, 80–85 years, Bafatá, 9 February 2007.

LFDA, female, 80–85 years, Bissau, 4 June and 20 November 2006.

LH, male, 55–60 years, Bissau, 5 February 2007.

LLDC, female, 90–95 years, Santa Luzia/Bissau, 3 May 2007.

LR, male, 40–45 years, Bissau, 22 February 2007.

M, male, 40–45 years, Bissau, 25 June 2006.

MASF and ERGM, female/male, 45–50 years, Bissau, 14 June 2006.

MB, female, 45–50 years, Bissau, 26 January 2007.

MC, female, ca. 85–90 years, Geba, 30 November 2006.

MCF, male, 45–50 years, Quinhamel, 25 April 2006.

MaCF, female, 70–75 years, Bissau, 2, 25, and 30 April 2007.

MCVE, female, 75–80 years, Bissau, 21 August 2006.

MDL, female, 80–85 years, Bissau, 26 March 2007.

MJ, female, 45–50 years, Dakar, 25 January 2007.

MuJ, female, 50–55 years, Bissau, 28 September 2006.

MM, male, 55–60 years, Bissau, 12 November 2006.

MN, male, 50–55 years, Bissau, 21 July 2006.

MV, female, 55–60 years, Bolama, 9 December 2006.

NGD, male, 45–50 years, Bissau, 16 May 2006.

NN, female, 60–65 years, Bafatá, 9 February 2007.

NR, female, 80–85 years, Bafatá, 13 April 2007.

PJV, male, 60–65 years, Bissau, 26 July and 8 August 2006.

PPB, male, 55–60 years, Bissau, 18 August 2006.

REMBDC, male, 50–55 years, Bissau, 21 November 2006.

SC, male, 45–50 years, Bissau, 11 August 2006.

SG, female, 95–100 years, Bissau, 26 March 2007.

SM, male, and IFS, female, 55–60 years, Bissau, 20 June 2006.

    SaM, female, 55–60 years, Bissau, 1 April 2006.

SeM, female, 25–30 years, Bafatá, 12 April 2007.

SiM and SN, male, 65–70 years, Geba, 30 November 2006.

TL, female, 75–80 years, Bissau, 21 and 26 March 2007.

UM, male, 25–30 years, Bafatá, 7 February 2007.

UW, female, 30–35 years, Chugué, 16 February 2007.

VDC, female, 30–35 years, Bafatá, 13 April 2007.

VFR, male, 90–95 years, Bissau, 3 May 2007.

Bibliography

Abrams, Philip. 1988. "Notes on the Difficulty of Studying the State." *Journal of Historical Sociology* 1: 58–89.

Acção para o Desenvolvimento. 1993. *O Movimento Associativo Rural na Guiné-Bissau. Evolução e Situação Actual.* Bissau: Acção para o Desenvolvimento.

Acôrdo Missionário entre a Santa Sé e a República Portuguesa. 1940. *Diário do Governo* 158 (1st series): 763–67.

Alexandre, Valentim. 1997. "Der Estado Novo und das Kolonialreich." In *Vom Ständestaat zur Demokratie: Portugal im zwanzigsten Jahrhundert,* edited by Fernando Rosas, 75–87. Munich: R. Oldenbourg.

Alkmin, Tania Maria. 1983. "Les 'Portugais' de Ziguinchor (Sénégal)" Approche sociolinguistique d'une communauté créolophone." PhD thesis, Université René Descartes.

Álvares, Manuel. 1990. "Ethiopia Minor and a Geographical Account of the Province of Sierra Leone (c. 1615). Translation and Introduction by Paul E. H. Hair." Manuscript. Liverpool: University of Liverpool, Department of History.

Amado, Leopoldo. 2011. *Guerra Colonial e Guerra de Libertação Nacional 1950–1974: O Caso da Guiné-Bissau.* Lisbon: Instituto Português de Apoio ao Desenvolvimento.

Amin, Ash, and Stephen Graham. 1997. "The Ordinary City." *Transactions of the Institute of British Geographers* 22: 411–29.

Amos, Alcione M. 2001. "Afro-Brazilians in Togo: The Case of the Olympio Family, 1882–1945." *Cahiers d'Études Africaines* 162: 293–314.

Anderson, Benedict R. 1999. *Imagined Communities: Reflections on the Origin and Spread of Nationalism.* London: Verso.

Andreini, Jean-Claude, and Marie-Claude Lambert. 1978. *La Guinée-Bissau: D'Amílcar Cabral à la Reconstruction Nationale.* Paris: Harmattan.

Annex No. 1. 1911. *Boletim Oficial da Guiné Portuguesa* 21.

Annex No. 2. 1911. *Boletim Oficial da Guiné Portuguesa* 39.

Annex No. 3. 1911. *Boletim Oficial da Guiné Portuguesa* 44.

Annex No. 4. 1911. *Boletim Oficial da Guiné Portuguesa* 52.

Ansaldo, Umberto. 2009. *Contact Languages: Ecology and Evolution in Asia.* Cambridge: Cambridge University Press.

Appaduarai, Arhun. 1996. *Modernity at Large: Cultural Dimensions of Globalization.* Minneapolis: University of Minnesota Press.

Araoye, Lasisi Ademola. 2014. *Sources of Conflict in the Post Colonial African State.* Trenton, NJ: Africa World Press.

Arassi Taveira, Maria. 1989. "A Importância de Cacheu e a Figura de Honório Barreto." In *Actas: I Reunião Internacional de História de África,* edited by Maria Emília Madeira Santos, 377–82. Lisbon: Instituto de Investigação Científica e Tropical.

Ardener, Shirley. 1964. "The Comparative Study of Rotating Credit Associations." *Journal of the Royal Anthropological Institute of Great Britain and Ireland* 94: 201–29.

AS/JUM. 2007. "Bairro de Míssira vence Carnaval 2007." In *Gazeta de Notícias* 284, p. 3.

Asad, Talal. 2006. "Trying to Understand French Secularism." In *Political Theologies: Public Religions in a Post-Secular World,* edited by Hent de Vries and Lawrence E. Sullivan, 494–526. New York: Fordham University Press.

Askew, Kelly M. 2002: *Performing the Nation: Swahili Music and Cultural Politics in Tanzania.* Chicago: University of Chicago Press.

Assmann, Jan. 2002. *Das kulturelle Gedächtnis: Schrift, Erinnerung und politische Identität in frühen Hochkulturen.* Munich: C. H. Beck.

Associação de Mandjuandades da Guiné-Bissau (AMT-GB). 2007. Estatuto Associação de Mandjuandades-Tina da Guiné-Bissau.

Associação de Mandjuwandades do SAB (AMSAB). 1993. Estatuto da Associação de Mandjuwandades do Sector Autónomo de Bissau (SAB).

Augel, Johannes. 1998. "Staatskrise, Ethnizität und Ressourcenkonflikte in Guinea-Bissau." University of Bielefeld, Faculty of Sociology, Sociology of Development Research Centre Working Papers 309.

Bakhtin, Mikhail M. 1993. *Rabelais and His World.* Bloomington: Indiana University Press.

Barreto, João. 1938. *História da Guiné 1418–1918.* Lisbon: self-published.

Barrington, Lowell W. 1997. "'Nation' and 'Nationalism': The Misuse of Key Concepts in Political Science." *Political Science and Politics* 30:712–16.

———. 2006. "Nationalism and Independence." In *After Independence: Making and Protecting the Nation in Postcolonial and Postcommunist States,* edited by Lowell W. Barrington, 3–30. Ann Arbor: University of Michigan Press.

Barros, Miguel de, and Redy Wilson Lima. 2012. "Rap Kriol(u): O Pan-Africanismo de Cabral na Música de Intervencao Juvenil na Guiné-Bissau e em Cabo Verde." *Realis-Revista de Estudos AntiUtilitaristas e Póscoloniais* 2: 88–116.

Barth, Fredrik. 1969. "Introduction." In *Ethnic Groups and Boundaries: The Social Organization of Culture Difference,* edited by Fredrik Barth, 9–38. Bergen: Allen and Unwin.

Batalha, Luis. 2007. "The Politics and Symbolics of Cape Verdean Creole." In *Creole Societies in the Portuguese Colonial Empire,* edited by Philip J. Havik and Malyn Newitt, 93–104. Bristol: Seagull/Faoileán.

Baxter, Alan N. 2005. "Kristang (Malacca Creole Portuguese): A Long-Time Survivor Seriously Endangered." *Estudios de Sociolingüística* 6: 1–37.

Bayart, Jean François. 2012. *The State in Africa: The Politics of the Belly.* Cambridge: Polity.

Bender, Gerald J. 1978. *Angola under the Portuguese: The Myth and the Reality.* Berkeley: University of California Press.

Bender, Wolfgang. 2000. *Sweet Mother: Afrikanische Musik.* Wuppertag: Peter Hammer Verlag.

Benson, Carol J. 1994. "Teaching Beginning Literacy in the 'Mother Tongue': A Study of the Experimental Crioulo/Portuguese Primary Project in Guinea-Bissau." PhD thesis, University of California, Los Angeles.

Berger, Stefan. 2008. "Narrating the Nation: Die Macht der Vergangenheit." *Aus Politik und Zeitgeschichte* 1–2: 7–13.

Berman, Bruce. 1998. "Ethnicity, Patronage and the African State: The Politics of Uncivil Nationalism." *African Affairs* 97: 305–41.

Bernatzik, Hugo Adolf. 1933. *Äthiopen des Westens: Forschungsreisen in Portugiesisch-Guinea.* 2 vols. Vienna: Verlag von L. W. Seidel and Sohn.

Bertrand-Bocandé, Emmanuel. 1849a. "Notes sur la Guinée Portugaise ou Sénégambie Méridionale." *Bulletin de la Société de Géographie* 11 (3rd series): 265–350.

———. 1849b. "Notes sur la Guinée Portugaise ou Sénégambie Méridionale." *Bulletin de la Société de Géographie* 12 (3rd series): 57–93.

Besley, Timothy, Stephen Coate, and Glenn Loury. 1994. "Rotating Savings and Credit Associations, Credit Markets and Efficiency." *Review of Economic Studies* 61: 701–19.

Bethencourt, Francisco 1998. "A Igreja." In *História da Expansão Portuguesa.* Vol. 1: *A Formação do Império (1415–1570),* edited by Francisco Bethencourt and Kirti Chaudhuri, 369–86. Lisbon: Círculo de Leitores.

Bethke, Felix S. 2012. "Zuverlässig invalide: Indizes zur Messung fragiler Staatlichkeit." *Zeitschrift für Vergleichende Politikwissenschaft* 6: 19–37.

Bettelheim, Judith. 1985. "The Lantern Festival in Senegambia." *African Arts* 18: 50–102.

Biasutti, Artur. 1987. *Kriol-Purtugîs: Esboço, Proposta de Vocabulário,* 2nd ed. Bubaque: Missão Católica.

Birmingham, David. 1987. "Carnival at Luanda." *Journal of African History* 29: 93–103.

Bittencourt, Marcelo. 2000. "A Resposta dos 'Crioulos Luandenses' ao Intensificar do Processo Colonial em Finais do Século XIX." In *A África e a Instalação do Sistema Colonial (c. 1885–1930),* edited by Maria Emília Madeira Santos, 655–71. Lisbon: Instituto de Investigação Científica Tropical.

Black, Christopher F. 1989. *Italian Confraternities in the Sixteenth Century.* Cambridge: Cambridge University Press.

Blanc, Serge. 1993. *Le Tambour Djembe: Percussions Africaines.* Epone: Hexamusic.

Boege, Volker, M. Anne Brown, and Kevin P. Clements. 2009. "Hybrid Political Orders, Not Fragile States." *Peace Review: A Journal of Social Justice* 21: 13–21.

Boletim Oficial da República da Guiné-Bissau. 1975 et seq. Bissau: Imprensa Nacional.

Borszik, Anne-Kristin. 2008. "Régulos in the Gabú Region: Power in Non-State Dispute Settlement." *Soronda-Revista de Estudos Guineenses (Número Especial: Experiências Locais de Gestão de Conflitos):* 57–89.

Bowman, Joye L. 1980. "Conflict, Interaction, and Change in Guinea Bissau: Fulbe Expansion and Its Impact, 1850–1900." PhD thesis, University of California.

———. 1986. "Abdul Njai: Ally and Enemy of the Portuguese in Guinea-Bissau, 1895–1919." *Journal of African History* 27: 463–79.

———. 1997. *Ominous Transitions: Commerce and Colonial Expansion in the Senegambia and Guinea, 1857–1919.* Aldershot: Avebury.

Braga da Cruz, Manuel. 1988. *O Partido e o Estado no Salazarismo.* Lisbon: Editorial Presença.

Braga, Teófilo. 1985–86. *O Povo Português: Nos Seus Costumes, Crenças e Tradições.* 2 vols. Lisbon: Dom Quixote.

Brandily, Monique. 2001: *Kora Kosi: Die Musik Afrikas.* Heidelberg: Palmyra Verlag.

Brant, Sebastian. 1962. *The Ship of Fools.* New York: Dover Publications.

Brásio, António Editor. 1964. *Monumenta Missionaria Africana. Africa Ocidentale (1570–1600).* Vol. 3. Lisbon: Agência Geral do Ultramar.

Bräuchler, Birgit, and Thomas Widlok. 2007. "Die Revitalisierung von Tradition: Im (Ver-) Handlungsfeld zwischen staatlichem und lokalem Recht." *Zeitschrift für Ethnologie* 132: 5–14.

Braun, Karl. 2002. "Karneval? Karnevaleske! Zur volkskundlich-ethnologischen Erforschung karnevalesker Ereignisse." *Zeitschrift für Volkskunde* 98: 1–15.

Brito-Semedo, Manuel. 2006. *A Construção da Identidade Nacional: Análise da Imprensa entre 1877 e 1975.* Praia: Instituto da Biblioteca Nacional e do Livro.

Britz, Rudolf G., Hartmut Lang, and Cornelia Limpricht. 1999. *Kurze Geschichte der Rehobother Baster bis 1990.* Windhoek, Göttingen: Klaus Hess Verlag.

Brooks, George E. 1984. "The Observance of All Souls' Day in the Guinea-Bissau Region: A Christian Holy Day, an African Harvest Festival, an African New Year's Celebration, or All of the Above?" *History in Africa* 11: 1–34.

———. 1993a. "Historical Perspectives on the Guinea-Bissau Region, Fifteenth to Nineteenth Centuries." In *Mansas, Escravos, Grumetes e Gentio. Cacheu na Encruzilhada de Civilizações: Actas do Colóquio "Cacheu, Cidade Antiga,"* edited by Carlos Lopes, 25–54. Bissau: Instituto Nacional de Estudos e Pesquisa.

———. 1993b. *Landlords and Strangers: Ecology, Society, and Trade in Western Africa, 1000–1630.* Boulder, CO: Westview Press.

———. 2003. *Eurafricans in Western Africa: Commerce, Social Status, Gender, and Religious Observance from the Sixteenth to the Eighteenth Century.* Athens: Ohio University Press.

Brubaker, Rogers. 2004a. *Ethnicity without Groups.* Cambridge, MA: Harvard University Press.

———. 2004b. "Ethnicity without Groups." In *Facing Ethnic Conflicts: Toward a New Realism,* edited by Andreas Wimmer, 34–52. Lanham, MD: Rowman and Littlefield.

Cabral, Amílcar. 1976. *Unidade e Luta: A Arma da Teoria.* Lisbon: Seara Nova.

———. 1977. *Unidade e Luta: A Prática Revolucionária.* Lisbon: Seara Nova.

———. 1990. "A Questão da Língua." *Papia-Revista Brasileira de Estudos Crioulos e Similares* 1: 59–61.

Cabral, Juvenal 2002. *Memórias e Reflexões.* Praia: Instituto da Biblioteca Nacional.

Caldeira, Alfredo (ed.). 2001. *Amílcar Cabral: Sou um Simples Africano* . . . 2nd ed. Lisbon: Fundação Mário Soares.

Campbell, Susan. 2014. "Calabash Culture." In *Nights Publications*. Retrieved 16 September 2015 from http://nightspublications.com/print/1172.

Cardoso, Carlos. 2002. "A Formação da Elite Política na Guiné-Bissau." *Centro de Estudos Africanos Occasional Paper* 5.

Cardoso, Hugo C. 2010. "The African Slave Population of Portuguese India: Demographics and Impact on Indo-Portuguese." *Journal of Pidgin and Creole Languages* 25: 95–119.

Carreira, António. 1947. *Vida Social dos Manjacos*. Bissau: Centro de Estudos Africanos da Guiné Portuguesa.

———. 1961a. "O Censo Geral da População de 1960." *Boletim Cultural da Guiné Portuguesa* 16: 125–37.

———. 1961b. "Organização Social e Económica dos Povos da Guiné Portuguesa." *Boletim Cultural da Guiné Portuguesa* 16: 641–736.

———. 1963. Aspectos da Influencia da Cultura Portuguesa na Área Compreendida entre o Rio Senegal e o Norte da Serra Leoa (Subsídios para o seu estudo). In *Actas do Congresso Internacional de Etnografia*, vol. 4, edited by Colóquio de Etnografia Comparada, 187–229. Lisbon: Junta de Investigações do Ultramar.

———. 1964. "Aspectos da Influencia da Cultura Portuguesa na Área compreendida entre o Rio Senegal e o Norte da Serra Leoa." *Boletim Cultural da Guiné Portuguesa* 19: 373–417.

———. 1967. "Manjacos-Brames e Balantas: Aspectos Demográficos." *Boletim Cultural da Guiné Portuguesa* 22: 41–92.

———. 1983. *Panaria Caboverdeana-Guineense*. Praia: Instituto Caboverdeano do Livro.

———. 1984. *Os Portugueses nos Rios de Guiné (1500–1900)*. Lisbon: self-published.

———. 2000. *Formação e Extinção de uma Sociedade Escravocrata (1460–1878)*, 3rd ed. Praia: Instituto de Promoção Cultural.

Carreira, António, and Fernando Rogado Quintino. 1964. *Antroponímia da Guiné Portuguesa*, vol. 1. Lisbon: Junta de Investigações do Ultramar.

Carta Orgânica da Província da Guiné, Decreto no. 3.168 (5 July 1917). *Boletim Oficial da Guiné Portuguesa* (1917) 27, supplement.

Carvalho, José Peixoto Ponces de. 1929. "Alguns Dados Estatísticos sôbre a Guiné." *Boletim da Agência Geral das Colónias* 44: 208–10.

Cassama, L. 2011. "Biombo vence Carnaval na Guiné-Bissau." In *Voz da América*. Retrieved 16 October 2015 from http://www.voaportugues.com/content/article-03-08-2011-bissau-carnival-117581848/1259713.html.

Castanheira, José Pedro. 1999. *Quem Mandou Matar Amílcar Cabral?*, 3rd ed. Lisbon: Relógio d'Água.

Castelo, Cláudia. 1999. *"O Modo Português de Estar no Mundo": O Luso-Tropicalismo e a Ideologia Colonial Portuguesa (1933–1961)*. Porto: Edições Afrontamento.

Censo da População Civilizada da Guiné. *Boletim Oficial da Guiné Portuguesa* (1916) 32: 461; 35: 496; 37: 531.

Chabal, Patrick. 1983. "Party, State and Socialism in Guinea-Bissau." *Canadian Journal of African Studies* 17: 189–210.

————. 1996. "The African Crisis: Context and Interpretation." In *Postcolonial Identities in Africa*, edited by Richard Werbner and Terence Range, 29–54. London: Zed Books.

————. 2002. *Amilcar Cabral: Revolutionary Leadership and People's War*. London: Hurst.

Chan, Kok Eng. 1983. "The Eurasians of Melaka." In *Melaka: The Transformation of a Malay Capital, c. 1400–1980*, vol 2, edited by Kernial Singh Sandhu and Paul Wheatley, 264–81. Kuala Lumpur: Oxford University Press.

Chan-Vianna, Adriana Cristina, and Maria Aparecida Curupaná da Rocha de Mello. 2007. "A Construção da Gramática Guineense: O Sufixo -ndadi." *PAPIA—Revista Brasileira de Estudos Crioulos e Similares* 17: 67–79.

Chauchadis, Claude. 1986. "Les Modalités de la Fermeture dans les Confréries religieuses espagnoles (XVIe–XVIIIe siècle)." In *Les Sociétés Fermées dans le Monde Ibérique, XVI-XVIIIe siècle: Définitions et Problématique*, edited by Joseph Perez, 83–105. Paris: Centre National de la Recherche Scientifique.

Chelmicki, José Conrado Carlos, and Francisco Adolfo de Varnhagen. 1841. *Corografia Cabo-Verdiana ou Descripção Geografico-Historica da Província das Ilhas de Cabo Verde e Guiné*, vol. 1. Lisbon: Typographia de L. C. da Cunha.

Chilcote, Ronald H. 1972. *Emerging Nationalism in Portuguese Africa Documents*. Stanford: University of California Press.

Chirikba, Viacheslav A. 2008. "The Problem of the Caucasian Sprachbund." In *From Linguistic Areas to Areal Linguistics*, edited by Pieter Muysken, 25–94. Philadelphia: John Benjamins Publishing Company.

"Circular" (9 November 1896). In *Colecção da Legislação Novíssima do Ultramar*, 567. Lisbon: Imprensa Nacional.

Coe, Cati. 2005. *Dilemmas of Culture in African Schools. Youth, Nationalism, and the Transformation of Knowledge*. Chicago: University of Chicago Press.

Coelho, Adolfo. 1993. *Obra Etnográfica*. Vol. 1: *Festas, Costumes e outros Materiais para uma Etnologia de Portugal*. Lisbon: Dom Quixote.

Cohen, Robin, and Paola Toninato. 2010. "The Creolization Debate: Analysing Mixed Identities and Cultures." In *Creolization: Studies in Mixed Identities and Cultures*, edited by Robin Cohen and Paola Toninato, 1–21. New York: Routledge.

Colónia da Guiné. 1944. *Conferência dos Administradores: Actas das Sessões realizadas em 1944, sob a Presidência do Governador da Colónia, Major de Artilharia Ricardo Vaz Monteiro*. Bolama: Imprensa Nacional.

Conceição das Neves Silva, M. da. 2002. "La Transition Politique en Guinée-Bissau: Les 'Sites de Mémoire' comme Points de Relais." In *Post-Socialisme, Post-Colonialisme et Postérité de l'Idéologie*, edited by T. Landry and C. Zobel, 97–121. Paris: École des Hautes Études en Sciences Sociales.

Constant, Fred P. 1997. "White Minority Power in Martinique and Guadeloupe." *Caribbean Affairs* 7(6): 115–28.

Cooper, Frederick. 2005. *Colonialism in Question: Theory, Knowledge History*. Berkeley: University of California Press.

Cornelißen, Christoph. 2010. Erinnerungskulturen, Version: 1.0. *Docupedia-Zeitgeschichte*, 11 February 2010. Retrieved 25 April 2016 from http://docupedia .de/zg/Erinnerungskulturen.

Corrado, Jacopo. 2010. "The Fall of a Creole Elite? Angola at the Turn of the Twentieth Century: The Decline of the Euro-African Urban Community." *Luso-Brazilian Review* 47(29): 100–19.

Correa e Lança, Joaquim da Graça. 1890. *Relatório da Província da Guiné Portugueza, referido ao Anno Económico de 1888–1889*. Lisbon: Imprensa Nacional.

Correia de Almeida, Januário. 1859. *Um Mez na Guiné*. Lisbon: Typographia Universal.

Costa Dias, Eduardo. 2000. "A Balantização da Guiné-Bissau." *Público*, 5 December 2000.

Couto, Hildo Honório do. 1989. "O Crioulo Guineense em Relação ao Português e às Línguas Nativas." *Linguistica* 29: 107–28.

———. 1990. "Política e Planeamento Lingüístico na Guiné-Bissau." *Papia-Revista Brasileira de Estudos Crioulos e Similares* 1: 47–58.

———. 1994. *O Crioulo Português da Guiné-Bissau*. Hamburg: Helmut Buske Verlag.

Couto, Hildo Honório do, and Filomena Embaló. 2010. "Literatura, Língua e Cultura na Guine-Bissau: Um Pais da CPLP." *Papia-Revista Brasileira de Estudos Crioulos e Similares* 20.

Crowley, Daniel J. 1989a. "Carnival as Secular Ritual: A Pan-Portuguese Perspective." In *Folklore and Historical Process*, edited by Dunja Rihtman-Auguštin, 143–48. Zagreb: Institute of Folklore Research.

———. 1989b. "The Carnival of Guinea-Bissau." *Drama Review* 33: 74–86.

Crowley, Eve Lakshmi. 1990. "Contracts with the Spirits: Religion, Asylum, and Ethnic Identity in the Cacheu Region of Guinea-Bissau." PhD thesis, Yale University.

Cultru, Prosper (ed.). 1913. *Premier Voyage du Sieur de la Courbe fait à la Coste d'Afrique en 1685*. Paris: Édouard Champion and Émile Larose.

Cunningham, James. 1980. "The Colonial Period in Guiné." *Tarikh* 6: 31–46.

Czarniawska, Barbara, and Bernward Joerges. 1996. "Travels of Ideas." In *Translating Organizational Change*, edited by Barbara Czarniawska, 13–48. Berlin: de Gruyter.

Davidson, Basil. 1981. "No Fist Is Big Enough to Hide the Sky: Building Guinea-Bissau and Cape Verde." *Race and Class* 23: 43–64.

Davidson, Joanna. 2003. "Native Birth: Identity and Territory in Postcolonial Guinea-Bissau, West Africa." *European Journal of Cultural Studies* 6: 37–54.

Dawson, Jane, 2010. "Thick Description." In *Encyclopedia of Case Study Research*, edited by Albert J. Mills, Gabrielle Durepos, and Elden Wiebe, 943–45. Thousand Oaks, CA: Sage Publications.

d'Costa, Adelyne 1977. "Caste Stratification among the Roman Catholics of Goa." *Man in India* 57: 283–92.

Decreto 13,698 (30 May 1927). *Boletim Oficial da Guiné Portuguesa* (1927) 29: 424–25.

Decreto-Lei 43,893 (6 September 1961). *Boletim Oficial da Guiné Portuguesa* (1961) 8, supplement: 1–3.

de Jong, Ferdinand. 1999. "Trajectories of a Mask Performance: The Case of the Senegalese Kumpo." *Cahiers d'Etudes Africaines* 153: 49–71.

———. 2000. "Secrecy and the State: The Kankurang Masquerade in Senegal." *Mande Studies* 2: 153–73.

———. 2007. *Masquerades of Modernity: Power and Secrecy in Casamance, Senegal.* Edinburgh: Edinburgh University Press for the International African Institute.

de Vlaminck, Nick. 2015. "A Fresh Start for Guinea-Bissau?" In *Global Risk Insights,* 10 May 2015. Retrieved 8 July 2016 from http://globalriskinsights .com/2015/05/a-fresh-start-for-guinea-bissau/.

Delfim da Silva, Fernando. 2003. *Guiné-Bissau: Páginas de História Política, Rumos da Democracia.* Bissau: Firquidja Editora.

Departamento Central do Recenseamento. 1979. *Manual de Codificação.* Bissau.

———. 1982. *Recenseamento Geral da População e da Habitação.* Vol. 5: *Reportório Nacional das Localidades Recenseadas.* Bissau: Departamento Central do Recenseamento.

Dhada, Mustafah. 1993. *Warriors at Work: How Guinea Was Really Set Free.* Niwot, CO: University Press of Colorado.

———. 1998. "The Liberation War in Guinea-Bissau Reconsidered." *Journal of Military History* 62: 571–93.

Dias de Carvalho, Henrique Augusto. 1944. *Guiné: Apontamentos Inéditos.* Lisbon: Agência Geral das Colónias.

Dias Vicente, João 1992. "Subsidios para a Biografia do Sacerdote Guineense Marcelino Marques de Barros (1844–1929)." *Lusitania Sacra* (2nd series) 4: 395–470.

———. 1993. "Quatro Séculos de Vida Crista em Cacheu." In *Mansas, Escravos, Grumetes e Gentio: Cacheu na Encruzilhada de Civilizações; Actas do Colóquio "Cacheu, Cidade Antiga,"* edited by Carlos Lopes, 99–133. Bissau: Instituto Nacional de Estudos e Pesquisa.

Dieterle, Gertrud. 1999. *Disionariu Kiriol-Inglis: Creole-English Dictionary.* Bissau: Igreâa Ivanjeliku ku Mison Ivanjeliku di Guine-Bisau.

Diploma Legislativo 535 (25 October 1930). *Boletim Oficial da Guiné Portuguesa* (1930) 45: 638.

Diploma Legislativo 1,364 (7 October 1946). *Boletim Oficial da Guiné Portuguesa* (1946) 40: 312–13.

Dirks, Nicholas. 2002. "Annals of the Archive: Ethnographic Notes on the Sources of History." In *From the Margins: Historical Anthropology and Its Future,* edited by Brian Keith Axel, 47–65. Durham, NC: Duke University Press.

Djaló, Ibrahima. 1987. "Contribuição para uma Reflexão: Educação, Multilinguismo e Unidade Nacional." In *II Encontro Nacional da Associação Portuguesa de Linguística,* edited by Direcção da Associação Portuguesa de Linguística, 242–59. Lisbon: Faculdade de Letras da Universidade de Lisboa.

Djaló, Tcherno. 2012. *O Mestiço e o Poder: Identidades, Dominações e Resistências na Guiné.* Lisbon: Nova Vega.

Doelter, Cornelio August. 1884. *Über die Cupverden nach dem Rio Grande und Futah Djallon: Reiseskizzen aus Nord-West-Afrika.* Leipzig: Verlag von Paul Frohberg.

Domingues, Maria Manuela Abreu Borges. 2000. "Estratégias Femininas entre as Bideiras de Bissau." PhD thesis, Universidade Nova de Lisboa.

———. 2005. "Carga e encargo da Empreitada Colonial Portuguesa no Atlântico Sul: Contribuição para o Estudo das Conexões Culturais entre a África e o Brasil." Paper presented at *Actas do Congresso Internacional O Espaço Atlântico de antigo Regime: Poderes e Sociedades, Lisbon, November 2005.* Retrieved 7 November 2017 from http://cvc.instituto-camoes.pt/eaar/coloquio/comunicacoes/maria_manuela_borges.pdf.

Domingues, Maria Manuela Abreu Borges, Joseania Manuela Freitas, and Luzia Gomes Ferreira. 2006. "Relações de Alteridades e Identidades: Mandjuandades na Guiné-Bissau e a Irmandade da Boa Morte na Bahia." *Impulso (Piracicaba)* 17: 91–103.

Dominguez, Virginia R. 1977. "Social Classifications in Creole Louisiana." *American Anthropologist* 4: 589–602.

Donelha, André. 1977. *Descrição da Serra Leoa e dos Rios de Guiné do Cabo Verde.* Lisbon: Junta de Investigações Científicas do Ultramar.

Duarte, Aristides, and Aquino Gomes. 1996. "O Sector Informal." In *O Programa de Ajustamento Estrutural na Guiné-Bissau: Análise dos Efeitos Sócio-Económicos,* edited by António Isaac Monteiro, 97–115. Bissau: Instituto Nacional de Estudos e Pesquisa.

Duarte, Fausto. 1934. *Auá: Novela Negra.* 2nd ed. Lisbon: Livraria Clássica Editora.

———. 1946. *Anuário da Guiné Portuguesa.* Bissau: Governo da Colónia da Guiné Portuguesa.

———. 1948. *Anuário da Guiné Portuguesa.* Bissau: Governo da Colónia da Guiné Portuguesa.

Duarte Silva, António E. 1997. *A Independência da Guiné-Bissau e a Descolonização Portuguesa: Estudo de História, Direito e Política.* Porto: Edições Afrontamento.

———. 2010. *Invenção e Construção da Guiné-Bissau: Administração Colonial, Nacionalismo, Constitucionalismo.* Lisbon: Almedina.

Dumas Teixeira, Ricardino Jacinto. 2008. "Sociedade Civil e Democratização na Guiné-Bissau, 1994–2006." Master's thesis, Universidade Federal de Pernambuco.

Dumont, Louis. 1986. *Essays on Individualism: Modern Ideology in Anthropological Perspective.* Chicago: University of Chicago Press.

Eckert, Andreas. 2006. *Kolonialismus.* Frankfurt am Main: Fischer Taschenbuch Verlag.

Eckert, Julia. 2002. "Der Hindu-Nationalismus und die Politik der Unverhandelbarkeit: Vom politischen Nutzen eines (vermeintlichen) Religionskonfliktes." *Politik und Zeitgeschichte* 42–43: 23–30.

Elwert, Georg. 1989. "Nationalismus und Ethnizität: Über die Bildung von Wir-Gruppen." *Kölner Zeitschrift für Soziologie und Sozialpsychologie* 41: 440–64.

———. 2002. "Switching Identity Discourses: Primordial Emotions and the Social Construction of We-Groups." In *Imagined Differences: Hatred and the Construction of Identity,* edited by Günther Schlee, 33–54. London: Lit Verlag.

Embaló, Filomena. 2008. "O Crioulo da Guiné-Bissau: Língua Nacional e Factor de Identidade Nacional." *Papia-Revista Brasileira de Estudos Crioulos e Similares* 18: 101–7.

Eriksen, Thomas Hylland. 1999. "Tu Dimunn pu Vini Kreol: The Mauritian Creole and the Concept of Creolization." *Transnational Communities Programme, Working Paper* 99.

———. 2007. "Creolization in Anthropological Theory and in Mauritius." In *Creolization: History, Ethnography, Theory,* edited by Charles Stewart, 153–77. Walnut Creek, CA: Left Coast Press.

Errante, Antoinette. 1998. "Education and National Personae in Portugal's Colonial and Postcolonial Transition." *Comparative Education Review* 42: 267–308.

Estatística. *Boletim Oficial da Guiné Portuguesa* (1901) 18, supplement: 23–24.

Estatuto Missionário / Decreto-Lei 31,207 (5 April 1941). *Boletim Oficial da Guiné Portuguesa* (1941) 25, supplement 13.

Estatuto Orgânico das Missões Católicas Portuguesas da África e Timor / Decreto 12,485 (13 October 1926). *Boletim Oficial da Guiné Portuguesa* (1927) 11, supplement 8.

Estatuto Politico, Civil e Criminal dos Indígenas de Angola e Moçambique / Decreto 12,533 (23 October 1927). *Boletim Oficial da Guiné Portuguesa* (1927) 23: 318–21.

Esteves, Maria Luísa. 1988. *Gonçalo de Gamboa de Aiala, Capitão-Mor de Cacheu, e o Comércio Negreiro Espanhol*. Lisbon: Centro de Estudos de História e Cartografia Antiga.

Evans-Pritchard, Edward Evan. 1940. *The Nuer: A Description of the Modes of Livelihood and Political Institutions of a Nilotic People*. Oxford: Clarendon Press.

Eyzaguirre, Pablo B. 1986. "Small Farmers and Estates in São Tomé, West Africa." PhD thesis, Yale University.

Falzon, Mark-Anthony (ed.). 2009. *Multi-Sited: Ethnography; Theory, Praxis and Locality in Contemporary Research*. Farnham: Ashgate.

Fanon, Frantz. 1963. *The Wretched of the Earth*. New York: Grove Press.

———. 2008. *Black Skin, White Masks*. London: Pluto Press.

Ferguson, James. 2002. "Of Mimicry and Membership: Africans and the 'New World Society.'" *Cultural Anthropology* 17: 551–69.

Fernandes, Gabriel. 2002. *A Diluição da África: Uma Interpretação da Saga Identitária Cabo-Verdiana no Panorama Político (Pós)Colonial*. Florianópolis: Editora da Universidade Federal de Santa Catarina.

———. 2006. *Em Busca da Nação: Notas para uma Reinterpretação do Cabo Verde Crioulo*. Florianópolis: Editora da Universidade Federal de Santa Catarina; Praia: Instituto da Biblioteca Nacional e do Livro.

Ferraz de Matos, Patrícia. 2006. *As Côres do Império: Representações Raciais no Império Colonial Português*. Lisbon: Imprensa de Ciências Sociais.

Figueira, Carla. 2013. *Languages at War: External Language Spread Policies in Lusophone Africa; Mozambique and Guinea-Bissau at the Turn of the 21st Century*. Frankfurt am Main: Peter Lang.

Fischer-Lichte, Erika, and Matthias Warstat. 2009. "Einleitung." In *Staging Festivity. Theater und Fest in Europa*, edited by Erika Fischer-Lichte and Matthias Warstat, 9–16. Tübingen and Basel: A. Francke Verlag.

Forrest, Joshua B. 1992. *Guinea-Bissau: Power, Conflict, and Renewal in a West African Nation*. Boulder, CO: Westview Press.

———. 1993. "Autonomia Burocrática, Política Económica e Política num Estado 'Suave': O Caso da Guiné-Bissau Pós-Colonial." *Soronda* 15: 57–95.

Foucault, Michel. 1995. *Discipline and Punish: The Birth of the Prison*. New York: Vintage Books.

Frahm, Ole. 2012. "Defining the Nation: National Identity in South Sudanese Media Discourse." *Africa Spectrum* 47: 21–49.

Fraunlob, Julia. 2004. *Die traditionellen Autoritäten und der Staat in Guinea-Bissau: Zum Beziehungsverhältnis seit Beginn des Demokratisierungsprozesses.* Hamburg: Verlag Dr. Kovac.

Frederiks, Martha. 2002. The Krio in the Gambia and the Concept of Inculturation. *Exchange* 31: 219–29.

Gabbert, Wolfgang. 1992. *Creoles: Afroamerikaner im karibischen Tiefland von Nicaragua.* Münster: Lit-Verlag.

Gable, Eric. 1990. "Modern Manjaco: The Ethos of Power in a West African Society." PhD thesis, University of Virginia.

———. 2002. "Bad Copies: The Colonial Aesthetic and the Manjaco-Portuguese Encounter." In *Images and Empires: Visuality in Colonial and Postcolonial Africa,* edited by Paul S. Landau and Deborah D. Kaspin, 294–319. Berkeley: University of California Press.

Gacitua-Mario, Estanislao, Sigrun Aasland, Hakon Nordang, and Quentin Wodon. 2006. "Institutions, Social Networks and Conflicts in Guinea-Bissau: Results from a 2005 Survey." In *Guinea-Bissau: Integrated Poverty and Social assessment (IPSA); Conflict Livelihood and Poverty in Guinea-Bissau (in two volumes).* Vol II: *Background Papers,* edited by the World Bank, 19–36, Washington, DC: World Bank.

———. 2007. "Institutions, Social Networks and Conflicts in Guinea-Bissau: Results from a 2005 Survey." In *Conflict Livelihood and Poverty in Guinea-Bissau,* edited by Barry Boubacar-Sid, Edward G. E. Creppy, Estanislao Gacitua-Mario, and Quentin Wodon, 23–41, Washington, DC: World Bank.

Galli, Rosemary E., and Jocelyn Jones. 1987. *Guinea-Bissau: Politics, Economics and Society.* Boulder, CO: Francis Pinter, Lynne Rienner.

Gamble, David P. 1989. "Source Material on the Fanaal (Lantern) in Senegambia." In *Verbal and Visual Expressions of Wolof Culture,* edited by David P. Gamble, 1–48. Bisbane, CA: The Editor.

Geertz, Clifford. 1962. "The Rotating Credit Association: A 'Middle Rung' in Development." *Economic Development and Cultural Change* 10: 241–63.

———. 1973. "Thick Description: Toward an Interpretive Theory of Culture." In *The Interpretation of Cultures: Selected Essays,* 3–30. New York: Basic Books.

Gellner, Ernest. 1998. *Nations and Nationalism.* Oxford: Blackwell Publishers.

Geschiere, Peter. 2009. *The Perils of Belonging: Autochthony, Citizenship, and Exclusion in Africa and Europe.* Chicago: University of Chicago Press.

Giesing, Cornelia, and Valentin Vydrine. 2007. *Ta:rik Mandinka de Bijini (Guinée-Bissau): La Mémoire des Mandinka et des Sòoninkee du Kaabu.* Leiden: Brill.

Girtler, Roland. 2001. *Methoden der Feldforschung.* Stuttgart: UTB.

Godinho Gomes, Patrícia. 2010. *Os Fundamentos de uma Nova Sociedade: O P.A.I.G.C. e a Luta Armada na Guiné-Bissau (1963–1973).* Turin: L'Harmattan Italia.

———. 2013. "Na Senda da Luta pela Paz e Igualdade: O Contributo das Mulheres Guineenses." Retrieved 27 February 2014 from http://www.buala.org/pt/mukanda/na-senda-da-luta-pela-paz-e-igualdade-o-contributo-das-mulheres-guineenses.

Goldberg, David T. 1997. *Racial Subjects: Writing on Race in America.* New York: Routledge.

Gomes, Bea. 2001. "'O Mundo que o Portugues Criou' — Von der Erfindung einer lusophonen Welt." *Wiener Zeitschrift für kritische Afrikastudien* 2: 27–43.

Gomes Viegas, Caterina, and Fafali Koudawo. 2000. "A Crise no PAIGC: Um Prelúdio à Guerra?" *Soronda Número Especial 7 de Junho* 4 (New Series): 11–24.

Gonçalves, Carlos F. 2006. *Kab Verd Band.* Praia: Instituto do Arquivo Histórico Nacional.

Gonzaga Ferreira, Luís. 1998. *Quadros de Viagem de um Diplomata: África: Senegal, Guiné, Cabo Verde.* Lisbon: Vega.

Governo da Guiné. 1952. *Guiné: Alvorada do Império.* Bolama: Imprensa Nacional da Guiné.

Graf, Friedrich Wilhelm. 2004. *Die Wiederkehr der Götter: Religion in der modernen Kultur.* Munich: C. H. Beck.

Grands Dossiers. 2012. "Réunion de la CEDEAO à Abidjan: Les Dirigeants des 15 Applaudiront-ils la Médiation d'Alpha Condé?" *Guineexpress,* 26 April 2012. Retrieved 12 February 2014 from http://www.guineexpress.com/index.php?option=com_content&view=article&id=136:grands-dossiers—reunion-de-la-cedeao-a-abidjan—les-dirigeants-des-15-applaudiront-ils-la-mediation-dalpha-conde—&catid=2:flahs-news.

Green, Toby. 2010. "The Evolution of Creole Identity in Cape Verde." In *The Creolization Reader: Studies in Mixed Identities and Cultures,* edited by Robin Cohen and Paola Toninato, 157–66. New York: Routledge.

Gromes, Thorsten. 2012. *Ohne Staat und Nation ist keine Demokratie zu machen: Bosnien und Herzegowina, Kosovo und Mazedonien nach den Bürgerkriegen.* Baden-Baden: Nomos.

Guran, Milton. 1999. *Agudás: Os "Brasileiros" do Benim.* Rio de Janeiro: Editora Nova Fronteira.

Halbwachs, Maurice. 1980. *The Collective Memory.* New York: Harper & Row Colophon Books.

Hannerz, Ulf. 1987. "The World in Creolization." *Africa* 57: 546–59.

———. 1992. *Cultural Complexity: Studies in the Social Organization of Meaning.* New York: Columbia University Press.

———. 1998. *Transnational Connections: Culture, People, Places,* reprinted ed. New York: Routledge.

———. 2002. "Notes on the Global Ecumene." In *The Anthropology of Globalization: A Reader,* edited by Jonathan Xavier Inda and Renato Rosaldo, 37–45. Malden: Blackwell.

Harasim, Linda M. 1983. "Literacy and National Reconstruction in Guinea-Bissau: A Critique of the Freirean Literacy Campaign." PhD thesis, University of Toronto.

Hauser-Schäublin, Birgitta. 2008. "Teilnehmende Beobachting." In *Methoden ethologischer Feldforschung,* edited by Bettina Beer, 37–59. Berlin: Reimer.

Havik, Philip J. 1995–1999. "Mundasson i Kambansa: Espaço Social e Movimentos Políticos na Guiné Bissau (1910–1944)." *Revista Internacional de Estudos Africanos* 18–22: 115–67.

———. 2004. *Silences and Soundbites: The Gendered Dynamics of Trade and Brokerage in the Pre-Colonial Guinea Bissau Region.* Münster: Lit-Verlag.

———. 2007a. "Kriol without Creoles: Afro-Atlantic Connections in the Guinea Bissau Region (16th to 20th Centuries)." In *Cultures of the Lusophone Black Atlantic, Studies of the Americas,* edited by Nancy Priscilla Naro, Roger Sansi-Roca, and Dave H. Treece, 41–73. New York: Palgrave Macmillan.

———. 2007b. "The Port of Geba: At the Crossroads of Afro-Atlantic Trade and Culture." *Mande Studies* 9: 21–50.

———. 2008. "Tributos e Impostos: A Crise Mundial, o Estado Novo e a Política na Guiné." *Economia e Sociologia* 85: 29–55.

———. 2011. "Traders, Planters and Go-Betweens: The Kriston in Portuguese Guinea." *Portuguese Studies Review* 19: 197–226.

Hawthorne, Walter. 2003. *Planting Rice and Harvesting Slaves: Transformations along the Guinea-Bissau Coast, 1400–1900.* Portsmouth: Heinemann.

Hayes, Carlton J. H. 1926. Nationalism as a Religion. In *Essays on Nationalism,* edited by J. H. Carlton, 93–125. New York: The Macmillan Company.

Hill, Jonathan. 2005. "Beyond the Other? A Postcolonial Critique of the Failed State Thesis." *African Identities* 3: 139–54.

Hobsbawm, Eric. 1999. *Nations and Nationalism since 1780: Programme, Myth, Reality.* Cambridge: Cambridge University Press.

Hobsbawm, Eric J., and Terence Ranger (eds.). 1983. *The Invention of Tradition.* Cambridge: Cambridge University Press.

Höhn, Stefanie. 1987. "Kreolisch, Portugiesisch oder Französisch in Guiné-Bissau?" *DASP-Hefte* 9–10: 3–5.

Højbjerg, Christian Kordt. 2007. *Resisting State Iconoclasm among the Loma of Guinea.* Durham, NC: Carolina Academic Press.

Hughes, Arnold, and David Perfect. 2006. *A Political History of the Gambia, 1816–1994.* Rochester, NY: University of Rochester Press.

Huria, Sonali. 2008. "Failing and Failed States: The Global Discourse." *Institute of Peace and Conflict Studies Issue Brief* 75.

Idahosa, Pablo Luke Ehioze. 2002. "Going to the People: Amílcar Cabral's Materialist Theory and Practice of Culture and Ethnicity." *Lusotopie* 9(2): 29–58.

Induta, Zamora. 2001. *Guiné: 24 Anos de Independência 1974–1998.* Lisbon: Hugin Editores.

Instituto Nacional de Estatística (Portugal). 1900. *Anuário Estatístico de Portugal.* Lisbon: Instituto Nacional de Estatística.

———. n.d. *Anuário Estatístico 1969.* Vol. 2: *Províncias Ultramarinas.* Lisbon: Instituto Nacional de Estatística.

Instituto Nacional de Estatística (Guinea-Bissau). 2009. *Kantu Djintis, kantu Kasas: Terceiro Recenseamento Geral da População Habitação. Características Socioculturais.* Bissau: Instituto Nacional de Estatística.

Instituto Nacional de Estatística e Censos. 1996. *Recenseamento Geral da População e Habitação 1991,* vol. 1. Bissau: Ministério do Plano e Cooperação Internacional.

Instrucções para o Recenseamento Geral da População da Guiné Portugueza. *Boletim Oficial da Guiné Portuguesa* (1893) 14: 65–66.

Instrucções para se Realisar o Recenseamento Geral da População da Província da Guiné. *Boletim Oficial da Guiné Portuguesa* (1900) 30: 170–71; 39: 212.

International Crisis Group. 2012. Au-Delà des Compromis: Les Perspectives de Réforme en Guinée-Bissau. In *Africa Report* 183.

Jacobs, Bart. 2009. "The Upper Guinea Origins of Papiamentu: Linguistic and Historical Evidence." *Diachronica* 26: 319–79.

Jao, Mamadú. 1989. "Estrutura 'Política' e Relações de Poder entre os Brâmes ou Mancanhas." *Soronda* 8: 47–61.

———. 1992. "Aspectos da Vida social dos Mancanhas: A Cerimónia do Ulém." *Soronda* 13: 59–66.

Jenkins, Richard. 1994. "Rethinking Ethnicity: Identity, Categorization and Power." *Ethnic and Racial Studies* 17: 197–223.

Jesus Tavares, Manuel de. 2005. *Aspectos Evolutivos da Música Cabo-Verdiana.* Praia: Centro Cultural Português, Associação de Escritores Cabo-Verdianos.

Junta de Investigações do Ultramar. 1959. *Província da Guiné: Censo da População de 1950.* Lisbon: Junta de Investigações do Ultramar.

Kasper, Josef Ernst. 1995. *Bissau: Existenzsichernde Strategien in einer westafrikanischen Stadt.* Bern: Peter Lang.

Kaufmann, Matthias, and Richard Rottenburg. 2012. "Translation als Grundoperation bei der Wanderung von Ideen." In *Kultureller und sprachlicher Wandel von Wertbegriffen in Europa: Interdisziplinäre Perspektiven,* edited by Rosemarie Lühr, Natalia Mull, Jörg Oberthür, and Hartmut Rosa, 219–33. Frankfurt am Main: Peter Lang.

Kawamura, Shinzo. 1999. "Making Christian Lay Communities during the 'Christian Century' in Japan: A Case Study of Takata District in Bungo." PhD thesis, Georgetown University.

Keese, Alexander. 2003. "'Proteger os Pretos': Havia uma Mentalidade Reformista na Administração Portuguesa na África Tropical (1926–1961)?" *Africana Studia* 6: 97–125.

———. 2007. "The Role of Cape Verdeans in War Mobilization and War Prevention in Portugal's African Empire, 1955–1965." *International Journal of African Historical Studies* 40: 497–511.

Kennedy, James C. 2008. "Religion, Nation and European Representation of the Past." In *The Contested Nation. Ethnicity, Class, Religion and Gender in National Histories,* edited by Stefan Berger and Chris Lorenz, 104–34. Basingstoke: Palgrave Macmillan.

Kersting, Norbert. 2009. "New Nationalism and Xenophobia in Africa: A New Inclination?" *Africa Spectrum* 44: 7–18.

Kertzer, David I., and Dominique Arel. 2002. "Censuses, Identity Formation, and the Struggle for Political Power." In *Census and Identity: The Politics of Race, Ethnicity, and Language in National Censuses,* edited by David I. Kertzer and Dominique Arel, 1–42. Cambridge: Cambridge University Press.

Kihm, Alain. 1994. *Kriyol Syntax: The Portuguese-Based Creole Language of Guinea-Bissau.* Philadelphia: John Benjamins Publishing Company.

Kirkendall, Andrew J. 2010. *Paulo Freire and the Cold War Politics of Literacy.* Chapel Hill, NC: University of North Carolina Press.

Knörr, Jacqueline. 1995. *Kreolisierung versus Pidginisierung als Kategorien kultureller Differenzierung: Varianten neoafrikanischer Identität und Interethnik in Freetown, Sierra Leone.* Münster, Hamburg: Lit-Verlag.

―――. 2007. *Kreolität und postkoloniale Gesellschaft: Integration und Differenzierung in Jakarta.* Frankfurt am Main: Campus.

―――. 2008. "Towards Conceptualizing Creolization and Creoleness." *Max Planck Institute for Social Anthropology Working Papers* 100.

―――. 2009. "Postkoloniale Kreolität versus koloniale Kreolisierung." *Paideuma* 55: 93–115.

―――. 2010a. "Creolization and Nation-Building in Indonesia." In *The Creolization Reader: Studies in Mixed Identities and Cultures,* edited by Robin Cohen and Paola Toninato, 353–63. New York: Routledge.

―――. 2010b. "Contemporary Creoleness; or, The World in Pidginization?" *Current Anthropology* 51: 731–59.

―――. 2014. "Creole Identity in Postcolonial Indonesia." New York: Berghahn Books.

Knörr, Jacqueline, Christian Kordt Højbjerg, Christoph Kohl, Anita Schroven and Wilson Trajano Filho. 2008. "Research Group 'Integration and Conflict in the Upper Guinea Coast': (Re-)Constructions of National Identity in the Upper Guinea Coast." In *Report 2006–2007,* edited by Max Planck Institute for Social Anthropology, 30–40. Halle (Saale): Max Planck Institute for Social Anthropology.

Kode, Johannes. 2013. "On the Social Conditions of Governance: Social Capital and Governance in Areas of Limited Statehood." *SFB 700-Governance in Areas of Limited Statehood Working Paper Series* 60.

Kohl, Christoph. 2007. "Um Encontro com Aliu Barri." *Ntama—Journal of African Music and Popular Culture.* Retrieved 1 April 2014 from http://www .uni-hildesheim.de/ntama/index.php?option=com_content&view=article &id=193:um-encontro-com-aliu-barri&catid=66:articles&Itemid=29.

―――. 2009a. "The Kristons de Gêba of Guinea-Bissau: Creole Contributions to Postcolonial Nation-Building." *Online Working Paper, Graduate School Society and Culture in Motion, Martin Luther University of Halle-Wittenberg,* vol. 9. Retrieved 18 May 2009 http://wcms-neu1.urz.uni-halle.de/download.php ?down=10474&elem=2088503.

―――. 2009b. "The Praça of Geba: Marginalisation Past and Present as Re-source." *Mande Studies* 11: 73–90.

―――. 2011b. "National Integration in Guinea-Bissau since Independence." *Cadernos de Estudos Africanos* 20: 85–109.

―――. 2016. "Limitations and Ambiguities of Colonialism in Guinea-Bissau: Examining the Creole and 'Civilized' Space in Colonial Society." *History in Africa* 43: 169–203.

―――. In print. "A Chamada 'Justiça Tradicional' na Guiné-Bissau: As Sombras do Passado no Presente." In *Antropologia de Direito,* edited by Vânia Ribeiro. Recife: Editora da Universidade Federal de Pernambuco.

Kohl, Christoph, and Anita Schroven. 2014. "Suffering for the Nation: Bottom-Up and Top-Down Conceptualizations of the Nation in Guinea and Guinea-Bissau." *Max Planck Institute for Social Anthropology Working Papers* 152.

Kopytoff, Igor. 1987. "The Internal African Frontier: The Making of African Political Culture." In *The African Frontier: The Reproduction of Traditional African Societies,* edited by Igor Kopytoff, 3–84. Bloomington: Indiana University Press.

Koudawo, Fafali. 1994. *Eleições e Lições: Esboços para uma Análise das Primeiras Eleições Pluralistas na Guiné-Bissau*. Bissau: Kusimon Editora.
———. 1996. "Sociedade Civil e Transição Pluralista na Guiné-Bissau." In *Pluralismo Político na Guiné-Bissau: Uma Transição em Curso*, edited by Fafali Koudawo and Peter Karibe Mendy, 67–120. Bissau: Instituto Nacional de Estudos e Pesquisa.
Lahon, Didier. 1999a. "As Festas Religiosas e Profanas das Confrarias." In *Os Negros em Portugal, Séculos XV a XIX*, edited by Ana Maria Rodrigues, 144–57. Lisbon: Comissão Nacional Para as Comemorações dos Descobrimentos Portugueses.
———. 1999b. *O Negro no Coração do Império: Uma Memória a Resgatar. Séculos XV–XIX*. Lisbon: Ministério de Educação.
———. 2000. "Exlusion, Intégration et Métissage dans les Confréries Noires au Portugal (XVIe–XIXe siècles)." In *Negros, Mulatos, Zambaigos. Derroteros Africanos en los Mundos Ibéricos*, edited by Berta Ares Queija and Alessandro Stella, 275–311. Seville: Escuela de Estudios Hispano-Americanos.
———. 2001. "Esclavage et Confréries Noires au Portugal durant l'Ancien Régime (1441–1830)." PhD thesis, Ecole des Hautes Etudes en Sciences Sociales.
———. 2003. "Esclavage, Confréries Noires, Sainteté Noire et Pureté de Sang au Portugal (XVIe et XVIIIe siècles)." *Lusitania Sacra* 2 (2nd Series): 119–62.
———. 2004. "Du Bateau de Thésée ou des Identités Esclaves au Portugal sous l'Ancien Régime: Confréries Noires, Kalunga, Calundu." In *Identités Périphériques: Péninsule Ibérique, Méditerranée, Amérique Latine*, edited by Marie-Lucie Copete and Raul Caplan, 53–81. Paris: L' Harmattan.
———. 2005. "Black African Slaves and Freedmen in Portugal during the Renaissance: Creating a New Pattern of Reality." In *Black Africans in Renaissance Europe*, edited by Thomas F. Earle and Kate J. P. Lowe, 261–81. Cambridge: Cambridge University Press.
Landerset Simões, A. de. 1935. *Babel Negra: Etnografia, Arte e Cultura dos Indígenas da Guiné*. Porto: self-published.
Lange, Katharina. 2005. "Biographische Methoden als Zugang zur Geschichte ehemaliger Nomaden in Syrien." In *Methoden als Aspekte der Wissenskonstruktion*, edited by Jörg Gertel, 43–54. Halle (Saale): SFB "Differenz und Integration."
Langewiesche, Dieter. 2000. *Nation, Nationalismus, Nationalstaat in Deutschland und Europa*. Munich: C. H. Beck.
Latour, Bruno. 2005. *Reassembling the Social: An Introduction to Actor-Network-Theory*. Oxford: Oxford University Press.
Lei Orgânica de Administração Civil das Províncias Ultramarinas / Lei 227 (15 August 1914). *Boletim Oficial da Guiné Portuguesa* (1914) 40. 329–43.
Leite de Vasconcellos, José. 1982. *Etnografia Portuguesa: Tentame de Sistematização*. Vol. 8. Lisbon: Imprensa Nacional-Casa da Moeda.
Lemos Coelho, Francisco de. 1953a. "Descrição da Costa da Guiné desde o Cabo Verde athe Serra Lioa com todas as Ilhas e Rios que os Brancos Navegam." In *Duas Descrições Seiscentistas da Guiné de Francisco de Lemos Coelho*, edited by Damião Peres, 1–88. Lisbon: Academia Portuguesa da História.

———. 1953b. "Descripção da Costa de Guiné e Situação de todos os Portos e Rios della, e Roteyro para se Poderem Navegar todos seus Rios." In *Duas Descrições Seiscentistas da Guiné de Francisco de Lemos Coelho,* edited by Damião Peres, 89–250. Lisbon: Academia Portuguesa da História.

Liebenow, Gus. 1969. *Liberia: The Evolution of Privilege.* Ithaca, NY: Cornell University Press.

Loff de Vasconcelos, Luiz. 1916. *A Defeza das Victimas da Guerra de Bissau: O Extermínio da Guiné.* Lisbon: Imprensa Libanio da Silva.

Lonsdale, John M. 1996. "Ethnicité, Morale et Tribalisme Politique." *Politique Africaine* 61: 98–115.

Lopes, Carlos. 1987a. "Guiné-Bissau: Crioulo, Português ou Francês?" In *II Encontro Nacional da Associação Portuguesa de Linguística,* edited by Direcção da Associação Portuguesa de Linguística, 279–85. Lisbon: Faculdade de Letras da Universidade de Lisboa.

———. 1987b. *Guinea Bissau: From Liberation Struggle to Independent Statehood.* London: Zed Books.

———. 1988. *Para uma Leitura Sociológica da Guiné-Bissau.* Lisbon: Editorial Economia e Socialismo, Instituto Nacional de Estudos e Pesquisa.

Lopes da Silva, Baltasar. 1984. *O Dialecto Crioulo de Cabo Verde.* Lisbon: Imprensa Nacional.

Lopes de Lima, José Joaquim. 1844. *Ensaios sobre Statística das Possessões Portuguezas na África Occidental e Oriental, na Ásia Occidental, na China, e na Oceânia.* Lisbon: Imprensa Nacional.

Lopes, José Vicente. 2002. *Cabo Verde: Os Bastidores da Independência,* 2nd ed. Praia: Spleen Edições.

Lourenço-Lindell, Ilda. 2002. *Walking the Tight Rope: Informal Livelihoods and Social Networks in a West African City.* Stockholm: Almqvist and Wiksell International.

Lundy, Brandon D. 2012. "Spiritual Spaces, Marginal Places: The Commodification of a Nalú Sacred Grove." In *Contested Economies: Global Tourism and Cultural Heritage,* edited by Sarah Lyon and Christian Wells, 121–42. Lanham, MD: Altamira Press.

Ly, Aliou. 2015. "Revisiting the Guinea-Bissau Liberation War: PAIGC, UDEMU and the Question of Women's Emancipation, 1963–74." *Portuguese Journal of Social Science* 14: 361–77.

Lyall, Archibald. 1938. *Black and White Make Brown: An Account of the Cape Verde Islands and Portuguese Guinea.* London: William Heinemann.

Lyon, Judson M. 1980. "Marxism and Ethno-Nationalism in Guinea-Bissau, 1956–76." *Ethnic and Racial Studies* 3: 156–68.

Mac Cord, Marcelo. 2005. *O Rosário de D. Antônio. Irmandades Negras, Alianças e Conflitos na História Social do Recife 1848–1872.* Recife: Editora Universitária UFPE.

Macedo, Francisco de 1978. "A Educação na República da Guiné-Bissau: O Passado, as Transformações no Presente, as Perspectivas do Futuro." *Itinerarium* 23: 158–94.

———. 1989. "O Problema das Línguas na Guiné-Bissau." *Humanidades* 22: 33–38.

Magalhães Ferreira, Patrícia. 2004. "Guinea-Bissau: Between Conflict and Democracy." *African Security Review* 13: 45–56.

Mamdani, Mahmood. 1996. *Citizen and Subject: Contemporary Africa and the Legacy of Late Colonialism*. Princeton, NJ: Princeton University Press.

Marbeck, Joan M. 1995. *Ungua Adanza: An Inheritence*. Melaka: Loh Printing Press.

Marcelino, Pedro F. 2016. "The African 'Other' in the Cape Verde Islands: Interaction, Integration and the Forging of an Immigration Policy." In *The Upper Guinea Coast in Global Perspective*, edited by Jacqueline Knörr and Christoph Kohl, 116–34. New York: Berghahn Books.

Mark, Peter. 1985. *A Cultural, Economic, and Religious History of the Basse Casamance since 1500*. Wiesbaden: Franz Steiner Verlag.

———. 1999. "The Evolution of 'Portuguese' Identity: Luso-Africans on the Upper Guinea Coast from the Sixteenth to the Early Nineteenth Century." *Journal of African History* 40: 173–91.

———. 2002. *"Portuguese" Style and Luso-African Identity: Precolonial Senegambia, Sixteenth-Nineteenth Centuries*. Bloomington: Indiana University Press.

Mark, Peter, and José da Silva Horta. 2011. *The Forgotten Diapora: Jewish Communities in West Africa and the Making of the Atlantic World*. Cambridge: Cambridge University Press.

Marques de Barros, Marcelino. 1882. "Guiné Portugueza: Ou Breve Notícia sobre Alguns dos seus Usos, Costumes, Línguas e Origens de seus Povos." *Boletim da Sociedade de Geographia de Lisboa* 12: 707–31.

———. 1897/99. "O Guinéense." *Revista Lusitana* 5: 271–300.

———. 1900. "Littératura dos Negros: Contos, Cantigas e Parabolas." Lisbon: Typographia do Commercio.

———. 1902a. "O Guineense (Conclusão)." *Revista Lusitana* 7: 268–82.

———. 1902b. "O Guineense (Continuado)." *Revista Lusitana* 7: 166–88.

Marques Geraldes, Francisco António. 1887. "Guiné Portugueza: Communicação à Sociedade de Geographia sobre esta Província e suas Condições Actuaes." *Boletim da Sociedade de Geographia de Lisboa* 7: 465–522.

Martinus, Efraim Frank. 1996. "The Kiss of a Slave: Papiamentu's West-African Connections." PhD thesis, University of Amsterdam.

Massa, J.-M. 1996. *Dictionnaire Bilingue Portugais-Français des Particularités de la Langue Portugaise en Guinée-Bissau*. Rennes: Université de Haute Bretagne.

Matos e Lemos, Mário. 1995. "A 'Revolução Triunfante.' Guiné 1931." *Revista de História das Ideias* 17: 303–47.

———. 1999. *Política Cultural Portuguesa em África: O Caso da Guiné-Bissau (1985–1998)*. Bissau: Banco Totta and Açores-Bissau.

Matos e Lemos, Mário, and Alexandre Ramires. 2008. *O Primeiro Fotógrafo de Guerra Português: José Henriques de Mello. Guiné: Campanhas de 1907–1908*. Coimbra: Imprensa da Universidade de Coimbra.

McCulloch, Jock. 1983. *In the Twilight of Revolution: The Political Theory of Amílcar Cabral*. London: Routledge and Kegan Paul.

McGilvray, Dennis B. 1982. "Dutch Burghers and Portuguese Mechanics: Eurasian Ethnicity in Sri Lanka." *Comparative Studies in Society and History* 24: 235–63.

Meeker, Michael E. 2004. "Magritte on the Bedouins: Ce n'est pas une Société Segmentaire." In *Segmentation und Komplementarität: Organisatorische, ökonomische und kulturelle Aspekte der Interaktion von Nomaden und Sesshaften*, edited by Bernhard Streck, 33–55. Halle (Saale): SFB "Differenz und Integration."

Meintel, Deirdre. 1984. *Race, Culture, and Portuguese Colonialism in Cabo Verde.* Syracuse, NY: Syracuse University.

Mello, Maria Aparecida Curupaná da Rocha de. 2007. "A Questão da Produtividade Morfológica no Guineense." PhD thesis, Universidade Nacional de Brasília.

Mendes, José Catengul. 2007. *Guinée-Bissau: Une Nouvelle Image S'Impose.* Paris: self-published.

Mendes, João Francisco. 1966. "Crónica da Província." *Boletim Cultural da Guiné Portuguesa* 21: 523–45.

Mendes, J. U. 2007. "Plan Organiza Carnaval Infantil 2007 na Região de Bafatá: Crianças Pedem Continuidade da Iniciativa." *Gazeta de Notícias* 284: 3.

Mendy, Peter Karibe. 1994. *Colonialismo Português em África: A Tradição de Resistência na Guiné-Bissau (1879–1959).* Lisbon: Instituto Nacional de Estudos e Pesquisa.

———. 1996. "A Emergência do Pluralismo Político na Guiné-Bissau." In *Pluralismo Político na Guiné-Bissau. Uma Transição em Curso*, edited by Fafali Koudawo and Peter Karibe Mendy, 11–65. Bissau: Instituto Nacional de Estudos e Pesquisa.

———. 2006. "Amílcar Cabral and the Liberation of Guinea-Bissau: Context, Challenges and Lessons for Effective African Leadership." *African Identities* 4: 7–21.

Mendy, Peter Karibe, and Richard A. Lobban Jr. 2013. *Historical Dictionary of the Republic of Guinea-Bissau.* 4th ed. Lanham, MD: Scarecrow Press.

Merry, Sally Engle. 2006. "Transnational Human Rights and Local Activism: Mapping the Middle." *American Anthropologist* 108: 38–51.

Mezger, Werner. 1980. "Fasnacht, Fasching und Karneval als soziales Rollenexperiment." In *Narrenfreiheit: Beiträge zur Fastnachtsforschung*, edited by Hermann Bausinger and Manfred Fuhrmann, 203–26. Tübingen: Tübinger Vereinigung für Volkskunde.

———. 2000. "Masken an Fastnacht, Fasching und Karneval: Zur Geschichte und Funktion von Vermummung und Verkleidung während der närrischen Tage." In *Masken und Maskierungen*, Alfred Schäfer and Michael Wimmer, 109–34. Opladen: Leske und Budrich.

Mills, Dorothy. 1929. *The Golden Land: A Record of Travel in West Africa.* London: Duckworth.

Ministério da Administração Interna. 1995. *Guiné-Bissau: Constituição, Lei Eleitoral e Legislação complementar.* Lisbon: Edições 70.

Ministério da Coordenação Económica e Plano. 1981. *Recenseamento Geral da População e da Habitação: Resultados Provisórios (Fase II).* Bissau.

Ministério das Obras Públicas, Commércio e Indústria. 1884. *Annuário Estatístico de Portugal 1884.* Lisbon: Imprensa Nacional.

Ministério de Educação, Cultura e Desportos. 1987. *Propostas de Uniformização da Escrita do Crioulo.* Bissau.

Miranda Freitas, Joseania and Maria Manuela Abreu Borges Domingues. 2005. "Perspectivas histórico-educacionais do Associativismo feminino na África e no Brasil: Memórias solidárias. Mandjuandades na Guiné-Bissau e a Irmandade da Boa Morte na Bahia." *Revista Educação em Questão* 22: 34–54.

Mitchell, Jon P. 2006. "Performance." In *Handbook of Material Culture*, edited by Christopher Tilley, Webb Keane, Susanne Küchler, Michael Rowlands, and Patricia Spyer, 384–401. London: SAGE.

Mollien, Gaspard-Théodore. 1820. *Voyage dans l'Intérieur de l'Afrique, aux Sources du Sénégal et de la Gambie*. Paris: Courcier.

Monteiro, Félix. 1948. "Tabanca: Evolução Semântica." *Claridade* 6: 14–18.

Monteiro, Fernando Amaro, and Teresa Vazquez Rocha. 2004. *A Guiné do Século XVII ao Século XIX. O Testemunho dos Manuscritos*. Lisbon: Prefácio.

Montenegro, Teresa. 1993. "Breve Notícia da Revolução Triunfante." *Soronda* 15: 139–49.

———. 2002. *Kriol Ten. Termos e Expressões*. Bissau: Ku Si Mon Editora.

Moreira, Adriano. 1951. "A Revogação do Acto Colonial." *Revista do Gabinete de Estudos Ultramarinos* 3: 3–38.

Moser, Dietz-Rüdiger. 1986. *Fastnacht, Fasching, Karneval. Das Fest der "verkehrten Welt."* Graz: Verlag Styria.

Mühlmann, Wilhelm Emil. 1964. *Chiliasmus und Nativismus: Studien zur Psychologie, Soziologie und historischen Kasuistik der Umsturzbewegungen*, 2nd ed. Berlin: Dietrich Reimer.

Nafafé, José Lingna. 2007a. *Colonial Encounters: Issues of Culture, Hybridity and Creolisation. Portuguese Mercantile Settlers in West Africa*. Frankfurt am Main: Peter Lang.

———. 2007b. "Lançados, Culture and Identity: Prelude to Creole Societies on the Rivers of Guinea and Cape Verde." In *Creole Societies in the Portuguese Colonial Empire*, edited by Philip J. Havik and Malyn Newitt, 65–91. Bristol: Seagull/Faoileán.

Nagel, Joane. 1995. "American Indian Ethnic Renewal: Politics and the Resurgence of Identity." *American Sociological Review* 60: 947–65.

Nassum, Manuel. 1994. "Política Linguística Pós-Colonial: Ruptura ou Continuidade?" *Soronda* 17: 45–78.

Nketia, J. H. Kwabena. 1979. *Die Musik Afrikas*. Wilhelmshaven: Heinrichshofen's Verlag.

Nobles, Melissa. 2002. "Racial Categorization and Censuses." In *Census and Identity: The Politics of Race, Ethnicity, and Language in National Censuses*, edited by David I. Kertzer and Dominique Arel, 43–70. Cambridge: Cambridge University Press.

Nobrega, Álvaro. 2003a. "Desejo de 'Cambança': O Processo Eleitoral de 1999." *Soronda* 7 (New Series): 7–81.

———. 2003b. *A Luta pelo Poder na Guiné-Bissau*. Lisbon: Universidade Técnica de Lisboa.

Nora, Pierre. 1989. "Between Memory and History: Les Lieux de Mémoire." *Representations* 26: 7–24.

Nunley, John W. 1982. "Images and Printed Words in Freetown Masquerades." *African Arts* 15: 42–92.

————. 1985. "The Lantern Festival in Sierra Leone." *African Arts* 18: 45–103.

Oram, Jenny. 1998. Float Traditions in Sierra Leone and the Gambia. *African Arts* 31: 50-96.

————. 2002. "Urban Float Traditions in West Africa." In *Museums and Urban Culture in West Africa,* edited by Alexis B. A. Adande and Emmanuel Arinze, 77–96. Oxford: James Currey.

Ortner, Sherry B. 1995. "Resistance and the Problem of Ethnographic Refusal." *Comparative Studies in Society and History* 37: 173–93.

Osterhammel, Jürgen. 2009. *Kolonialismus. Geschichte, Formen, Folgen.* 9th ed. Munich: C. H. Beck.

Ostheimer, Andrea E. 2001. "The Structural Crisis in Guinea-Bissau's Political System." *African Security Review* 10: 45–57.

Parente Augel, Moema. 1997. *Ora di kanta tchiga. José Carlos Schwarz e o Cobiana Djazz.* Bissau: Instituto Nacional de Estudos e Pesquisa.

————. 1998. *A Nova Literatura da Guiné-Bissau.* Bissau: Instituto Nacional de Estudos e Pesquisa.

————. 2006. O Crioulo Guineense e a Oratura. *Scripta* 10: 69–91.

Parés, Luis Nicolau. 2013. *A Formação do Candomblé: História e Ritual da Nação Jeje na Bahia.* Campinas: Editora da Unicamp.

Pattee, Richard. 1974. "Portuguese Guinea: A Microcosms of a Plural Society in Africa." *Plural Societies* 4 (4): 57–64.

Peck, Stephen Madry, Jr. 1988. "Tense, Aspect and Mood in Guinea-Casamance Portuguese Creole." PhD thesis, University of California.

Pélissier, René. 1989. *Naissance de la Guiné: Portugais et Africains en Sénégambie (1841–1936).* Orgeval: Editions Pélissier.

Pereira, Aristides. 2003. *O meu Testemunho: Uma Luta, um Partido, dois Países. Versão Documentada.* Lisbon: Editorial Notícias.

Pereira, Dulce. 2006. *Crioulos de Base Portuguesa.* Lisbon: Editorial Caminho; Luanda: Editorial Nzila.

Pereira Barreto, Honório. 1843. *Memoria sobre o Estado actual de Senegambia Portugueza, Causes de sua Decadência, e Meios de a Fazer Prosperar.* Lisbon: Typ. da Viuva Coelho and Comp.

Perfect, David. 1991. "The Political Career of Edward Francis Small." In *The Gambia: Studies in Society and Politics,* edited by Arnold Hughes, 64–79. Birmingham: Centre of West African Studies, University of Birmingham.

Person, Yves. 1968. *Samori: Une Révolution Dyula,* part 1. Dakar: Institut Fondamental d'Afrique Noire.

Pink, Sarah. 1999. "Panos for the Brancus: Interweaving Cultures, Producing Cloth, Visualizing Experience, Making Anthropology." *Journal of Material Culture* 4: 163–82.

————. 2001. "Sunglasses, Suitcases and Other Symbols: Intentionality, Creativity and Indirect Communication in Festive and Everyday Performances." In *An Anthropology of Indirect Communication,* edited by Joy Hendry and C. W. Watson, 101–14. New York: Routledge.

Pinto Bull, Benjamin. 1989. *O Crioulo da Guiné-Bissau: Filosofia e Sabedoria.* Lisbon, Bissau: Instituto de Cultura e Língua Portuguesa, Instituto Nacional de Estudos e Pesquisa.

Pinto Rema, Henrique. 1971. "A Segunda Missão Franciscana da Guiné Portuguesa." *Boletim Cultural da Guiné Portuguesa* 26: 653–749.
————. 1982. *História das Missões Católicas da Guiné.* Braga: Editorial Franciscana.
Pirio, Gregory Alonso. 1983. "Race and Class in the Struggle over Pan-African-
ism: A Working Paper on the Partido Nacional Africano, the Liga Africana and
the Comintern in Portuguese Africa." Paper presented at the Class Basis of
Nationalist Movement in Angola, Guinea Bissau and Mozambique conference,
University of Minnesota.
Ponte, Nunes da. 1953. *Honório Pereira Barreto: Heróico Governador Negro da Guiné.*
Lisbon: Sociedade de Geografia de Lisboa.
Portaria 10 (11 February 1946). *Boletim Oficial da Guiné Portuguesa* (1946) 6.
Portaria 38 (9 February 1917). *Boletim Oficial da Guiné Portuguesa* (1917) 6: 41.
Portaria 39 (10 April 1928). *Boletim Oficial da Guiné Portuguesa* (1928) 15: 181–82.
Portaria 136 (18 September 1940). *Boletim Oficial da Guiné Portuguesa* (1940) 20,
supplement 38: 1–10.
Portaria 177 (8 October 1925). *Boletim Oficial da Guiné Portuguesa* (1925) 42: 555–56.
Portaria 495 (9 November 1921). *Boletim Oficial da Guiné Portuguesa* (1921) 46: 443.
Portaria 1,301 (18 January 1961). *Boletim Oficial da Guiné Portuguesa* (1961) 2,
supplement.
Portuense, Vitoriano. 1974. "Carta do Bispo de Cabo Verde D. Fr. Vitoriano
Portuense para sua Majestade El-Rei D. Pedro II, em que dá Conta da Missão
e Visita ao Sertão, Cacheo e Reino de Bissao—1694." In *As Viagens do Bispo D.
Frei Vitoriano Portuense à Guiné e a Cristianização dos Reis de Bissau,* edited by
Avelino Teixeira da Mota, 67–77. Lisbon: Junta de Investigações Científicas do
Ultramar.
Proença Garcia, Francisco. 2000. *Guiné 1963–1974: Os Movimentos independentistas,
o Islão e o Poder Português.* Lisbon: Comissão Portuguesa de História Militar,
Universidade Portucalense Infante D. Henrique.
Província da Guiné. 1961. *Anuário Estatístico 1956–1958.* Lisbon: Tipografia
Portuguesa.
————. 1978. *IX Recenseamento Geral da População 1960: Resumo Geral.* Lisbon:
Ministério dos Negócios Estrangeiros.
————. n.d. *Censo da População de 1950.* Vol. 2: *População Não Civilizada.* Lisbon:
Tipografia Portuguesa.
Rambout Barcelos, Manuel, Nicolau Fara Gomes, Félix Sigá, Harriet C. McGuire,
and Simon Ottenberg. 2006. "Masked Children in an Urban Scene: The Bissau
Carnival." In *African Children's Masquerades: Playful Performers,* edited by Si-
mon Ottenberg and David A. Binkley, 181–206. New Brunswick: Transactions
Publishers.
Ranger, Terence. 1993. "The Invention of Tradition Revisited. The Case of Co
lonial Africa." In *Legitimacy and the State in Twentieth-Century Africa,* edited
by Terence Ranger and Olufemi Vaughan, 62–111. New York: Palgrave
Macmillan.
Reade, W. Winwood. 1864. *Savage Africa: Being the Narrative of a Tour in Equatorial,
South-Western, and North-Western Africa.* 2nd ed. London: Smith, Elder, and Co.
Reginaldo, Lucilene. 2011. *Os Rosários dos Angolanos: Irmandades de Africanos e
Crioulos na Bahia Setecentista.* São Paulo: Alameda.

Regulamento das Circunscrições Civis da Província da Guiné (7 September 1912). *Boletim Oficial da Guiné Portuguesa* (1913) 18.

Regulamento de Transito, Fixação e Deslocação dos Indígenas / Diploma Legislativo 827 (27 January 1934). *Boletim Oficial da Guiné Portuguesa* (1934) 5: 41–46.

Regulamento do Trabalho dos Indígenas (9 November 1899). *Boletim Oficial da Guiné Portuguesa* (1900) 1.

Regulamento do Trabalho das Indígenas das Colónias Portuguesas (27 May 1911). *Boletim Oficial da Guiné Portuguesa* (1911) 32.

Reis, João José. 2003. *Rebelião Escrava no Brasil: A História de Levante dos Malês em 1835*. Rev. ed. São Paulo: Companhia das Letras.

Reuter, Jens. 2000. "Serbien und Kosvo: Das Ende eines Mythos." In *Der Kosovo-Konflikt: Ursachen, Verlauf, Perspektiven*, edited by Jens Reuter and Konrad Clewing, 139–55. Klagenfurt: Wieser Verlag.

Ribeiro, Carlos Rui. 1986. "A Sociedade Crioula na Guiné Portuguesa (1900–1960)." Thesis, Instituto Superior de Ciências do Trabalho e da Empresa.

———. 1993. "Personalidades crioulas em Contextos Ideológicos Específicos: Os Casos de Honório Pereira Barreto e Amílcar Cabral." In *Mansas, Escravos, Grumetes e Gentio: Cacheu na Encruzilhada de Civilizações. Actas do Colóquio "Cacheu, Cidade Antiga,"* edited by Carlos Lopes, 275–303. Bissau: Instituto Nacional de Estudos e Pesquisa.

———. 1994/95. "Os Crioulos, as Leis e a Participação Comunitária." Manuscript. Bissau.

Robertson, Roland. 1945. "Globalisation or Glocalisation?" *Journal of International Communication* 1: 33–52.

Rocha, Leopoldo da. 1973. *As Confrarias de Goa, Séculos XVI–XX: Conspecto Histórico-Jurídico*. Lisbon: Centro de Estudos Históricos Ultramarinos.

Rodrigues Zeverino, Guilherme Jorge. 2005. *O Conflito Politico-Militar na Guiné-Bissau (1998–1999)*. Lisbon: Instituto Português de Apoio ao Desenvolvimento.

Rogado Quintino, Fernando. 1969. "Os Povos da Guiné." *Boletim Cultural da Guiné Portuguesa* 24: 861–915.

———. n.d. *Eis a Guiné: Breve Notícia da sua Terra e da sua Gente*. Lisboa: Sociedade de Geografia de Lisboa.

Rosa Pereira, Isaías da. 1972. "Dois Compromissos de Irmandades de Homens Pretos." *Arqueologia e Historia* 3: 9–47.

Ross, Doran H. 1993. "Carnaval Masquerades in Guinea-Bissau." *African Arts* 26:64–71+88.

Rougé, Jean Louis. 1986. "Uma Hipótese sobre a Formação do Crioulo da Guiné-Bissau e da Casamansa." *Soronda* 2: 28–49.

———. 1988. *Petit Dictionnaire Etymologique du Kriol de Guinée-Bissau et Casamance*. Bissau: Instituto Nacional de Estudos e Pesquisa.

Rudebeck, Lars. 1974. "Guinea-Bissau: A Study of. Political Mobilization." Uppsala: Scandinavian Institute of African Studies.

———. 2001. *Colapso e Reconstrução Política na Guiné-Bissau 1998–2000: Um Estudo de Democratização Difícil*. Uppsala: Nordiska Afrikainstitutet.

Sand, Shlomo. 2013. *Die Erfindung des jüdischen Volkes: Israels Gründungsmythos auf dem Prüfstand*. Berlin: List.

Santo Vaz de Almeida, Sabou Espírito. 1991. _Crioulo Grammar Made Simple_. US Peace Corps.

Sarmento Rodrigues, Manuel Maria. 1947. "Prefácio." In _Honório Pereira Barreto: Biografia, Documentos, "Memoria sobre o Estado actual de Senegambia Portuguesa,"_ edited by Jaime Walter, vii–xv. Bissau: Centro de Estudos da Guiné Portuguesa.

Scantamburlo, Luigi. 1981. _Gramática e Dicionário da Língua Criol da Guiné-Bissau_. Bologna: Editrice Missionaria Italiana.

———. 1999. _Dicionário do Guineense_. Vol. 1: _Introdução e Notas Gramaticais_. Lisbon, Bubaque: Edições Colobri, Fundação para o Apoio ao Desenvolvimento dos Povos do Arquipélago de Bijagós.

———. 2002. _Dicionário do Guineense_. Vol. 2: _Dicionário Guineense-Português_. Bubaque: Edições Fundação para o Apoio ao Desenvolvimento dos Povos do Arquipélago de Bijagós.

———. 2005. "O Ensino Bilingue nas Escolas primárias das Ilhas Bijagós: Crioulo Guineense-Português." In _Língua Portuguesa e Cooperação para o Desenvolvimento_, edited by Maria Helena Mira Mateus and Luísa Teotónio Pereira, 63–78. Lisbon: Edições Colibri, CIDAC.

Schaumloeffel, Marco Aurelio. 2009. _Tabom: The Afro-Brazilian Community in Ghana_. Bridgetown: Schaumloeffel Editor and Custom Books Publishing.

Schiefer, Ulrich. 2002. _Von allen guten Geistern verlassen? Guinea-Bissau: Entwicklungspolitik und der Zusammenbruch afrikanischer Gesellschaften_. Hamburg: Institut für Afrika-Kunde.

Schieffelin, Edward L. 1985. "Performance and the Cultural Construction of Reality." _American Ethnologist_ 12: 707–24.

Schramm, Katharina. 2000. _Dancing the Nation: Ghanaische Kulturpolitik im Spannungsfeld zwischen Nation und globaler Herausforderung_. Münster: Lit.

Scott, James C. 1998. _Seeing like a State: How Certain Schemes to Improve the Human Condition Have Failed_. New Haven, CT: Yale University Press.

Seibert, Gerhard. 2012. "Creolization and Creole Communities in the Portuguese Atlantic: São Tomé, Cape Verde, the Rivers of Guinea and Central Africa in Comparison." _Proceedings of the British Academy_ 178: 29–51.

Semedo, José Maria, and Maria R. Turano. n.d. _Cabo Verde: O Ciclo Ritual das Festividades da Tabanca_. Praia: Spleen Edições.

Semedo, Maria Odete da Costa Soares. 2007. "As Cantigas Medievais e as Cantigas de Dito: Uma Leitura Comparada Possível." _SCRIPTA (Belo Horizonte)_ 11:57–78.

———. 2010. "As Mandjuandadi. Cantigas de Mulher na Guiné-Bissau: Da Tradição Oral à Literatura." PhD thesis, Pontifícia Universidade Católica de Minas Gerais.

Semedo, Rui Jorge. 2011. "O Estado da Guiné-Bissau e os Desafios Político-Institucionais." _Tensões Mundiais_ 7/13: 95–115.

Senna Barcellos, Christiano José de. 1905. _Subsídios para a História de Cabo Verde e Guiné_. Part 3. Lisbon: Typographia da Academia.

Serviços de Estatística. n.d. _Anuário Estatístico 1948_. Lisbon: Sociedade Industrial de Tipografia.

Sigá, Félix. 1995. "Carnaval: A Maior Manifestação Popular da Guiné-Bissau." _Tcholona. Revista de Letras, Artes e Cultura_ 1: 11–14.

Silva, Tomé Varela da. 1998. "Crenças e Religiões." In *Descoberta das Ilhas de Cabo Verde,* edited by Arquivo Histórico Nacional, 153–75. Praia: Arquivo Histórico Nacional, Sépia.

Silva Cunha, J. M. da. 1959. *Missão de Estudo dos Movimentos Associativos em África: Relatório da Campanha de 1958 (Guiné).* Lisbon: Junta de Investigações do Ultramar.

Silva Horta, José da. 2000. "Evidence for a Luso-African Identity in 'Portuguese' Accounts on 'Guinea of Cape Verde' (Sixteenth–Seventeenth Centuries)." *History in Africa* 27: 99–130.

———. 2011. *A "Guiné do Cabo Verde" Produção Textual e Representações (1578– 1684).* Lisbon: Fundação Calouste Gulbenkian, Fundação para a Ciência e a Tecnologia.

Simmons, William S. 1971. *Eyes of the Night: Witchcraft among a Senegalese People.* Boston: Little, Brown and Company.

Skinner, David, and Barbara E. Harrell-Bond. 1977. "Misunderstandings Arising from the Use of the Term 'Creole' in the Literature on Sierra Leone." *Africa: Journal of the International African Institute* 47: 305–20.

Soares, Maria João. 2000. "Contradições e Debilidades da Política Colonial Guineense: O Caso de Bissau." In *A África e a Instalação do Sistema Colonial (c. 1885–1930),* edited by Maria Emília Madeira Santos, 123–56. Lisbon: Instituto de Investigação Científica Tropical.

Soares Sousa, Julião. 2012. "Amílcar Cabral (1924–1973)." *Vida e Morte de um Revolucionário Africano.* 2nd ed. Lisbon: Vega.

Sociedade de Geográfia de Lisboa. 1939. *Monografia-Católogo da Exposição da Colónia da Guiné. Semana das Colónias de 1939.* Lisbon: Sociedade Industrial de Tipografia.

Sousa Monteiro, Jozé Maria. de 1853. "Estudos sobre a Guiné de Cabo Verde IV." *O Panorama* 10(55–56): 230–31.

Starr, Paul. 1987. "The Sociology of Official Statistics." In *The Politics of Numbers,* edited by William Alonso and Paul Starr, 7–57. New York: Russell Sage Foundation.

Stewart, Charles. 2007. "Creolization, History, Ethnography, Theory." In *Creolization: History, Ethnography, Theory,* edited by Charles Stewart, 1–25. Walnut Creek, CA: Left Coast Press.

Stoler, Ann Laura. 2009. *Along the Archival Grain: Epistemic Anxieties and Colonial Common Sense.* Princeton, NJ: Princeton University Press.

Stoler, Ann Laura, and Frederick Cooper. 1997. "Between Metropole and Colony: Rethinking a Research Agenda." In *Tensions of Empire. Colonial Cultures in a Bourgeois World,* edited by Ann Laura Stoler and Frederick Cooper, 1–56. Berkeley: University of California Press.

Strauss, Anselm L. 1987. *Qualitative Analysis for Social Scientists.* Cambridge: Cambridge University Press.

Sundhaussen, Holm. 2000. "Kosovo: Eine Konfliktgeschichte." In *Der Kosovo-Konflikt: Ursachen, Verlauf, Perspektiven,* edited by Jens Reuter and Konrad Clewing, 65–89. Klagenfurt: Wieser Verlag.

Sundiata, Ibrahim K. 1972. "The Fernandinos: Labor and Community in Santa Isabel de Fernando Poo, 1827–1931." PhD thesis, Northwestern University.

————. 1996. *From Slaving to Neoslavery: The Bight of Biafra and Fernando Po in the Era of Abolition, 1827–1930*. Madison: University of Wisconsin Press.

Tambiah, Stanley J. 1990. "Presidential Address: Reflections on Communal Violence in South Asia." *Journal of Asian Studies* 49: 741–60.

Teixeira da Mota, Avelino. 1951. "Contactos Culturais Luso-Africanos na 'Guiné do Cabo Verde.'" *Boletim da Sociedade de Geografia de Lisboa* 69: 659–67.

————. 1954. *Guiné Portuguesa*. 2 vols. Lisbon: Agência Geral do Ultramar.

Teixeira, Manuel. 1963. *Macau e a sua Diocese*. Vol. 6: *A Missão Portuguesa de Malaca*. Lisbon: Agência Geral do Ultramar.

Teixeira da Silva, Francisco. 1889. *Relatório do Governo da Província da Guiné Portugueza, 1887–1888*. Lisbon: Typographia Minerva Central.

Temudo, Marina Padrão. 2008. "From 'People's Struggle' to 'This War of Today': Entanglements to Peace and Conflict in Guinea Bissau." *Africa* 78: 245–63.

Thomaz, Luís Filipe Ferreira Reis. 1981–82. "Goa: Une Société Luso-Indienne." *Bulletin des Etudes Portugaises et Brésiliennes* 42/43: 15–44.

Thompson, Robert Wallace. 1961. "O Dialecto Português de Hongkong." *Boletim de Filologia* 19: 289–93.

Trajano Filho, Wilson. 1993. "Rumores: Uma Narrativa da Nação." *Série Antropologia* 143.

————. 1998. "Polymorphic Creoledom: The 'Creole' Society of Guinea-Bissau." PhD thesis, University of Pennsylvania.

————. 2001a. "Manjuandadis e Tabancas: Duas Formas Associativas em Duas Sociedades Crioulas." *Artiletra* 36/37: x–xi.

————. 2001b. "Manjuandadis e Tabancas: Duas Formas Associativas em Duas Sociedades Crioulas (Continuação)." *Artiletra* 38: xx–xxii.

————. 2002. "Narratives of National Identity in the Web." *Ethnográfica* 6: 141–58.

————. 2005. "A Construção da Nação e o Fim dos Projetos Crioulos: Os Casos de Cabo Verde e da Guiné-Bissau." In *"Lusofonia" em Africa: Historia, Democracia e Integração Africana*, edited by Teresa Cruz e Silva, Manuel G. Mendes de Araújo, and Carlos Cardoso, 95–120. Dakar: CODESRIA.

————. 2006a. "Por uma Etnografia da Resistência: O Caso das Tabancas de Cabo Verde." *Série Antropologia* 408.

————. 2006b. "Some Problems with the Creole Project for the Nation: The Case of Guinea Bissau." Paper presented at the Powerful Presence of the Past: Historical Dimensions of Integration and Conflict in the Upper Guinea Coast conference, Max-Planck Institute for Social Anthropology, Halle (Saale), October 19–21, 2006.

————. 2007. "A Cooperação Internacional e a Consciência Infeliz: O Caso da Guiné-Bissau." In *Timor-Leste por Trás do Palco. Cooperação Internacional do Estado*, edited by Kelly Cristiane da Silva and Daniel Schröter Simião, 365–82. Belo Horizonte: Editora Universidade Federal de Minas Gerais.

————. 2009a. "The Conservative Aspects of a Centripetal Diaspora: The Case of the Cape Verdean 'Tabancas.'" *Africa* 79: 520–42.

————. 2009b. "Os Cortejos das Tabancas: Dois Modelos da Ordem." In *As Festas e os Dias: Ritos e Sociabilidades Festivas*, edited by Maria Laura Viveiros de Castro Cavalcanto and José Reginaldo Santos Gonçalves, 37–73. Rio de Janeiro: Contra Capa.

————. 2010. "Território e Idade: Ancoradouros do Pertencimento nas Manjuan-dadis da Guiné-Bissau." In *Lugares, Pessoas e Grupos: As Lógicas do Pertencimento em Perspectiva Internacional,* edited by Wilson Trajano Filho, 225–55. Brasília: Athalaia Gráfica e Editora.

————. 2012. "As Cores nas Tabancas: Sobre Bandeiras e seus Usos." In *Travessias Antropológicas: Estudos em Contextos Africanos,* edited by Wilson Trajano Filho, 339–66. Brasília: ABA Publicações.

————. 2016. "'Tabanka': Semantic Fluctuations in the Atlantic World." In *The Upper Guinea Coast in Global Perspective,* edited by Jacqueline Knörr and Christoph Kohl, 157–73. New York: Berghahn Books.

Travassos Valdez, Francisco. 1864. *Africa Occidental: Noticias e Considerações,* vol. 1. Lisbon: Imprensa Nacional.

Turner, Victor. 1979. "Dramatic Ritual/Ritual Drama: Performative and Reflexive Anthropology." *Kenyon Review* 1 (New Series): 80–93.

————. 1995. *The Ritual Process: Structure and Anti-Structure.* New York: Aldine de Gruyter.

————. 1996. *Dramas, Fields, and Metaphors: Symbolic Action in Human Society.* Ithaca, NY: Cornell University Press.

UDEMU—União Democrática das Mulheres da Guiné. n.d. Retrieved 2 April 2008 from http://www.paigc.org/udemu1.htmH.

Urdang, Stephanie. 1979. *Fighting Two Colonialisms: Women in Guinea-Bissau.* New York: Monthly Review Press.

Vail, Leroy. 1989a. "Introduction: Ethnicity in Southern African History." In *The Creation of Tribalism in Southern Africa,* edited by Leroy Vail, 1–19. Berkeley: University of California Press.

————. 1989b. "Preface." In *The Creation of Tribalism in Southern Africa,* edited by Leroy Vail, ix–xii. Berkeley: University of California Press.

Vale de Almeida, Miguel. 2007. "From Miscegenation to Creole Identity: Portuguese Colonialism, Brazil, Cape Verde." In *Creolization: History, Ethnography, Theory,* Charles Stewart, 108–32. Walnut Creek, CA: Left Coast Press.

————. 2008. "Portugal's Colonial Complex: From Colonial Lusotropicalism to Postcolonial Lusophony." Paper presented at the Queen's Postcolonial Research Forum, Queen's University, Belfast.

Valkhoff, Marius François. 1966. *Studies in Portuguese Creole: With a Special Reference to South Africa.* Johannesburg: Witwatersrand University Press.

————. ed. 1972. *New Light on Afrikaans and "Malayo-Portuguese."* Leuven: Éditions Peeters.

van der Drift, Roy. 2000. "Democracy: Legitimate Warfare in Guinea-Bissau." *Soronda Número Especial 7 de Junho* 4 (New Series): 37–65.

Vansina, Jan. 1985. *Oral Tradition as History.* London, Nairobi: James Currey, Heinemann Kenya.

————. 1990. *Paths in the Rainforest: Toward a History of Political Tradition in Equatorial Africa.* London: James Currey.

Vaz, Nuno, and Iris Cordelia Rotzoll. 2005. "Presidential Elections in Guinea Bissau 2005: A Stabilizing Factor in a Fragile Democracy or Only a Spot Test of the State of Affairs?" *Afrika Spectrum* 40: 535–46.

Veiga de Oliveira, Ernesto. 1984. *Festividades cíclicas em Portugal*. Vol. 6: *Portugal de Perto*. Lisbon: Publicações Dom Quixote.

Velez Caroço, Jorge Frederico. 1923. *Relatório Annual do Governador da Guiné (1921-1922)*. Coimbra: Imprensa da Universidade.

Vieira Có, Joãozinho. 2001. *As Consequências jurídico-constitucionais do Conflito Político-Militar da Guiné-Bissau*. Verona: Associação Rete Guinea Bissau.

Vigh, Henrik E. 2006. *Navigating Terrains of War: Youth and Soldiering in Guinea-Bissau*. New York: Berghahn Books.

Vögelin, Eric. 2007. *Die politischen Religionen*. 3rd ext. ed. Paderborn: Fink.

Voz di Paz. 2010. *Roots of Conflicts in Guinea-Bissau: The Voice of the People*. Bissau: Voz di Paz.

Walker, Iain. 2005. "Mimetic Structuration: Or, Easy Steps to Building an Acceptable Identity." *History and Anthropology* 16: 187–210.

Weber, Eugen. 1976. *Peasants into Frenchmen: The Modernization of Rural France, 1870–1914*. Stanford, CA: Stanford University Press.

Weber, Max. 1978. *Economy and Society: An Outline of Interpretive Sociology*. 2 vols. Berkeley: University of California Press.

Wehler, Hans-Ulrich. 2001. *Nationalismus: Geschichte, Formen, Folgen*. Munich: C. H. Beck.

Weichlein, Siegfried. 2006. "Nationalbewegungen und Nationalismus in Europa." Darmstadt: Wissenschaftliche Buchgesellschaft.

Weil, Peter M. 1971. "The Masked Figure and Social Control: The Mandinka Case." *Africa* 41: 279–93.

Wick, Alexis. 2006. "Manifestations of Nationhood in the Writings of Amilcar Cabral." *African Identities* 4: 45–70.

Wyse, Akintola J. G. 1989. *The Krio of Sierra Leone: An Interpretative History*. London: Hurst.

York, Luís de. 1959. "O Nosso Irmão Honório." *Bolamense* 32.

Young, Crawford. 1988. "The African Colonial State and its Political Legacy." In *The Precarious Balance: State and Society in Africa*, edited by Donald Rothchild and Naomi Chazan, 25–66. Boulder, CO: Westview Press.

———. 2007. "Nation, Ethnicity and Citizenship: Dilemmas of Democracy and Civil Order in Africa." In *Making Nations, Creating Strangers. States and Citizenship in Africa*, edited by Sara Dorman, Daniel Hammett, and Paul Nugent, 241–64. Leiden: Brill.

Index